Gu mo dheagh c
Iain Urchada
J
24/10/16

St Paul In Roman

Asia Minor

E Lennox Manton

Author of "Roman North Africa"

Shield **Crest**

© Copyright 2015 E. Lennox Manton

All rights reserved

This book shall not, by way of trade or otherwise, be lent, re-sold, hired out, or otherwise circulated without the prior consent of the copyright holder or the publisher in any form of binding or cover other than that in which it is published and without a similar condition including this condition being imposed on the subsequent purchaser. The use of its contents in any other media is also subject to the same conditions.

ISBN   978-1-911090-06-9

MMXV

A CIP catalogue record for this book
Is available from the British Library

Published by
ShieldCrest
Aylesbury, Buckinghamshire, HP22 5RR
England

www.shieldcrest.co.uk

Contents

ACKNOWLEDGEMENTS i

LIST OF FIGURES AND ILLUSTRATIONS: iii

    The Years Before Antioch iii

    Antioch And The First Missionary Journey iii

    The Second Missionary Journey iv

    The Third Missionary Journey iv

    The Final Journey to Rome and Martyrdom v

PREFACE vii

CHAPTER 1 - The Years before Antioch. 1

CHAPTER 2 - Antioch and the First Missionary Journey. 44

CHAPTER 3 - The Second Missionary Journey. 105

CHAPTER 4 - The Third Missionary Journey 128

CHAPTER 5 - The Final Journey to Rome 208

POSTSCRIPT 229

ABOUT THE AUTHOR 231

CHRONOLOGY OF ST PAUL'S MISSIONARY JOURNEYS 232

INDEX 233

ACKNOWLEDGEMENTS

I must acknowledge in no small measure my indebtedness to the late Reverend Alwyn Wragg. We discussed St Paul on many occasions, not the least when we enjoyed the hospitality of Father Christopher Fuze and his fellow Rosminians in their Monastery by the Porta Latina in Rome. He was in accord with many of my conclusions regarding Onesimus and Paul's early life in Jerusalem under Gameliel. We discussed little of Paul's theology for I am far from qualified to appreciate the finer points, but I am sure that he was not of the opinion of some who assert that Paul did little for Christianity. I am also more than indebted to Professor G Stanton then of King's College London for his guidance and unstinting help, especially with regard to the many hidden pitfalls in the New Testament!

So too I am indebted to Dr French of the British Institute of Archaeology in Ankara. On the occasions when I saw him in Ankara he was very generous with details and information regarding his work on the roads that were extant in Asia Minor during the Pauline period, especially in respect of those Paul might have used. Aerial survey could well have helped him to trace more of these ancient routes but was not permitted by the military establishment, thus making his project more difficult than need be. I am also indebted, and in no small measure, to my daughter, Deirdre, and David Farnen for their unstinting help in the final editing of the manuscript, and for their suggestions regarding illustrations.

I must express my thanks to the Turkish Government too for their also unstinting hospitality, and particularly to Caglar Yasal Bey for arranging no less than four protracted tours of Asia Minor, and to all those who were involved. Here I must mention Ibrahim Buyukbenli of Antalya, an old friend who has in the past given me a great deal of valuable advice, and one who is an authority on the history of Pamphylia and Cilicia; an outstanding memory is a lunch that we had in the harbour restaurant on the quay at Kas. Here he spent a very considerable amount of time assessing the merits of the lobsters that were biding their time in a tank by the kitchen, before choosing the victims destined to end up on our platters.

Not least, however, must I express my appreciation of the kindness of Mrs Gulsen Karaman of the Ministry of Tourism in Ankara, and that of her husband, both of them having given me invaluable help when on my journeys, especially the last in June 1989 when I drove some three thousand miles from Istanbul to Ankara, Pontus, and over the Pontic Alps to the ruins of the Armenian churches at Ani. Paul did not come this way though the Christian Church spread rapidly throughout Georgia and Armenia; it is doubtful if Paul ever ventured further to the East than the Caesarea of Cappadocia, today's Kayseri.

The Reverend Canon Colin Semper, formerly of Westminster Abbey was with me on two of the journeys that were sponsored by the Turkish Government. He went to record letters from the Pauline cities to be broadcast on B.B.C. Radio 4, and I to obtain photographs for a series of Epilogues on St Paul and the Rupestral Churches of Cappadocia for Southern Television. The monuments in many of the ancient cities of Asia Minor have undergone sympathetic restoration, but there is still a great deal to be done and much to be discovered, a slow process hampered by the lack of funds.

Those who visit these sites today should also visit their excellent museums and keep in mind a passage from the preface that, as far back as the year 1887, Amelia B. Edwards wrote for Professor Maspero's 'Treatise on Egypt'. She was a remarkable woman who founded in 1885 the Chair of Egyptology at University College London, once held by Sir Flinders Petrie, and she wrote, 'As regards the practical side of Archaeology, it ought to be unnecessary to point out that its usefulness is strictly parallel with the usefulness of public museums. To collect and exhibit objects of ancient art and industry is worse than idle if we do not also endeavour to disseminate some knowledge of the history of those arts and industries, and of the processes employed by the artists and craftsmen of the past. Archaeology, no less than love, adds a precious seeing to the eye; and without that gain of mental sight, the treasures of public collections are regarded by the general visitor as mere 'curiosities' -- flat and stale for the most part, and wholly unprofitable'. How right she was, for this not only applies to the museum collections but also to the sites from whence they came.

LIST OF FIGURES AND ILLUSTRATIONS:

Cover Image. St Paul, the Chora Museum, Istabul – photographed by David Farnen

The Years Before Antioch

1. Weighing grain in the corn market in old Tarsus.

2. Street vendor in old Tarsus.

3. Communal fountain in old Tarsus.

4. The Way of Life in Old Damascus.

5. Roman Damascus.

6. The Forum in Jerash.

7. The Granite Bowl Jerash Nymphaeum.

8. The Siq, Petra.

9. Tomb facades in the mountain sides that climatic conditions have eroded over the centuries.

10. The El Khasneh, known as Solomon's Treasury.

11. The Deir. Petra.

12. The Mountains of Seir.

Antioch And The First Missionary Journey

13 A and B. Life today in old Antioch.

14. Cave Church of St Peter in Antioch.

15. Interior of the Church.

16. Mosaic of a Negro Slave, Antioch.   )

17. Mosaic of the Happy Hunchback, Antioch.   )   Depictions

18. Orpheus.   )   Showing

19. Pompeian Couple.   )   Pompeian

20. Mosaic of Neptune, Antioch.   )   Influence

21. Mosaic floor with the symbol of a cross.   )

22. A section of the conduit cut by Trajan to divert storm water from flooding Lower Seleucia.

23.24.25. Examples of marble decoration that once embellished the Public buildings of Perga.

26. Bas relief of an Actor's mask and that of a winged Harpie.

27. The main colonnaded street of Perga with the central water course fed from the Nymphaeum.

28 A similar water course in the main street of Antalya that has since been covered over.

29. The Agora with shop fronts that is reminiscent of the Georgian Period.

30. Relief of a cleaver and meat hook on the plinth of a butcher's counter.

31. The Hellenistic Theatre.

32. Marble Bas relief of Dionysus in his chariot in the Theatre at Perga.

33. Remains of the Aqueduct that brought water to Pisidian Antioch.

34. The site of the Temple to Augustus at Pisidian Antioch.

35. Part of a marble frieze from the Proplyon that gave onto the Temple of Augustus showing the relief of a poppy head.

36. Detail of the poppy head.

37. A field of opium poppies growing in a field near Pisidian Antioch.

38. A capitol lying amongst the corn stubble at Lystra. All that is left in situ of the Ancient city.

39. The site of ancient Derbe.

40. The inscription found by the Director of the Karaman Museum, the ancient Laranda, and now in the museum confirming that this was once the site of ancient Derbe.

41. One of the remote chapels of the Bin Bir Kilise on the summit of the Kara Dag Mountains.

42. Ruins of the Basilica of the Monastery at Alahan.

The Second Missionary Journey

43. The Periene Fountain at Corinth.

The Third Missionary Journey

44. The white calcified falls of Pammukale, the ancient Hierapolis.

45. Ruins of the great Theatre at Laodicea.

46. All that remains of the Nymphaeum that once lay at the junction of the two main streets of Laodicea.

47. The Martyrium of the Apostle Phillip who died in A.D. 80 at Hierapolis.

48. A section of marble frieze that fell from one of the lorries that took the treasures of Colossae for a hard core for the railway that was then being built through the Konya Plain.

49. The site of ancient Colossae.

50. Remains of the small Theatre or Odeon at ancient Colossae.

51. Statue of the Ephesian Diana.

52. Obverse and reverse of a silver tetradrachm showing the Bee as the emblem of the City, enlarged twice.

53. Curetes Street in Ephesus.

54. The Corinthian Temple to Hadrian in Curetes Street.

55. The Gate of Hercules and the Ram that was once the entrance to the Stata Agora but now separates the upper from the lower town.

56. The Sign cut into the paving of the Marble Street that slows the way to the Brothel.

57. The central Lavatories.

58. The Library of Celsus and the Triple Gate of Mazeus and Mithradates.

59. The Great Theatre.

60. The Chapel to the Virgin in the hills above Ephesus.

61. Interior of the Chapel.

62. The Tomb of St John.

63. The Basilica of St John built by Justinian.

64. The site of the Artemision.

65. The Agora at Miletus.

66. The Theatre at Miletus.

67. One of the two lions still in situ at the entrance to the Lion harbour at Miletus. A chain was slung from their mouths to protect the harbour when Miletus was threatened from the sea.

68. The Lion Harbour at Miletus.

69. The Arch of Modestus at Patara.

70. Two of five Portrait Busts from Ephesus

71. Two further Portrait Busts from Ephesus

72. The Tablet of the Tenth Legion still in situ in the ruins of their barracks by the Jaffa Gate in Jerusalem.

The Final Journey to Rome and Martyrdom

73. The vandalised tomb of St Nicholas at Demre.

74. The Lycian Tombs at Demre the ancient Myra that were antiquities in the days of St Paul.

75. The Statue of St Peter ~~Paul~~ in St Peters in Rome.

PREFACE

St Paul's letters which are generally considered to have been written between A.D. 40 and his death are largely in their original state and predate Acts and the Gospels. Of the Synoptic Gospels that of St Mark could have had its origins when Mark was with St Peter in Rome, but not written until after the death of St Peter, possibly around A.D. 70. The earliest passages in Greek from St Matthew's Gospel are recorded on fragments of papyri that were once a part of an early codex, and these are now in the possession of Magdalen College Oxford and could date to sometime before A.D. 90.

The Acts and the Gospels owe much to each other and to oral tradition, and also to a possible lost source known as 'Q', an abbreviation of 'Quelle'. However, they still have sufficient historical and archaeological truth for them to be taken at their face value. The letters of St Paul have been annotated and his every thought dissected by many scholars, possibly to the extent that even he would not have recognised some of their conclusions. But leaving all theological considerations to one side there are many questions that arise when endeavouring to correlate his Missionary Journeys with the various world events in his life, and the overall history of the period. In this respect it is helpful to try and picture the everyday existence and the lot of those who lived in the cities of Greece and Asia Minor at that time. The problems of everyday life that confronted Paul confront us today, possibly even more so, but contained in his letters there is a deal of advice and comment that is just as applicable to society today as it was to the Churches and his 'Saints'.

At that time the towns in Asia Minor were mostly the equivalent of small city states that had their own traditions and administration which, following the conquest of Alexander The Great, reflected their Hellenistic backgrounds. The Romans adapted much of these cultures to their own precepts whilst at the same time absorbing much of their indigenous religious heritage. This was the normal procedure after a Roman conquest. The Romans had a deal of religious tolerance which is reflected in the Temples of the Egyptian deities, Isis and Serapis; their ruins to be seen in many of the cities of the Empire, including Ephesus. These alien cults attracted many devotees as demonstrated in a painted frieze to be seen in the Villa of the Mysteries in Pompeii, one that depicts the Egyptian goddess Isis.

After the crucial defeat of Antony and Cleopatra at the battle of Actium in 31 B.C., the Roman Empire had many years of peace and prosperity under the administration of Augustus, and a prosperity that was reflected in the cities of Asia Minor where Greek was regarded as a second tongue. Many philosophers went from Asia Minor to Rome where they often made a name for themselves and inspired a considerable following. A case in point was that of the Sceptics who came from Scepsis, a city that lay in the hills a little to the East of the port of Alexander Troas. It was the Greek influence and culture in these old cities of Asia Minor that produced the philosophic turn of mind, in contradistinction to the number of eminent lawyers who came to Rome from many of the old established families of the Roman expatriates in North Africa. Possibly one of the most notable being Marcus Cornelius Fronto who was born in Cirta, to graduate from Carthage University, and finally end his days in a luxurious villa in

Pompeii that had scenes from North Africa frescoed on its garden walls. It is noteworthy that St Paul was born when Augustus was Emperor and lived under the rule of four succeeding Emperors, namely, Tiberius, Caligula, Claudius and finally that of Nero.

The Jews of the Diaspora were to be found in increasing numbers in the cities of the Empire where they enjoyed a religious tolerance and a degree of authority that the Roman administration allowed and this they exploited to the full. They could be numbered in their thousands and were so widespread that Seneca later wrote, 'The customs of these most infamous people have already gained such influence that they have been introduced into all countries; they the conquered, have given laws to the conquerors and so they remained in their communities well into the fourth century A.D., jealously guarding their rights'.

During the first century A.D., the Jewish communities in Palestine fell into various sects and parties that had differing religious views. Of these the two most important were the Sadducees and the Pharisees, and those who belonged to the Qumran and Samaritan communities.

The Sadducees organised and were responsible for the Temple affairs and from this community the High Priests were elected. They considered their interpretation of the Law to be fundamental and correct and that resurrection of the dead was not an option to be considered. Those who fell foul of their code could not expect any excess of charity from them and they were, more often than not, cruelly dealt with; it was they who brought their grievances before the Roman administration, often not to be dealt with to their entire satisfaction. Generally they were from the wealthy and select families of Jerusalem, and what could well be the ruins of six of their opulent dwellings have been excavated in the Herodian district of Jerusalem. They still have the remnants of frescos on their ruined walls that are indicative of what was once a sophisticated way of life.

On the other hand the Pharisees had a broader outlook and did believe in the concept of Resurrection; one of the major differences of opinion to be aired when Paul, as a Pharisee, confronted the Sanhedrin when attending for the last time the Feast of Pentecost in Jerusalem. It was the Pharisees, however, who were more spiritually inclined and the pillars of the Synagogues whom Paul set out to influence with the Gospel. The Scribes were the doctors of the Law who arbitrated on the more remote aspects of Judaism, and as such were not at all popular. Mark records in XII 38-40 'As he taught, he said, Beware of the Scribes, who like to walk around in long robes, and be greeted with respect in the marketplaces, and to have the best seats in the synagogues and places of honour at banquets! They devour widows' houses and for the sake of appearance say long prayers. They will receive the greater condemnation'. Not an unfamiliar picture in some sections of society today! The Essenes of Qumran were those who led an ascetic and reclusive life in the wilderness, patiently waiting the coming of the Messiah, whilst the Samaritans quietly went their own way.

They all conducted their lives by the Law of Moses, and all observed the rite of Circumcision that was fundamental to their religious identity. To the Jews it was the rigid observance and the importance of the rite that was the major cause of the difficulties that Paul had throughout his life with the Diaspora. Juvenal wrote of the Diaspora, 'The Jews refuse to point the way to anyone not worshipping with the same rites, and will conduct none but the circumcised to the desired fountain'; when it came to the conversion of the Gentiles this, for Paul, was the great stumbling block.

However, it seems that there could have been a number of the younger Jews amongst the Grecian families who did not accept circumcision, no doubt preferring the easier way of life that was open to them in the Baths and the Palestrae where they could disport themselves, in the nude, without fear of embarrassment. There were also the Proselytes, those who were not of Jewish lineage but had fully accepted the Jewish faith, and on their conversion had endured the rite of circumcision. There were then the 'God fearers', others too who were not of Jewish stock but remained on the fringes of the Jewish Law by refusing to submit to circumcision, observing only the Dietary restrictions.

Paul's attitude to the Dietary laws is reflected in his comment on the question of what the Jews regarded as impure food, and is recorded in Romans 14. 14. 'I know and am persuaded in the Lord Jesus that nothing is unclean in itself, but it is unclean for anyone who thinks it unclean', and he goes on to say 'For the kingdom of God is not food and drink but righteousness and peace and joy in the Holy Spirit'. This echoes a passage in St Mark VII, 15, 'There is nothing outside a person that by going in can defile, but the things that come out are what defile', i.e. his thoughts and deeds.

The dates of Paul' s missionary journeys, his conversion on the Damascus road, his stay in Ephesus, and his trial, or trials, before Nero in Rome cannot be accurately determined, and though various authorities differ as to the actual dates concerned there cannot be a great discrepancy in their various conclusions, for certain fixed points in History give a guide. For instance Festus, who replaced Felix as procurator of Judaea, died in Caesarea when on his tour of duty in A. D. 62. Nero then sent Albinus from Rome to replace him, a factual appointment that has been recorded by both Eusebius and the historian Josephus; but there was a lapse of time between the death of Festus and the arrival of Albinus to take up the appointment, a time when Judaea had no authoritative administration. During this hiatus Ananias, the then High Priest in Jerusalem, seized the opportunity to bring James, the leader of the Jerusalem Church and the brother of Jesus, before the court of the Sanhedrin on charges of breaking the Jewish Law. The outcome was inevitable, he was martyred: it was about this time too when Paul was in his hired house in Rome awaiting the pleasure of Nero.

There are strong indications that Paul was released on this occasion, to be brought before Nero at a later date for a second trial. Eusebius, who was bishop in Caesarea in A.D. 315, was of this opinion and quotes 11 Timothy IV. 16-l7. 'At my first defense no one came to my support, but all deserted me. May it not be counted against them! But the Lord stood by me and gave me strength, so that through me the message might be fully proclaimed and all the Gentiles might hear it, so I was rescued from the lion's mouth'. The lion's mouth being Paul's reference to Nero himself, and possibly an oblique reference to the games in the amphitheatres where criminals were savaged by lions and other beasts.

Luke ends the Acts without any mention or comment on Paul's trial, and omits to give any indication as to its outcome; this begs the question as to whether he was present at the hearing, or not? If not was he still in Rome? For if he had been it is not likely that he would not have supported Paul. However, in 11 Timothy IV, 11, which could refer to his second imprisonment, he mentions the fact that Demas has left the Church altogether preferring the delights of the world, and records that Titus was in Dalmatia and Crescens in Galatia, possibly on Church business. Here he states that Luke is with him and asks Timothy, who was then bishop in Ephesus, to come to him and bring Mark with him.

These are not the only questions that arise. One wonders why he confided so little to Luke regarding the years he spent between his escape from Damascus and his Joining Barnabus in Antioch. He merely records having spent three years in Arabia. In 11 Corinthians XI. 25. he recounts having been beaten with rods and stoned, incidents documented as having occurred at Lystra and elsewhere, but he also records having been shipwrecked three times, on one occasion being 'a night and a day I was adrift at sea'. Luke has described the shipwreck on the rocks of Malta in graphic detail, but the other two incidents must have occurred when Paul was travelling alone, and it is frustrating that he doesn't give any details as to when and where they occurred.

Some have suggested that Onesimus, after having gone back to Colossae with the letter from Paul to Philemon, returned to Rome to help Paul with his ministry. However, this supposition is not entirely logical for it is patent that Onesimus, whilst undergoing his conversion, spent some time with Paul in Rome. His Journey back to Colossae would have taken some time, as would his return Journey to Rome had Philemon been willing, by which time Paul could well have been brought before Nero and acquitted. After his acquittal it is not feasible that Paul would have remained in Rome. In his letter to Philemon, taken by Onesimus on his return to Colossae, Paul states his intention of visiting Colossae on his acquittal, Philemon 22, 'one thing more- prepare a guest room for me, for I am hoping through your prayers to be restored to you'. Obviously the goings on in the Galatian Churches, as reported by Epaphras when he especially went to Rome to see Paul, needed his attention to bring them into line. Onesimus, after his leaving Rome with the letter to Philemon, in which Paul says I would have, 'wanted to keep him with me, so that he might be of service to me in your place during my imprisonment for the Gospel' (Philemon 13). He is at pains to name in his letters those who loyally helped him in his ministry; had Onemisus returned from Colossae after giving the letter to Philemon he would have surely mentioned the fact. The site of Colossae was rarely visited in years past, being somewhat remote, but now it figures on the itinerary of several tours, in spite of the fact that next to nothing remains to be seen, but its location and the nature of the site must surely stir the imagination.

These are only a few of the many questions that cannot be answered with any degree of certainty, but they do give rise to a great deal of interesting speculation.

CHAPTER 1

The Years before Antioch.

I t is only in recent years that the antiquities of Turkey, the Asia Minor of the Bible, have become more familiar to the world at large. Even in the late fifties and early sixties it is debatable if many knew the exact location of Ephesus, let alone Tarsus. It was the antiquities of Greece, Turkey's near neighbour, that were renowned for their grandeur in spite of the fact many of those in Turkey were as equally impressive. It is the present day phenomenon of the 'Package Tour' that has done much to bring about Turkey's inclusion on the Tourist agenda, and made the many interesting aspects of the country more accessible.

The aura of remoteness to Western eyes had much to do with the 1914- 1918 war; possibly it was the battle of Gallipoli in 1915, and the exploits of Lawrence of Arabia, that did much to put Turkey in a bad light; in the aftermath of the war their peoples being prone to unfavourable comments in the press and apt to be treated with a degree of suspicion, an atmosphere that took some generations to alter for the better. I can well remember in my childhood being told by my mother, having erred to her extreme exasperation, that I was 'As Wiley as a Turk'.

In common with many other countries today Turkey is not alone in having its problems, and these have become more apparent in the far Eastern sector. However, when travelling in this region in the past I have had few difficulties, apart from the roads: throughout my many journeys in Turkey I have experienced nothing but kindness and hospitality. But it has been difficult at times when accepting this hospitality, and other spontaneous desires to help, to know when to avoid a difficult situation and not to offend by proffering some monetary recompense. A case in point occurred when on a journey from Ani, on the Russian border, to Dogubayazit where I arrived with a boiling engine, the fan belt having melted when crossing by Mount Ararat. The local mechanic diagnosed a faulty thermostat and his friend, who was sitting in his workshop chatting and sipping a glass of hot apple tea, took endless trouble in taking me to the various depots in the somewhat rural town to search for a replacement. Having finally found one and having had it fitted I paid the mechanic and offered to take his friend for a non alcoholic drink.

This generated the utmost fury as I had unwittingly abused his code of hospitality to one in need, and had insulted him by offering something that in his eyes amounted to a monetary recompense: highly indignant be went back to sit and sulk on a stool outside his own small shop that was further up the street. His friend, the mechanic, was very amused at his antics so I left some money for them to have a mutual drink later, and then followed him up the street to explain myself and the concept of English hospitality. In the end we parted friends, and early next day when I passed his shop on the way to lake Van, I saw him stand on his stool to wave me off and shout his wishes for a safe journey.

Made up roads in the country some twenty five years ago were few and far between. The one from Anamur to Mersin eventually branched to Antioch in the South, with the other going North through the Taurus Mountains to Kayseri, one of the many ancient Caesareas, and

Ankara. The main highway from Istanbul to Ankara had to be avoided at all costs; it was narrow and lethal and monopolised by incessant heavy transport that brooked no argument. No road existed along the South coast from Bodrum to Fethiye, nor was there one between Kas and Antalya, only tracks that Dame Freya Stark covered by horse when writing her book on Alexander the Great.

There are vast differences in the country terrain and its scenery. Around Adiyaman in Commagene, and Harran beyond Salinurfa in the Far East, are vast plains that once were harvested by families camping out amongst the crops in straw huts, something of the past for all is now reaped with the aid of the John Deere harvesters. In contrast are the weird landscapes of Cappadocia with their numerous cave monasteries and churches that date from the ninth to the twelfth centuries; all the work of dedicated monks and anchorites who have laboriously hewn them into the tufa cones and cliffs, then to decorate them with frescoed scenes from the New Testament and make them veritable museums of early Byzantine art. They now lie amongst the vineyards and some do service as pigeon lofts.

Tea and nuts, and now coffee, are grown along the Black Sea coast to be sold in the markets of Trabizond, a fascinating and historic city that is the gateway to the incomparable scenery of the Pontic Alps. Apple orchards abound; Napoleon cherries that yearly flood the barrows of Istanbul street traders have now found their way to our supermarket shelves. Though the South coast is still rich with citrus groves many by Mersin have been grubbed out for urban development. But the banana plantations to the East of Alanya have spread almost down to the sea. Wild flowers abound, spectacular are the tracts of large pale blue iris that grow in droves by Ararat, and the acres of rose fields by Isparta that give a heady scent in summer and go into the production of rose liquor and jam.

The archaeological sites are all too numerous to mention but stretch from Hattusas, the Hittite capital that Tutmosis failed to subdue in 1459 B.C. at Kadesh, to the tomb of King Midas in Gordium where his skull has been found. There are the ruins of Sardis, Capital of the wealthy Croesus of Lydia until he died in 546 B.C, and his riches from the particles of gold brought down from the mountains by the local river, and trapped in the fleece of sheep that he suspended in it; at least so it is said. The river still flows, and the site of the furnaces where the first ever coinage was minted can still to be seen.

But of all it is the many ruins of the Greco Roman cities that litter the Western seaboard, together with those in Cilicia and elsewhere, that are impressive and testify to the might of Rome. Sites despised in the past and so neglected that much of their important and irreplaceable artefacts have been destroyed. Now those such as Aphrodisias are being brought back to something akin to their erstwhile splendour; not a few of them, such as Ephesus, having been once a part of a life that was familiar to St Paul.

It was early in September and the weather unusually hot for the time of year; in spite of being high up in the Taurus Mountains travelling was still not very comfortable. The journey from England through the Balkans in a Morris 1100 had not been without incident: I had previously found out from the Turkish Authorities in London that car hire in Turkey was not then available, and I was now on my way to Cappadocia to satisfy a long felt ambition to see the early Byzantine frescoes in the cave churches of Goreme and Urgup. The journey from Ephesus had had its moments. The Authorities in London had also seen fit not to warn me that many of the roads in Turkey were nothing but dirt tracks, and the one between Ephesus and Antalya was not an exception, some four hundred and seventy kilometres of a track that produced clouds of dust.

Shortly after leaving Denizly, some many kilometres from Antalya, the accelerator cable snapped; almost the last straw for there was obviously no hope of having any help available for miles. However, a piece of stick from the roadside was enough to wedge the throttle open, but this meant the engine then had to be controlled by the ignition switch. After a tedious journey Antalya was finally reached in the early hours of the morning, but luckily enough a 'Pension' in the municipal gardens was keeping late hours and gave me a meal and a room. The cable was repaired the next day, but between Antalya and Alyana the engine began to seriously overheat, and this not due to the hot weather. A local mechanic working in a tin shed in Alanya gave his considered opinion that 'the car was sick', but after having worked on it all night, and all for the princely sum of five pounds, it was produced the next morning with the warning that, as no replacement gasket was available he had had to make do with the old one and this necessitated the oil level having to be watched.

I had been told by the authorities before leaving Ephesus that the section of road between Alanya and Anamur through the Taurus mountains was open, had this not been the case a considerable detour inland from Antalya to Kanya would have been necessary in order to reach Cappadocia. The coastal road from Antalya to Alanya was surfaced and in good order and so it remained to a little beyond the town of Dirmitash, but when it began to ascend into the Taurus the inevitable dirt track took over. This, however, was negotiable until I came up to the backside of a bulldozer that was carving from the hillside the last stretch of track necessary to join that pushed through from Annamur. To enable the low clearance of the Morris to get through this section the large clods of earth turned up by the bulldozer had to be flattened with a spade loaned by the driver, who had pulled off as far as he could into the cliff side. Since then I have used the road on many occasions when on the way to Antioch; it has magnificent views and is an essential link between Eastern and Western Turkey. Prior to its construction travellers to the West from Antioch, Adana, and Mersin had of necessity to go by sea; failing that by Tarsus and the Cilician Gates, or by Silifke through Karaman to Konya.

Those travelling throughout Turkey today do not have to face the hazards of some thirty years ago, but in some small measure they then did bring to mind the difficulties that must have been the normal lot for those who ventured abroad in the first century A.D., not the least of them St Paul while on his missionary journeys. A mission that culminated some two centuries, in A.D. 325, with the convocation of Nicaea where a conclave of Metropolitan Bishops, brought together by Constantine the Great, passed the edict where by the Christian Church was to finally displace the many Pagan Cults that had, until then, been the way of life for the Greeks and Romans of the ancient world.

However, in spite of the often bitter arguments that came about in the following years as to the nature of Christ's divinity and his teaching, arguments that resulted in the formation of many various schisms each proclaiming their infallibility as to the truth, the message of St Paul still remains loud and clear throughout the world today. Through the ages the Pauline letters have been a source of great inspiration for many, but equally disregarded by countless others. His tendentious and difficult character can still provoke feelings of profound irritation for in many instances he is obscure and ambiguous; at times almost hysterical in moods that could swing from compassion for those of his loyal followers, many of them to be named in his letters with the condemnation of those who would not see eye to eye with his tenets and his teaching. For many others he has short shrift but constantly exhorts those who follow him to lead a better life, and for those who desert him and fall by the wayside he castigates in no small measure. He appears to have little sense of humour and is sometimes tactless in his behaviour, yet his message to his 'Saints' is as applicable today as it was then.

To wander through the ruins of the ancient cities of Asia Minor, Greece, Syria, and elsewhere is to appreciate the way of life that was then familiar to Paul, and the benefits brought by the Roman administration. The mosaics that once graced the floors of public institutions and the villas of the wealthy, together with the many inscriptions that have survived the centuries are indications of the fact that human behaviour has not changed one whit in any walk of life. As has been said the problems that beset the ancient world are still with us today, and no doubt they will continue to beset the generations of the future.

The Crucifixion might possibly have seen the end of a local and bitter dispute between Christ and the Jewish factions in Palestine; the end of one of the many religious confrontations that were then commonplace in Judaea and apt to break out periodically during the Roman occupation when Tiberias, Vespasian, and Titus were the Emperors; disputes that, before they got out of hand, had to be contained and put down in order to preserve Roman law and order. But for Paul it is possible that the concept of the Church would have taken a great deal longer to spread abroad, and furthermore would not have embraced the Gentiles in the way and to the extent that it did, for those who accepted the teachings of the Apostles would then have been tied inevitably to the more fundamental aspects of the Jewish Law.

It is very noticeable too that at this time in Palestine the Sadducees and the Pharisees, who made up the greater part of Jewish society, were not at all prone to conduct their lives with any excess of charity. Doubtless it was this pervading social climate that prompted the Parable of 'The good Samaritan'. This lack of charity on the part of a great majority of the Sadducees and the Pharisees, also apparent in other sections of the populace, is demonstrated in the story of Christ's encounter with the woman at the well in Nablus. Fallen women and others beyond the pale such as tax collectors were the outcasts of Jewish society and Jesus was open to vindictive criticism for consorting with them, even from his own Apostles when they took him to task for allowing himself to be anointed by such a one, according to St. Luke VIII 37, with a costly spikenard, a woman whom St John pinpoints as being Mary the sister of Martha, St. John XII 3.

For the most part it would appear that the Samaritan Jews, despised by the Sadducees and the Levites who were responsible for the rituals of the sanctuary and had charge of the Tabernacle, were the few who were capable of showing a degree of compassion for others.

Jesus also had little regard for the Samaritans, feeling his mission to the Jews was not applicable to their religious tenets, and went so far as to warn the Apostles not to associate with them; but in spite of this he made the good Samaritan in Luke 10, 30-36. the centre figure in his parable, this possibly to demonstrate that, in His estimation, The Sanhedrin and their associates were an even lower form of life than the Samaritans themselves.

The descendants of these Samaritan Jews are still to be found In Nablus, the ancient Neapolis and Old Testament Sechem, living quietly in an enclosed community in a small Ghetto where they are very hospitable. They still dress in their traditional way and keep the Passover on the hills above the town; but their most treasured possession is a Pentateuch inscribed on a lengthy roll of sheepskin enclosed in an elaborate silver case. This they keep in a small and unpretentious Synagogue and firmly believe it to date from the fifth generation after Aaron; but be that as it may they are more than willing to show the ancient scroll to any who are interested and take the trouble to visit them.

Life also had its problems for the Gentiles. Those Greeks and Romans who lived in the Hellenistic Cities of the Empire during the last centuries B.C. and the first centuries A.D. At this time the gladiatorial contests and the gory spectacles in the amphitheatres were an essential part of life, though these were not as popular with the Greeks as they were with the Romans. Here scant regard was shown for life both human and otherwise; scenes that often culminated in acts of barbaric cruelty and slaughter.

In 1 Cor VII 1 to 16. Paul gives his views on marriage and begins by answering certain questions put to him. 'Now concerning the matters about which you wrote. It is well for a man not to touch a woman, but because of cases of sexual immorality each man should have his own wife and each wife her own husband'. He then at length discusses the marriage state and gives his observations as to the behaviour of those who are committed and those who are not. However, to the unmarried and widows in verses 7 and 8 he extols his own celibacy and then recommends them to do likewise. He again comes back to the subject in Ephesians V. where he once more deplores and warns against the vices of the world and gives his advice to wives and husbands.

In general Paul seems to have had little in common with the opposite sex. Does he sum up his attitude in 1 Cor VII 14 35 where he remarks that 'women should be silent in the churches and not permitted to speak, but should be subordinate. If there is anything they desire to know, let them ask their husbands at home'. However there are instances where he shows affection and regard such as in the cases of Thecla, Priscilla, Phoebe of Cenchrea, and Aphia of Colossae.

There is the question as to whether Paul had taken a wife at some time or other. Jewish males were expected to marry between the ages of eighteen and twenty, if by then they had not done so they were deemed to be somewhat peculiar. There are no indications in his letters, or in Acts, of his having embraced the married state. However, after the Crucifixion his close involvement with the Sanhedrin in the persecutions of the followers of Jesus brooks the further question as to whether he was, in fact, a member of that body. That he could have been a member is hinted at in Acts XXVI 10 and possibly elected in recognition of the part he played in the martyrdom of Stephen, with authority from the chief priests, 'I not only locked up many saints in prison, but I also cast my vote against them when they were condemned to death- I tried to force them to blaspheme; and being furiously enraged at them, I pursued them to foreign cities'. Following the stoning of Stephen, to which he consented (Acts VIII 1), he went to the High Priest asking 'for letters to the Synagogues at Damascus' to authorise his investigations there, and to bring back to Jerusalem in bondage for trial those unfortunates he might have found wanting (Acts IX 1 & 2).

If a member of the Sanhedrin it follows that Paul must have had a wife, for it was a statutory requirement of the Sanhedrin that all their members should have the blessings of a wife and children, and this on the assumption that It might encourage them to exhibit more compassion for others. For the most part it was a premise that seemed not to work out when it came to the point, for any considered by the Sanhedrin to have transgressed the Law, or thought to have been guilty of even a whiff of a blasphemy, was swiftly brought before them, tried, and if found guilty the subject of a swift and summary retribution, and this was universal and not solely confined to the Jerusalem Synagogues for the Sanhedrin claimed authority over all Synagogues and Jewry however widespread. There were, however, a few significant members of that body, such as Nicodemus and Joseph of Aramathea, who were cast in a different mould. Paul makes little reference to his personal life; it is what he has left unsaid that is intriguing and irritating. However, he does give the impression that he never entertained the marriage state for he makes no mention of a possible wife or a family anywhere in Acts or his letters; as has been noted in Cor VII 1 - 17 he records his celibacy when he gives advice to couples on how they should behave together, and to those who feel that celibacy is not for them.

In 2 Cor XII 7, together with his other infirmities, he complains about his 'Thorn in the Flesh' and this too has given rise to a deal of speculation. Here again it has been suggested that it might refer to some repressed sexual hang up with its attendant frustrations, and of this there are hints to be found in 1 Cor 7. There could have been a latent and suppressed tendency to homosexuality that was his undisclosed 'Thorn in the flesh'. In the Greek culture homosexuality and sexual variety were ways of life that spilled over into the Roman world as described in the Satyricon of Petronicus, one who was a native of Bithynia and a friend of Nero. But for the Jews it was a practice that could merit a sojourn in Hell. This would have been quite enough to deter Paul and give him mental anguish. He did, however, have a very close relationship with Timothy of Lystra, and to a certain extent with Titus, but there are not the slightest grounds in Acts or the letters to suggest any impropriety. In 11 Cor he almost revels in his other infirmities and regards them as a warning not to be too confident whilst further passages hint at periods of depression. The various maladies to which he alludes were obviously a periodic source of trouble.

Sir William Ramsay has suggested that Paul's ill health could have been due to recurrent bouts of malaria. Outbreaks of malaria were a part of life in much of Asia Minor at that time, and these can still occur for one broke out in and around Adana when I was there in the late nineteen seventies. These bouts would have left him very debilitated after periods of unpleasant rigors with attendant acute headaches, and the fact that he did suffer such headaches has been mentioned in the writings of Tertullian: however, he does not substantiate this in any way and it could be merely surmise on his part.

Paul also mentions having trouble with his eyes but does not describe the symptoms; it could be the bouts of acute headaches, if they did occur, that affected his sight. On the other hand one must not rule out the fact that this ailment might have been the result of the many arduous Journeys that be undertook in all weathers, especially and mostly during the summer months when the intense glare of the sun was reflected back from what must, on many occasions, have been harsh landscapes.

The Acts of Paul and Thecla, thought to have been written by a church proselyte in the late second century A.D. but now considered for the most part to be legendary, describes him as, 'A man of moderate stature, with scanty hair and crooked legged, having blue eyes with bushy eyebrows that met above a large long nose'. It was John Malais, an historian of the sixth century who also recorded the fact that his eyes were blue, that he had a ruddy complexion together with a full grey beard, and added the fact that his nose was hooked. Nicephorus Callistus writing in the fourteenth century mentioned that his beard was pointed, and he added the details that he was slightly built and a little bent. All in all a not a very prepossessing picture of the Saint, but in spite of these disadvantages it seems that he had at times the expression of an angel and was blessed with a grace and poise. These descriptions are very late, but it could be that his likeness in gold, as well as the traditional likeness of St Peter, has been recorded on many of the glass tablets that were buried with the dead in the catacombs in Rome. This general likeness, easily recognisable, can also be seen in frescos dating from the ninth to twelfth centuries that decorate the interiors of many of the cave churches of Cappadocia where he is often portrayed in conjunction with Peter.

It is known that Paul was born in Tarsus in the Province of Cilicia and Syria, and is thought to have taken place around 2 or 1 B.C. when Augustus was Emperor; if this was so it would then make him, more or less, a contemporary of Jesus. It is, however, quite impossible to date accurately the birth of Jesus[1], or for that matter the Crucifixion, but the Nativity must have taken place at some time before 4 B.C., for the death of Herod the Great occurred in the early part of that year[2]. Thus an approximate date of 5-6 B.C. for the Nativity would seem to be reasonable. The reference in the Gospels to the star of Bethlehem could be a pointer and of some significance. The German astrologer John Kepler noted on 17th Dec 1603 the conjunction of the planets Saturn and Jupiter In the constellation of Pices, and calculated that this could also have occurred in 7 B.C. However, more recently astronomers from the Royal Greenwich Observatory, The Mullard Space Science Laboratory in Dorking and Newcastle University have suggested that the Star of Bethlehem was a Nova, an exploding star that was recorded by the

---

[1] Though early on in his Gospel St Luke records the fact that Jesus was born during the reign of Herod the Great his statement that it also took place at the time when the census of the population of Judaea was being taken for tax purposes, when Qurinius was governor of Syria, is not accurate. Here St Luke has muddled the dates with the census that took place around A.D. 6 and not 6 B.C. a date confirmed by Josephus who has been proved very accurate in his historical observations. However, some astronomers have suggested that the Star of Bethlehem could have been the Nova that was visible to the Chinese for some two months during the Han dynasty, around 5 B.C.

[2] Jesus. Ian Wilson.

Chinese during the Han Dynasty in 5 B.C. If this happened to be the case it would then make Jesus the senior by a few years[3].

Paul's family were prominent members of the Jews of the Diaspora who lived in Tarsus. Jews of the Diaspora were to be found in all the cities of the Roman Empire where there was an assured potential for trade. From the early part of the second century B.C. they were an integral part of their populations and they often exerted a great deal of influence on the financial prosperity of the cities they inhabited; but they were not universally popular communities and tended to be disliked, in spite of many of them having absorbed the Hellenic culture to such an extent that the rest of Jewry referred to them as, 'The Grecians'.

In the main the Diaspora kept themselves to themselves and made very little effort to mix culturally with those who were not of the Jewish Faith and they would, moreover, go to any lengths to maintain what they considered to be their rights. An edict of Augustus gave them exemption from being conscripted into the Legions, possibly because of their dietary restrictions which could well have made them something of a liability when on active service, and this coupled with their strict observation of the Law[4]. They were also given a complete religious tolerance that enabled them to go their own way, regardless of Roman or Greek susceptibilities and the inherent cultural faiths of the State; and they were also allowed to raise monies for the Jerusalem Temple tax. These privileges were at times apt to make them a source of profound irritation to those Greeks and Romans who were their contemporary citizens. However, though they could not be conscripted for military service a number of them were employed in the Legions as slaves, many of them eventually being able to buy their freedom, or have it granted to them in various other circumstances. The Jewish community that appeared in Rome in the last centuries B.C. could well have had their origins in those who had thus gained their independence and with their freedom had opted to make their homes in the city.

It was unfortunate that the dissensions of the Diaspora would end, more often than not, in rioting, incidents borne out by inscriptions that are still extant and relate to their disputes. One such upheaval occurred in the year A.D. 115 when Trajan was Emperor. The very large Jewish community then living in Cyrene in Libya, the home town of Simon who carried the Cross, began a riot that escalated to such an extent it bordered on civil war. In the process the greater part of Cyrene was destroyed and it fell to Hadrian, who succeeded Trajan, to spend vast sums of money on rebuilding the devastated areas, a project that was necessary to bring Cyrene back into a habitable state. This event took place some forty five years after the death of Paul in Rome. To the governors who administered the far flung Colonies of the Empire and to the Gentile peoples who were part of their populations the antics of the Diaspora could be a periodically recurring nuisance.

Paul refers to his lineage in Phil 3:5 and records that his family were dedicated Pharisees and descendants of the Tribe of Benjamin. It is possible that his father was a maker of tents, or

---

[3] David Clark. Royal Greenwich Observatory. John Parkinson, Mullard Space Laboratory, Dorking. Richard Stephenson, Newcastle University.

[4] It was not unknown, but a very unusual occurrence, for Jews to be enlisted into the Legions; as a result religious tensions could very well have developed. As a whole the Legions were devoted to the god Mithras, one of his Temples having been discovered in London and one that was obviously used by the Roman occupation in the first and second centuries.

a cloth merchant with a family textile business that manufactured Cilicium; a much sought after cloth that was peculiar to the Province of Cilicia and a thriving industry in Tarsus. This was woven from goats' hair and of this there was an abundant supply from the herds that grazed the Cilician plains. They still do.

The tents of the present day Bedouin are made from a similar material, and when Morton visited Tarsus in 1933 the cloth was still being manufactured on ancient and primitive looms in the street of the weavers. The looms were of a type that was common to the Greeks and the Romans of the early centuries and their construction is known from paintings to be seen on much of the pottery of the period. But in spite of making numerous enquiries in 1984 and searching for the street that Morton described it could not be found, and no one appeared to have any knowledge of its whereabouts: I could only conclude that it must have disappeared into the limbo of the past. Sadly, an unfortunate occurrence for the design of these looms and their method of use was something that had survived from remote antiquity. There must still be a few weavers still plying their skills somewhere in Tarsus even though they seem to have become relics of the past since Morton described them.

However, there were still those in old Tarsus who carried on their respective trades in time honoured fashion. Vendors of spices sat on chairs with their goods displayed on the pavement about their feet and nearby the grain merchants congregated around their antique scales, busily absorbed in weighing out the harvest before filling the sacks held open by their fellow workers **(Figure 1)** the spilled grains glittering gold in shafts of fierce sunlight as they fell to the floor.

The streets of shut up shops looked much as they could have done in Roman times, bright with garments hung beneath striped canvas awnings, and brilliant too with rolls of coloured cloths stacked by the shutters in gaudy heaps. In the street of the copper smiths the artisans were melting down copper from piles of antique Ottoman dishes preparatory to hammering the recovered metal into new cauldrons and cooking pots, and at a nearby corner, in the shade of a tattered awning that had seen better days, an itinerant cobbler was doing his utmost to repair a heap of ancient foot wear. Others pushed their barrows loaded with oranges and purple aubergines through the streets, a vivid splash of colour in the bright sunlight **(Figure 2)**, and all this intermingled with the clinking cups and the brass trappings of the water sellers, the bicycles and the popping motor scooters.

The welcome in the streets was open and friendly, and those who saw your interest in their wares would want to know your history and be eager to tell you about themselves. This was the old Tarsus of a few years ago **(Figure 3)**. By 1988 it too was rapidly becoming a thing of the past though one was still made very welcome. Tarsus now has an industrial population of 160,000 and has succumbed in no small measure to the developer syndrome. The old road through the Taurus Mountains and the Cilician Gates, once trod by Xenophon and Alexander the Great, is today a busy motor way that has swept history irreverently aside. Tarsus is still 'No mean city', but not as Paul meant in the words that Luke records in Acts XXI 39, 'I am a man, a Jew of Tarsus, a City in Cilicia, a citizen of no mean City' and this to the chief Captain of the Guard in Jerusalem.

In the first century A.D. Tarsus was one of the major cities in Asia Minor that had a Hellenistic culture with Greek as the predominant tongue, a fact brought out in Acts 21 37-38 when Paul said unto the chief captain 'may I say something to you'? to have the reply 'Do you know Greek'? The town's administration was the responsibility of the City Fathers, for being a 'Civitas Libra' a free city like Antioch it had the right of self government without the presence of a Roman garrison. However, the Jewish community enjoyed all the privileges that were open to the citizens but they could not be elected to any Municipal office, nor could they take part in any aspect of the administration. Paul's family must have fallen into a slightly different category and had some considerable means for, even though the male members could not be elected to any official position they all had, by inheritance, the rare privilege of full Roman citizenship, including Paul.

Quite how it came about has not been recorded and remains a mystery, it may have been granted for some outstanding services to the Empire[5], but for all that many Romans had to acquire this privilege for a considerable sum of money thus Paul, not only being a Jew of the Diaspora but also a citizen of Rome, could enjoy all the advantages of that status. Being a Jew he could not be conscripted into the Legions and as a Roman citizen could not be flogged: as distinct from Jesus who was so abused by the Romans. Furthermore, being a Jew he was not obliged to pay homage to any of the Pantheon of Roman deities, advantages he made full use of and with some pride, as is apparent in Acts XXIII 28 where he tells the chief captain that 'I was born free'.

In Corinthians II 11, 24, he records having been beaten by the Jews on five occasions receiving forty strokes save one. It was the custom to Inflict 39 strokes to ensure there was no miscount and to avoid the infliction of 41 strokes in an enthusiastic error. But in the instance described in Acts XVI 37 Paul, when beaten by the Romans and thrust into prison Invokes his Roman citizenship and here, with his hackles up, he indignantly insists that the Magistrates came in person to release him and his companions. His Roman citizenship was a problem for the Roman administration. It prevented them from taking instant action against him, as they could with other erring members of the populace, including Jesus, who were not citizens of Rome.

When on his journeys his somewhat lack of tact in the Synagogues and his militant approach when spreading the Gospel were major factors in provoking the riots that often ensued, events that usually ended with his expulsion from the cities concerned. He must thus have acquired a considerable reputation with the Roman authorities in his ability to disrupt the peace of the Jewish communities concerned.

---

[5] The Libertines and Paul's Roman citizenship. During the Civil Wars a great number of Jews became slaves, to be later manumitted and given Roman citizenship. Acts 6.9. records "Then some of those who belonged to the synagogue of the Freedmen, as it was called, (in other words The Libertines), Cyrenians, Alexandrians, and others of those from Cilicia and Asia, stood up and argued with Stephen". Both Philo and Tacitus record how numerous the Libertini were throughout the Empire, and it is possible that Paul, together with other Cilician Jews, was one of the 'Libertino patre natus', the Cilician Libertines. (See Dr Wieseler, Chronology of the Apostles, Gottingen 1848). It has been estimated by some early writers that there were some 480 synagogues in Jerusalem and the environs, quite possibly an exaggeration, the more important having their own schools located apart from the place of worship but in the same building. Some were renowned Schools of Divinity.

Both Strabo and Cicero have left accounts of Tarsus as it was in the last centuries B.C. Cicero in particular for he lived there when governor of the Province of Cilicia in 50, B.C., and both he and Strabo have recorded the city as being one of Colonnaded streets, Market places, Marble Temples, Nymphaeums, and Public baths with their associated Palestrae. Every city had its public baths, and often more than one establishment, for they were popular centres where the citizens could congregate, relax, and indulge in idle gossip. Apart from the bath facilities many had libraries and rest rooms where the more elderly could spend their leisure whilst the young, the adolescent, and the more mature who were still active, disported themselves, usually in the naked state, in the Palestrae. Life as it was in the baths during the last centuries B.C. and the first centuries A.D. is graphically illustrated in the mosaic floors of these establishments in Ostia, the Port for Rome; they were in fact an essential institution throughout the cities of the ancient world. But life in the baths could be noisy and raucous, and not only in the daylight hours for Seneca, who lived adjacent to one of them in Italy, wrote bitterly about the perpetual cacophony that went on from dusk till dawn, thus giving him endless nights of little sleep.

Though Paul was a native of Tarsus and able to speak Greek it is doubtful if he was Hellenised enough to be classed as 'Grecian', and it is also doubtful if he ever visited these establishments. Being brought up as a strict Pharisee It is not likely that he would have enjoyed life in the Palestra and his circumcised state would have been as conspicuous as a sore thumb, for the Greeks considered such a condition an unforgivable mutilation of the body. However some of the more Hellenised and emancipated of the Jewish youth did go to the baths and took part in, and enjoyed, the activities in the Palestrae; but in order to conform with their Greek counter parts and make their condition less obvious they often endured a painful cosmetic operation that they hoped might reverse their circumcised state.

All cities of any standing had their theatres where the itinerant companies of actors presented their mimes and plays, and some had smaller odeons that were the venue for concerts, or reserved for the meetings of the Town's Elders; and there were the Law Courts where litigants could interminably argue their cases, Tarsus was also fortunate in that it had a University with a reputation making it one of the most respected in the ancient world, in Strabo's opinion it was the equal to that of Athens. Most of the students came from Cilicia and Syria, and as graduates were to be found throughout the Empire in all walks of life. One such, a native of Tarsus, was so highly regarded for his learning and ability he was destined to become the Tutor to the young Augustus, and when Augustus became Emperor, Athenodorus, who was the graduate in question, remained his confidant and mentor for the rest of his life. The greatest piece of advice he is said to have given Augustus was 'When in anger think twice before you speak'.

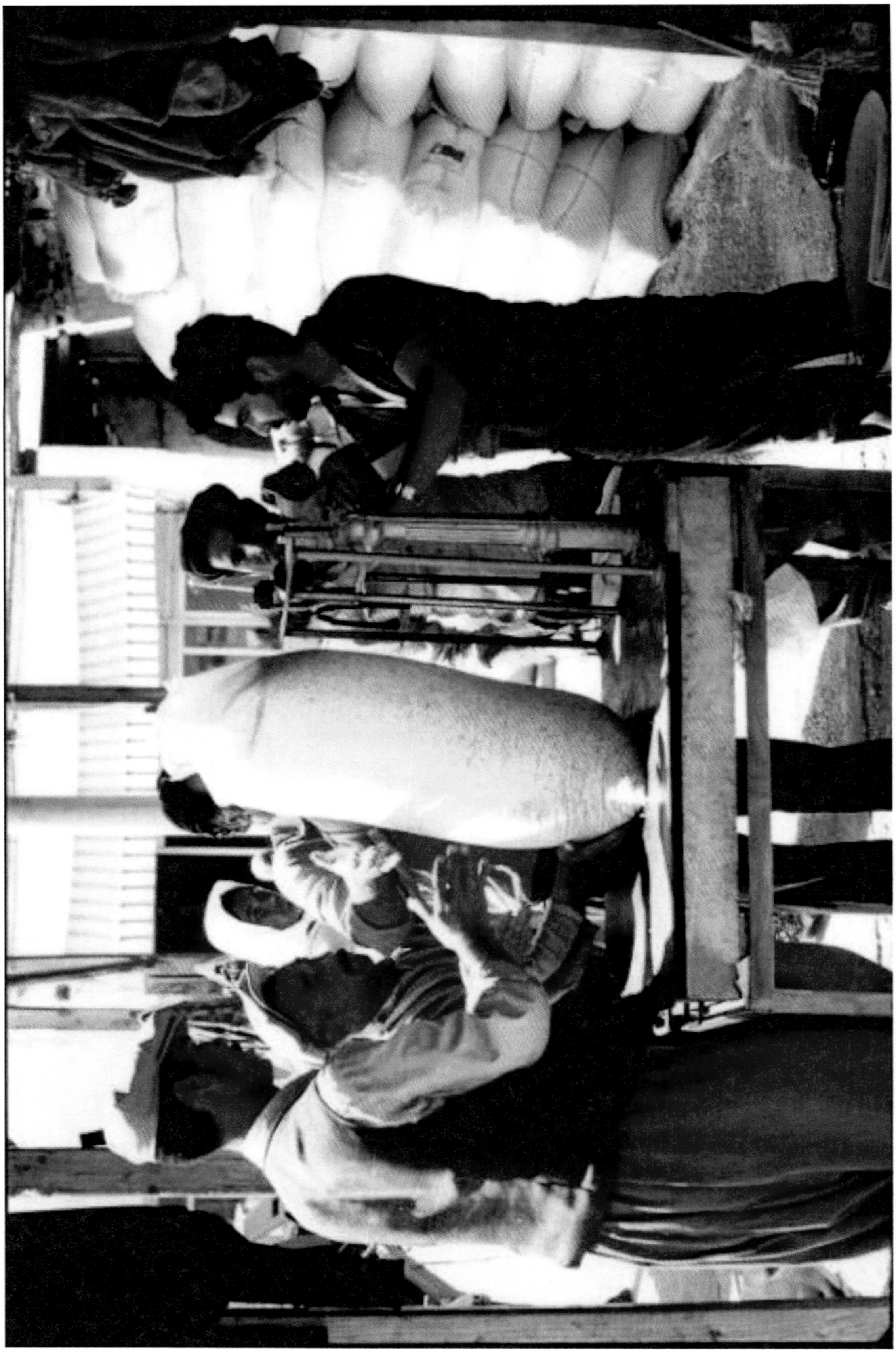

Figure 1: Weighing Grain in the Corn Market in Old Tarsus.

Figure 2: Street Vendor in Old Tarsus.

Figure 3: Communal Fountain in Old Tarsus.

Finally Athenodorus left Rome to go back to Tarsus in order to undertake the thankless task of reorganising the municipal administration that had, over the years, become riddled from top to bottom with graft and intrigue. His impact was such that many of those who had been responsible for this state of affairs were either banished or lost their citizenship. In the later decades their unfortunate descendants were destined to become the dregs of society and poverty stricken, and as a result were treated as second class citizens to be known disparagingly as 'The linen workers'. Athenodorus died before Paul was born, but his was a name that future generations always respected.

The river Cydnus was another asset that undoubtedly contributed a great deal to the prosperity of Tarsus for its course went through the City, said to have been some two hundred feet across, to a lake that lay some five miles inland from the sea. Here the important harbour of Rhegma, one of the largest in that part of the Mediterranean had its wharfs, quays, and warehouses, and an outlet from the lake, that was some thirty miles wide, reached the sea by a channel that had to be constantly dredged. However, in the later years this essential work was neglected to the extent that, by the fifth century, the whole had reverted to a swamp. Today all that remains of that great harbour is nothing but a vast area where groves of eucalyptus trees have been planted in an effort to drain it. In the days of Paul, the lake and harbour area would certainly have had malarial problems for areas of stagnant water would have been ideal breeding grounds for the Anopheles mosquito, and this could well have subjected the citizens of Tarsus to periodic epidemics of the disease and bouts of malaria might well have been responsible for much of Paul's ill health.

There was always the danger of the Cydnus overflowing and thereby flooding Tarsus which meant the river also had to be dredged at regular intervals, but at some time after A.D. 527, the date when Justinian became Emperor in Constantinople, a lateral canal was cut to the East of the town to counter this hazard and to become its future course. Today it remains a stream on the outskirts by Justinian's bridge thus freeing Tarsus from the threat of inundation.

Colourful tales of the junketings of Antony and Cleopatra must have been a feature of Paul's childhood for their visit to Tarsus could not have been more than some forty years back in time prior to his birth, reverberations of that great event must still have had its echoes for it was a sight that his grandfather could surely have witnessed. The barge of Cleopatra coming slowly up the river Cydnus would have been as spectacular an event today as it then was, it is unlikely that memories of such an event would have completely faded within the space of two or three intervening generations.

The ruins of ancient Tarsus now lie buried some feet under the modern city and as such they are beyond excavation. The only monument of any note today features the somewhat dilapidated remains of a town gate of the Roman period, known either as St Paul's Gate or Cleopatra's Arch. There is also the so called House of Paul that may, but more likely may not, be the original site. However, an ancient well in the court yard marks a spring that could have been the water source for an old dwelling; springs can often defy the passing centuries. Not far away and giving rise to further speculation is the site of the 'Dunuk Tas', where two extensive foundations of Roman concrete could have been the podiums of temples, enclosed as they are by thick walls that might once have been the boundaries of a sanctuary.

This was the Tarsus that Paul knew in the first century A.D. Though there are no records extant of him being a student at the University, and little is known of his early years the fact remains that he was well educated. This possibly either at home or in the Synagogue Schools for it is unlikely that he would have been entrusted to any Gentile foundation. On his own admission he learnt the family business and he must therefore have spent his early youth in Tarsus before going to Jerusalem to study the Law under Gamaliel. This could have been about the age of thirteen years. At ten years of age a Jewish child was obliged to learn and be conversant with the Mishna, and at thirteen had to be the subject of a ceremony, not unlike that of Confirmation, where he was pronounced a 'Filius Praecepti' and became responsible for his sins. It is likely that Paul was sent to Jerusalem at some time following this ceremony to study the Law under Gamaliel.

Gamaliel was one of the foremost Rabbis of the day, so much so in fact that he was given the prestigious title of 'Rabban'[6]. There were two eminent Rabbinical Schools for the Pharisees in Jerusalem at that time; those of Shammai and Hillel. That of Schammai contended the Law was subservient to tradition, that of Hillel thought otherwise and of the two was the more influential. Gamaliel was the grandson of Hillel by his son Simeon, the same it is thought who officiated at the presentation of the infant Christ in the Temple. Be that as it may Gamaliel was not of a fundamental turn of mind and had a liberal outlook that is shown in his attitude to the Apostles and their mission: clearly demonstrated in Acts 5 38-40 where he points out to the council 'keep away from these men and let them alone; because if this plan or this undertaking is of human origin it will fail; but if it is of God, you will not be able to overthrow them- in that case you may even be found fighting against God'[7]. However, in spite of Gamaliel's tolerant outlook Paul himself admits to his early fundamentalism in 1 Gal 14 'I advanced in Judaism beyond many among my people of the same age, for I was far more zealous for the traditions of my ancestors'. It is in Acts XXII 3 where Paul remarks 'I am a Jew born in Tarsus in Cilicia, but brought up in this city at the feet of Gamaliel, educated strictly according to our ancestral law'. This could be something of a literal statement and is a phrase rooted in custom where it describes how pupils had their education. Luke 10 39 records 'She had a sister named Mary, who sat at the Lord's feet and listened to what he was saying'. There is also the Jewish maxim, 'Place thyself in the dust at the feet of the wise'. Some years ago when in north Africa I saw a teacher seated on a low stool in a remote village school reciting the Koran to groups of young children sitting cross legged on the ground around his feet, all intoning the passages after him[8].

---

[6] Rabban is said to have been the title that was given to seven famous teachers of whom Gamaliel was one. Mary Magdalen once addressed Jesus as Raboni, the same as Rabban.

[7] Gamaliel had a broad mind that harboured little prejudice where Greek tradition was concerned. He died eight years before the fall of Jerusalem in which his son, also called Simeon, died.

[8] According to St Ambrose, in his commentary on the first Epistle to the Corinthians, it was the custom for the Elders when teaching to sit on a chair whilst their students sat on the pavement or on low stools. Philo also records the fact that the students of the Essenes sat at the feet of their Masters when being taught the law.

Certain authorities maintain that Paul did not go to Jerusalem to study but remained in Tarsus till being sent by the Sanhedrin to carry out their persecutions in Damascus. The passage quoted to support this hypothesis is based on Galatians 1 22 'And I was still unknown by sight to the Churches of Judaea that are in Christ; they only heard it said'. But this must be taken in context for, even if one allows for Paul's ambiguity, the passage must refer to the period when Paul, shortly after his return from Arabia, went from Damascus to Jerusalem as in 1 Galatians 17-20 'nor did I go up to Jerusalem to those who were already Apostles before me, but I went away at once into Arabia, possibly Petra(?), and afterwards I returned to Damascus. Then after three years, those that he could well have spent in Arabian Petra,' I did go up to Jerusalem to visit Cephas and stayed with him fifteen days; but I did not see any other Apostle except James the Lord's brother'.

It is then that he remarks in verse 22 that he was unknown by sight to the Judean Churches that are in Christ. This would not be at all surprising, for he had been in Arabia for the past three years; he was in fact referring to the many new converts who had joined the Churches in Judaea during the time he was away. He would have had very little time to see the new converts in Judaea in the two weeks he spent in Jerusalem on his return, when endeavouring to persuade the Apostles Peter and James that he had had a change of heart. That the Apostles were still not convinced at this time as to whether Paul's conversion was genuine or not is bourne out in Gal 1 23 'The one who formerly was persecuting us is now proclaiming the faith he once tried to destroy'. There are other factors to indicate that Paul did in fact go to Jerusalem to study under Gamaliel, not the least being the fact that the renowned Rabbi must certainly have been living in Jerusalem whilst teaching at the school of Hillel, and not in provincial Tarsus in Central Asia Minor, well known though Tarsus might have been.

Dr Coggan has suggested the possibility of the whole family moving to Jerusalem for the period of Paul's further education under Gamaliel, There were certainly family connections with Jerusalem for Paul's married sister could have been living there with her husband and son; whether she was older or younger than Paul is not known there being no indications as to her age, nor are there any references to her husband. However, there is the suggestion that he could have been one of the Sanhedrin. Her existence is known only from the casual reference by Paul to his nephew in Acts XXIII 16 where he is described as being a young man who, according to Sir William Ramsay, could in Biblical terms be any age between twenty to forty years. However, Tarsus is some distance from Jerusalem and it would have meant leaving the cloth business without any family direction and Paul does not record any other siblings apart from his sister.

After he had completed his education with Gamaliel, it seems that it took some ten years in order to become a Rabbi, it is more than likely that be returned to Tarsus in that capacity and possibly also to help with the family business. As has been said there is little reason to doubt that the family were anything but prosperous, and it is more than likely that he was in Tarsus during the Ministry of Jesus. It is significant that Paul does not refer to, or comment on, many of the individual episodes that took place during the years of Christ's Ministry, but he does where the Crucifixion is concerned though he fails to record any details of the event. In 1 Cor 1 23, he says after his conversion 'but we proclaim Christ crucified a stumbling block for

Jews and foolishness to Gentiles', and in 1 Cor II he discusses the institution of the Lord's Supper and its abuses. In 1 Cor XV he discusses the Resurrection and describes Christ's subsequent appearance to the Apostles and notes in verse 8. 'Last of all, as to one untimely born, he appeared also to me. For I am the least of the Apostles, unfit to be called an Apostle, because I persecuted the Church of God', but in 1 Cor IX 1 he writes 'Am I not free? Am I not an Apostle? Have I not seen Jesus our Lord?' This last statement would seem to hint at Paul being in Jerusalem around the time of the Crucifixion. However, on both counts it is more than likely that he is referring to visions and his crisis on the Damascus road. However, it is still an intriguing question as to whether Paul was actually in Jerusalem around the time of the Crucifixion, a question he does not decisively resolve[9]. However, if he was not in Jerusalem during the period of the crucifixion he must have been at some later date to have become a very willing agent in helping the Sanhedrin further their persecutions. The stoning of Stephen was an important incident in this campaign against the Church. Accused by the Sanhedrin of a major blasphemy he was immediately brought before them for trial, Acts. VII 58 with Paul being an active participant in his prosecution and consenting to his death as recorded in Acts; VIII 1 and XXII 20. It seems that members of the Cilician Synagogue in Jerusalem, compatriots of Paul, were some of the most outspoken in his condemnation and were supported amongst others by those of the Synagogues of the Alexandrians, the Cyrenians, and the Asians, denoting the fact that these factions had their separate establishments in Jerusalem Acts VI 9, 10[10].

Stephen, having enraged the Sanhedrin with his spirited defence was summarily executed. Stoning of victims always took place outside the city walls and it is thought that Stephen could have been taken through the gate named after him to a site by the Kedron brook near Gethsemane. It was the prerogative of the victim's accusers to cast the first stones, and in the case of Stephen those who did so laid their outer clothes at the feet of Paul, Acts VII 58. The complete truth of this narrative is in question for some consider it a coloured version of the event designed to indicate that Paul was present at the time, when in actual fact he was not. However, the detail in the narrative with the description of those who left their garments with Paul before the execution could well be a true account of what happened on that occasion. If Paul had not been present at the death of Stephen but in far off Tarsus, his stoning and death would have been a second hand item of news, if indeed the Jewish community ever realised it had taken place, and it would not then have had the profound effect on Paul that It latterly seems to have done.

After the death of Stephen there was a general dispersion of those of the Church to Cyprus, Antioch, Phoenicia, and Syria (Acts XI 19) but Paul records in Acts XXVI 11 'By punishing them often in all the synagogues I tried to force them to blaspheme; and since I was

---

[9] If Paul had been in Jerusalem at any time during the ministration of Christ he would almost certainly have mentioned the fact. It has been suggested by some that he was in Jerusalem at the time as a young student but not aware of the situation, however, this hardly seems to be likely.

[10] The death of Stephen gave the Sanhedrin and Paul the impetus to carry out the most ferocious persecutions of the church, a course of events that could have lasted over a period of some two years. The death of Stephen could have been a watershed in the early history of the Church, resulting as it did in many of the disciples leaving Jerusalem to take the Gospel to other cities of the Empire. It could have been the dignity and the peaceful resignation with which Stephen met his death that haunted Paul in his later years. In Acts VII. 60. Paul refers to those who had 'fallen asleep' more peaceably than Stephen. Then be knelt down and cried out in a loud voice, "Lord do not hold this sin against them".

so furiously enraged at them, I pursued them even to foreign cities'. It was his militant attitude towards the Church in Jerusalem and elsewhere that the Sanhedrin appreciated in Paul, and made him an ideal agent in his zeal for his proposed mission to Damascus[11].

Paul had the choice of one of two routes from Jerusalem to Damascus. One from Jerusalem went down to Jericho and then North by way of the Jordan valley to the river crossing at Beth She'an, the ancient Scythopolis that, judging from the extensive foundations of its Synagogue complete with a magnificent mosaic floor, must have had a notable population of the Diaspora. Scythopolis, like Damascus, was one of the ten cities of the Decapolis, and from there the road crossed over the Jordan at the South end of Lake Tiberias before it went through the hills to Gadara, also a city of the Decapolis. From there it passed by the Golan Heights to reach El Qunaytirah and finally Damascus. However, a somewhat longer journey, and the most likely route of choice, went through Samaria to today's Jenin on the edge of the Esdraelon plains. Though a little longer the journey would have been far less hot and a good deal more pleasant, avoiding as it did the rigours of the Jordan Valley. From Jenin the road would have crossed the Esdraelon plains to Sepphoris, an important market town that had a Roman garrison and was some five kilometres from Nazareth and the Horns of Hattim, where the Crusaders lost their cause to Saladin, to then drop down to Tiberias on Galilee.

In the nineteen thirties Tiberias was a sleepy old town where the boats of Galilee were still being built on primitive stocks by the quay, much as they had been for centuries past. The steep hills that go down to the lake were always a vast blue haze of wild lupine in the spring, but all that now is a thing of the past. What was once a centuries old pastoral landscape is an endless litter of shabby high rise flats, their drab and grubby exteriors looking like a forest of giant dead weeds, and all that is left of old Tiberias is the battered mosque with its drunken minaret, pock marked with a myriad shell holes.

Paul could have passed by the shores and the villages of Galilee till he came to Capernaum, where the road later passes north of the Lake to twist and turn in the hills before reaching the ford of the Seven Sisters of Jacob. In antiquity this was the crossing of the Jordan used by travellers and merchants when on their way from Palmyra, the cities of the Euphrates and Northern Lebanon, to Egypt and Palestine It was a frontier and customs post when the Lebanon was under the French mandate and still to be negotiated before entering or leaving Palestine. The road rises steeply from the Ford to a point where there are splendid views over Galilee and the distant Mountains of Moab and from here it would pass by towering snow capped Hermon to the North to cross flat uplands before dropping down to Damascus. Regardless of the route of choice Paul would have had to pass through Neapolis, the Nablus of today. The distance of some one hundred and thirty six miles would have taken the caravans some six or more days to make the journey. Paul would have had his first glimpse of Damascus as it lay some ten or more miles out of the city in a green haze in a sandy landscape, and

---

[11] After the death of Stephen the extent and vigour of Paul's persecutions as an agent of the Sanhedrin is vividly described by Paul himself in Acts VIII. 3. XXVI. 9,10. XXII.4. and XXVI. 10. This has led some to think that Paul could have been made a member of the Sanhedrin as a result of his complicity in the death of Stephen. If so it follows that he must have had a wife at that time and, if so, what became of her? Neither Luke nor Paul have ever made any reference to a wife, and nowhere in the New Testament is there a hint of Paul ever having been married, or having had a family. Was he a member of the Sanhedrin at the time of his mission to Damascus? On balance it would seem not and that he was merely a dedicated agent of the Sanhedrin before his conversion on the Damascus road.

blotched with the sun's glare from its white buildings; today it is marked by its domes and minarets, and sadly by its modern architecture, but in the same pool of shimmering greenery that is still a magical sight that can call to mind the Arabian Nights.

Approaching from the direction of Beirut it is the sudden appearance of the fruit trees on the banks of the Barada River, a little before one reaches the village of Doummar, that herald the nearness of civilization. The Arabs have a saying 'Boukra fil mish mish,' 'Tomorrow there will be apricots' and from here they thicken and grow more closely until the first houses of the Damascus suburbs appear amongst them. To Damascus the waters of the Barada are the blood of life. They nourish the multitude of orchards that have made the city famous since Roman times. Apricots abound, as do citrus, apples, grapes, figs, olives, nuts, and mulberries. Damascus has always been renowned for its fruits, its dried figs and plums were luxuries that were exported wholesale by the Damascenes to Rome where, as a part of life, they graced the tables in the households of the wealthy. Some even found their way to Britain as evidenced by the plum or 'pruna' stones that have turned up in various ancient middens. Damascus was famous also for its roses, cultivated for the perfumes considered by those who occupied the boudoirs of the Roman world to be more than a necessity; and today for the legions of shady poplars that march and push the desert aside, an integral feature of the landscape.

The circumstances of Paul's conversion have been the subject of a deal of speculation on the part of many academics, Professor C.H. Turner considers the date to be somewhere between A.D. 30-35: On the other hand Michael Grant has pinpointed it to A.D. 36. Ian Wilson has pointed out the fact that Pontus Pilate was the governor of Judaea between A.D. 27 - 36, a fact confirmed by Josephus, so that the Crucifixion must have taken place between these dates. According to John it took place on the 14th day of Nisan, the Passover preparation day equivalent to April 14th. Taking into account all the various possibilities and the premise that the Ministry of Christ lasted some three years, or there about, an average date for Paul's conversion on the Damascus road could have been towards the end of Pilate's tenure in office, possibly between A.D. 33-36. If Paul's conversion had taken place much earlier it would have been around the date of the Crucifixion, but from Acts it appears that Paul was in Jerusalem furthering the persecutions of the Sanhedrin for at least two years after the Crucifixion, and that he was present at the death of Stephen before he went to Damascus, thus this could bring the date of his crisis when on the Damascus road to A.D. 35-36, the last year of Professor Turner's bracket and the year suggested by Michael Grant. If in fact Paul had been born around A.D. 2 his age at the time would have some 38 years.

The actual details of his conversion have been narrated in Acts. IX 3-9, XXII 6-11, and XXVI 13-16, and traditionally it is said to have occurred on the Kaukab Hill, the hill of Celestial Light, some few miles out of Damascus and it is this first glimpse of Damascus that could well have been the catalyst that triggered his crisis, for by then, and following the stoning of Stephen, it is possible that he was having doubts as to the policies of the Sanhedrin in their persecutions, coupled with the realisation that he was now nearing Damascus where he was ordained to carry them out.

The first account states that, after being struck blind, he was led by the hand to the house of Judas, and this possibly because those conducting the caravans knew all the aspects of Damascus and Judas to be a physician, but even if this had been so it was left apparently to Ananias to cure Paul's blindness.

Morton's suggestion that a delegation of the Sanhedrin were with him on the journey does not, in the circumstances, seem to have been likely for, if so, they would have been a distinct embarrassment when the party reached the house of Judas. All accounts describe the bright light and hearing the voice of God with the last two accounts mentioning the fact that it took place at midday, which is significant for this would have been when the sun was at its zenith, but is only in Acts 26, 14, where the account gives the detail 'When we had all fallen to the ground, I heard a voice saying to me in the Hebrew language, Saul, Saul, why are you persecuting me? It hurts you to kick against the goads'. The phrase is interesting for it describes a Biblical way of life that was still a common sight throughout the dusty roads of Palestine up to the end of the Second World War, one that has now vanished.

The nineteen thirties saw the end of an era in the Middle East, a way of life that remained little changed for centuries and one that echoed much of the Biblical past. It was an everyday occurrence around the villages of Esdraelon to see an Arab astride a diminutive donkey, bolt upright with his feet scarce missing the ground as it laboured under his weight. His wife on foot behind him bent double under the faggots on her shoulder; in a shapeless black shroud she had the appearance of a large black crow. Inevitably she had with her a long pointed staff that was thrust periodically into the donkey's rump to spur its flagging to greater efforts. Violently protesting at this indignity it usually lashed out with its hind leg; hence the long staff, lurch on for a few more quickened paces to the discomfort of the rider, and then settle back to its previous staggering gait. Women's liberation was never ever an issue in the Middle East and this must have been a sight familiar to Paul, but it is odd that the voice he heard should so succinctly have likened his attitude to the Apostolic Church in terms of an occurrence that was common to everyday life.

Several theories regarding Paul's conversion have been put forward. Stuart Perowne suggested that the onset of a sudden and severe tropical storm might have been the reason for the intense flashes of light, but this does not seem to fit in very well with the account. The very bright light Paul saw could have been due to a medical phenomenon known as Photism, a hallucination that is manifested in seeing bright lights and hearing voices, a condition that can be brought about when the subject is in a physically and mentally exhausted state. It can occur in periods of acute mental stress brought on by a traumatic experience, or a long standing problem that has been buried in the depths of the mind. In the case of Paul, the stoning of Stephen and the circumstances of his journey to Damascus could have been a factor that contributed to the onset of his crisis, but, even so, this does not rule out a Divine intervention. Photism is a condition that many of a deeply religious and mystical turn of mind could have experienced in the past, and in many susceptible subjects it is accompanied by visions and the hearing of voices. St. Catherine and St. Teresa of Avila are amongst those who are thought to have had this condition.

In spite of Paul's attitude towards the Apostolic Church he must latterly have been having doubts regarding the policies of the Sanhedrin, and his increasing dissatisfaction with the Jewish teaching is very clear in his letter to the Philippians 111 8, where he dismisses the Law as 'so much dung'. The boundless energy he had once employed in the furtherance of the persecutions of the Sanhedrin was now used in his frenetic efforts to convert the Jews to a new way of thinking; and when they would have none of it he took his ministry to the Gentiles

The references to Ananias are also somewhat contradictory. In Acts IX 10, he is represented as one who has Joined the Church and queries the fact that Paul is other than one sent by the Sanhedrin to exact retribution on them, but in a vision is reassured and told to go to the house of Judas in the Street called Straight to cure Paul's blindness, a condition of an hysterical nature that could have been the result of his crisis on the Damascus road. But in Acts XXII 12, Ananias is described as 'a devout man according to the Law being well known to all the Jews of Damascus'.

Paul's zealous approach in proclaiming the Church in the Synagogues of Damascus was now as fanatical as it was in his former persecutions, and for this affront to the Damascene Jews he became for the first time the subject of their combined wrath and hostility, a phenomenon that was to dog him for the rest of his ministry.

Damascus is still a Capital city in spite of being founded before those of Palmyra and Baalbek, cities which now lie in splendid ruins. It was Ben Haddad, about 853 B.C., who was the first King of note to rule Damascus, and to be warned of his own murder by the Prophet Elisha who was then being held in custody by Naaman, the King's general. It was Elisha too who, as legend would have it, cured Naaman of leprosy by instructing him to bathe in the waters of the Jordan. Ezekiel has left a letter to Tyre, the port used by Damascus for its exports, in his book XXVII 16-25 in which he vividly describes the wealth in trade of all commodities, both luxury and otherwise, that obtained in the Middle East at that time, and in it he records the mercantile importance of Damascus as it was then, 'Damascus traded with you for your abundant goods - because of your great wealth of every kind- wine of Helbon, and white wool'.

Around 732 B.C. the wealth of the City was plundered by the Assyrians who also destroyed most of the orchards, to be restored and replanted under a later Persian domination when Damascus once again achieved prosperity. However, the tangible history of the City really begins with Alexander the Great who defeated the Persians on the plains of Issus near Antioch in 333 B.C. to then become the master of the vast wealth in gold and other possessions that Darius had accumulated and been forced to leave behind in Damascus.

The death of Alexander brought about a further period of unrest and depression until 64 B.C. when Damascus passed to a Roman administration and further prosperity as a result of an improvement in the trade routes. But Roman Damascus was still to have a chequered career for a besotted Mark Antony in blind generosity saw fit to give it to Cleopatra together with much of Syria, and this after Herod the Great had improved its amenities with the donation of a Theatre.

It was Roman Damascus that Paul would have known, and though most of it still lies fifteen feet or more under the Damascus of today there is much that remains in the shape of odd columns, the remnants of arches **(Figure 4)**, and blocks of masonry that have been incorporated into, the Arab architecture **(Figure 5)** . An impressive group of these columns can be seen at the entrance to the covered bazaar of the Suq el Hamidieh.

The Street called Straight was the Decumanus Maximus of the Romans, the main street that went from the Jupiter Gate to the Bab Charki, or Gate of the Sun. Today it begins with the Suq el Kumeileh and after that becomes the Midhat Pasha, but in the time of Paul the street was almost a mile long and had three wide thoroughfares. The centre for chariots and other wheeled traffic, whilst those on either side were flanked with shops and porticos for the pedestrians; apart from these facilities there were the Municipal Buildings, the Theatre, and the Palace of the Governor. The seven gates of Damascus gave on to more wide streets with shady colonnades, mostly put up in the time of Severus, but always alive and colourful with a cosmopolitan throng of peoples from North Africa, Egypt, Asia Minor, Greece and Rome, merchants, peasants, buskers with their repertoire of tricks and songs, and those who just sauntered along to waste their time.

Life was not much different in the Damascus of the nineteen thirties, in spite of having lost much of its classical heritage to an Arab culture. The Suqs still had their elegant shops, notably that of Asfar and Sarkis, where a myriad of fine rugs and carpets, jewellery, and sumptuous brocades were displayed. Damascus has a long history of expertise in this craft, and one that stems back in time from the Persian occupation; and there were also the textiles that came in by way of the caravans on the Silk Road from China. Today the raw silk for the Damascus brocades is the product of farms located high up in the hills above Beirut; they are still there in spite of the recent troubles that have devastated much of Beirut itself. Here long sheds that sprawl in the shade of dense mulberry groves have endless tier upon tier of racks that are cluttered full of pale yellow cocoons awaiting the spinning. The brocades of Damascus were much to be treasured. The wealth and variety of goods being traded then in Damascus could not have fallen far short of the description given in the past by Ezekiel.

The East Gate that gives on to the Street called Straight is the only one of the seven to retain anything of the original Roman structure, and most of this is now obscured by ramshackle buildings. But the Northern Gate, in Roman times reserved solely for pedestrians, is still in use and this in contrast to the Jupiter Gate that retains nothing of its Roman origin and is today immured in the darkness of its surrounding markets. It was a favourite place for pedlars to tout a motley of useless impedimenta from trays slung from cords about their necks, a motley that often included worn out razor blades.

It is almost impossible to denote with a degree of certainty the site of any Biblical event in the Middle East, and this is specifically true of Palestine. After Constantine adopted Christianity as the state religion St Helena, his Mother, in a frenzied activity toured the Holy Land in an effort to determine and build Basilicas on the numerous sites that she considered authentic. Many of them were decreed by persistent legend and some few have since been confirmed by archaeological investigation. A case in point is the House of Judas that was certainly in the Street called Straight, but the site as known today is open to conjecture. Both Moslems and Christians are of the opinion that its remains lie under a small and somewhat shabby mosque that lacks a minaret, but has a balcony of a dubious standard of safety that overlooks the street itself. However, a Franciscan tradition going back to A.D. 1616 could be significant for it records the fact that a Greek church to St Judas was there for many years before the mosque was built.

The site of the House of Ananias is also conjectural but is thought to lie not far from the Street called Straight, a little way from the corner where Hananya Street Joins Azaryeh Street, and here at the Roman level of Damascus, some fifteen feet down, is a chapel that has obvious Roman work in its fabric. There are a few pews, an altar and a side chapel that is thought to be all that remains of a larger Byzantine structure, but the interior is dark being very ill lit from two openings in the roof. Excavations in the nineteen twenties uncovered an altar with a dedication to Jupiter Haddad; the style of its inscription is such that it could date to some two hundred years after the Crucifixion; but this does not rule out the possible authenticity of the site.

Traditionally Paul's escape from Damascus took place over the wall near the Kaysan Gate where a nearby shrine commemorates the event. The Church and then the Mosque that used to occupy the site have long since disappeared, but a window above the Gate is said to mark the place of Paul's descent. The Damascenes though have a theory that Paul's escape was not by a basket over the wall, but through the efforts of an Abysinnian who smuggled him through the gate one night. Georgious was a Christian Abysinnian on guard duty that night and he was executed for his pains by the governor of Damascus on the following day. He is the St George of the Abyssinians and his tomb outside the Gate has been revered ever since: here the Damascenes still burn candles to his memory and place them in front of his Icon that stands a little forlorn on the shrine's primitive altar.

There appear to be two schools of thought as to when Paul made his escape from the outraged Jews of Damascus. One that it took place at some time after his baptism by Ananias. It was then he infuriated the Jews with his preaching of the new doctrine instead of persecuting the new Church as was his original intention. The passage in Acts IX 18-25, reads:

'And immediately something like scales fell from his eyes, and his sight was restored. Then he got up and was baptised, and after taking food, he regained his strength. For several days he was with the disciples in Damascus, and immediately he began to proclaim Jesus in the synagogues saying, "He is the Son of God". All who heard him were amazed and said 'Is not this the man who made havoc in Jerusalem among those who invoked this name? And has he not come here for the purpose of bringing them bound before the chief priests?'

Saul became increasingly more powerful and confounded the Jews who lived In Damascus by proving that Jesus was the Messiah. After some time had passed the Jews plotted to kill him, but their plot became known to Saul. They were watching the gates day and night so that they might kill him; but his disciples took him by night and let him down through an opening in the wall, lowering him in a basket.

Figure 4: The way of Life today in Old Damascus.

Figure 5: Roman Damascus.

The foregoing does seem to indicate that Paul's teaching in the Synagogues of Damascus had so infuriated the Jews that Ananias and the disciples had had to organise his escape into Arabia and this would have been logical for the Jews were expecting him to seek out and denounce all those who had joined the Church, and would not have envisaged him preaching them the Gospel. Paul records his decision in Gal 1 17-22 'Nor did I go up to Jerusalem to those who were already apostles before me, but I went away at once into Arabia, and afterwards I returned to Damascus'. He then goes on to say in verse 18 'Then after three years I did go up to Jerusalem to visit Cephas and stayed with him fifteen days; but I did not see any other apostle except James the Lord's brother'. The period of three years would no doubt be the time that elapsed between Paul's conversion and this visit.

However, there is a more accepted line of thought that Paul's escape from Damascus took place after his return from Arabia, when he had again upset the Jews with his teaching and they sought to kill him. Having made his escape he would then have gone back to Jerusalem. In Acts IX 26 Luke writes, ' When he had come to Jerusalem he attempted to join the disciples and they were all afraid of him, for they did not believe that he was a disciple' and in verse 27 Luke records that Barnabas was with Paul on that occasion and spoke up for him. The visit described by Paul in Galatians is possibly the same as the one described by Luke in Acts, but if so it is odd that Paul has not mentioned Barnabas. He surely would have done so if he had been with him on that occasion. The account of the visit as described by Luke appears to have been of duration of more than fifteen days. Whatever the circumstances it is certain that Paul on leaving Damascus, if not over the wall in a basket but at his own volition, went into Arabia. To have returned to Jerusalem in so short a space of time as a dedicated convert to the cause he had set out to persecute would have been out of the question. On the part of Paul it would have required some explanation to the Sanhedrin and would have been a confrontation to be avoided at all cost.

In Paul's account of his escape in 11 Cor XI, 11 32-33 he casually mentions the fact that it was not only the Jews who sought him but also the troops of Aretas: 'In Damascus the governor, or Ethnarch, under King Aretas guarded the city of Damascus in order to seize me, but I was let down in a basket through a window in the wall and escaped his hands'. The Aretas in question was Aretas IV, the King of the Nabateans whose Capital was Petra in Arabia. This appears to be the only historical reference to the effect that Damascus was then under the control of the wealthy Nabateans, confirmation of their occupation being the coinage they minted in Damascus. The time when Paul was in Damascus and Arabia is generally accepted as being between A.D. 36-39 and this would certainly fit in with the dates of Aretas who ruled between B.C. 8 and A.D. 40 which indicates that he must then have died shortly after Paul left Arabia.

It has been questioned why Damascus was under the control of the Nabateans and not the Romans at that time, a possible explanation being the death of Tiberius in A.D. 37. For some years before the death of Tiberius there had been an acrimonious border dispute between Aretas and Herod Antipas, the Tetrarch of Galilee and also his son in law. To aid Herod in this dispute Tiberias eventually decided to send an army from Syria under the command of the Governor, Vitellius. However, whilst the army was on its way through Judaea to reach its objective Tiberias unfortunately died, to be succeeded by Caligula. Caligula was not in accord with the policies of Tiberias and ordered Vitellius with his legions to return to Syria, and it is thought that he then ceded the administration of Damascus to Aretas[12].

The fact that there are no references to any of Paul's activities after his escape from Damascus brooks the question as to his final destination in Arabia. The clue could well lie with Aretas. The caravans that plied the trade routes of the Middle East went regularly from Petra to Damascus with government papers and to barter their exotic goods from the Orient. These were exchanged for perfumes, textiles, the purple dye from Tyre and other commodities such as silver and lead from the West. The caravans often numbered over a thousand beasts and left the city Hahns at dawn in order to reach the next caravansary, and safety, by night fall. When it became an urgent necessity for Paul to leave Damascus it could possibly have been Ananias who made the arrangements for him to join such a caravan outside the City walls and well away from the City gates.

The trade routes South from Damascus to Arabia would pass through the cities where they could break their journey for the night, and these could include those of the Decapolis such as Gerasa, today's Jerash, Pella, and Philadelphia, today's Amman, and also Bosra.

Jerash was a Jewish city before it became a member of the Decapolis and was then under the control of Alexander Jannaeus from 102 to 76 B.C., but in later years both it and Philadelphia developed trade relations with Aretas and the Nabateans. Many of the coins found in these Cities have a Nabatean connotation and their influence is reflected in some of the inscriptions of which a few refer to the Nabatean god Dusares.

Jerash was situated in good agricultural country not far from a river and above all was a city of some splendour. Its most impressive feature today lies in the unique and spacious elliptical Forum that is bordered by a magnificent colonnade. This gives onto the Decumanus Maximus, a street that went the length of the city with more impressive columns and flanked on either side with shops and temples together with another of the city's architectural gems, a Nymphaeum profuse with the decoration of the Corinthian order and rich with marble statues. In its forecourt and hewn from a single block of granite is a vast shallow bowl supported on a pedestal that is even now miraculously intact, in spite of the many centuries that have passed it by. All this was overlooked and dominated by a hill having a theatre built into it that was so orientated it gave a wide ranging view over the city expanse from the auditorium (**Figures 6 and 7**).

---

[12] The question of the importance of Paul's mention of Aretas in 2 Corinthians II 3-33 has been discussed at length by Douglas A. Campbell of King's College London in an article published in the 'Journal of Biblical Studies' 2002, p279-302. The importance of Paul's reference to Aretas lies in the fact that it could form a chronological date base framework for dating his journeys. Several opinions are discussed as to how Aretas gained control of Damascus in order to appoint an Ethnarch. To have troops under his command he must have had considerable authority. The option of choice appears to be the one cited above. Control of Damascus passed to Aretas on the death of Tiberius.

Roman architecture of the period together with the coins of Augustus and Tiberias that have been found confirm that Damascus at that time was administered by Rome. Coins of Nero have also been found but none of Caligula, only those minted by Aretas. This would seem to indicate that Caligula did hand over the administration to Aretas on the death of Tiberius and that by the time Nero was Emperor Damascus had again come under Roman domination. That Aretas was responsible for the administration of Damascus under his Ethnarch when Paul was there is confirmed by Paul's statement in 2 Corinthians XI. 32. At that time communications with Petra were good and the considerable population of Damascene Jews must have had good relations with the administration, favouring Aretas rather than Herod. In spite of the political situation it is not likely that Aretas would have usurped the administration from Roman power but that it was ceded to him. All in all it should not be discounted that Paul, when he went into Arabia, did in fact go to Petra.

The Greek and Roman influence also made Philadelphia a city of some consequence with more colonnaded streets and a theatre that was possibly more sophisticated in its decoration than that of Jerash and could seat some 6000: all this together with a small Odeon for concerts. These fine cities where life was gracious and pleasant had all the amenities, but for Paul there could have been one significant disadvantage. They were all too near Jerusalem for his comfort. By now, as far as the Sanhedrin was concerned, Paul must have become the ultimate blasphemer to be dealt with at all costs, and it must not be forgotten that they exercised jurisdiction over all synagogues wherever situated and over all those who transgressed the Law. Paul's whereabouts would soon have become known to them and it would not have been difficult to apprehend him and bring him to Jerusalem for trial.

Damascus being under the control of the Nabateans it follows that communications with Petra must have been frequent and well organised by making use of the trade routes. These trade routes were the main source of Solomon's wealth that came up with the caravans from the Biblical port of Ezion Geber In the Gulf of Aquaba, the haven for the fleets of Tarshish. The route extended from Ezion Geber to Petra, and then by way of Rabbath Amon, the Biblical name for Philadelphia, to Damascus; or by a second route that went west from Petra to its terminus at the Port of Gaza, the Capital of Idumea. Thus the merchandise that came into Ezion Geber went up to Petra where much of it was stored prior to being distributed to destinations throughout the Middle East. Ezion Geber is mentioned in 1 Kings IX 26 and it is apparent that Solomon had extensive shipyards there where his 'many ships beside Eloth' were built.

Eloth was probably near the site of today's Eliat, and in Biblical times there were a number of furnaces in the district used for smelting ore from the nearby copper mines. These were so arranged that they took advantage of the prevailing and constant winds that gave them the draft for their fires. They were extensively worked by the Pharaoh Seti I and Ramses III, and some in the time of Solomon. The book of Kings records a visit made by Solomon to Ezion Geber, and this quite possibly was to welcome the Queen of Sheba for the account of her arrival comes after that of his visit, and it is echoed in the Songs of Solomon, 'Who is this that cometh out of the wilderness like pillars of smoke, perfumed with myrrh and frankincense, and with all the powders of a merchant'.

Her route to Jerusalem would have taken her through the Wadi Musa to go West through Hebron to Jerusalem. In the time of Solomon the nature of the cargoes coming into Ezion Geber were far reaching and not only included vast quantities of gold, to the tune of some hundreds of shekels a year, but spices, incense, sugar and significant quantities of ivory. All this passed up to Petra with the caravans and the graffiti and signatures of the caravaneers are still to be seen on many of the rocks that lie along the way. Apart from this route another crossed the desert expanse lying West of Kuwait on the Persian Gulf, and this supplied Petra with a multitude of other exotic goods from India and the Far East.[13]

Petra was the Edom of the Biblical Edomites who were in fact a very civilised society it was Job, almost certainly an Edomite, who narrates that the men wore gold earrings: 'Every man

---

[13] See Petra, Iain Browning. The Antiquities of Jordan, Kester Harding.

gave him a piece of money and every man an earring of gold' - recorded when his family and friends came to see him at the end of his tribulations. David sought sanctuary in Edom to escape the wrath of King Saul, and later repaid their hospitality with a massacre that numbered in their thousands, no doubt in his effort to gain possession of the copper mines of Eloth; an act of treachery that the Edomites never forgot or forgave. When Jerusalem and the Temple of Solomon fell in 588 B.C., to Nebuchadnezzar the Edomites, in their loathing of Judaea, celebrated the event with a song of triumph that has unfortunately been lost, but its echoes and traces can be found in Psalm 137: 'Remember o Lord The children of Edom in the day of Jerusalem; how said they down with it, down with it even to the ground'.

The Nabateans who took over Petra from the Edomites went to great lengths to preserve and exploit the ancient trade routes, so much so that Petra became the clearing house for the merchandise that came in with the caravans, The Nabateans were quick to exploit any potential for making money, and to this effect they levied customs duties on the goods that passed through on the way to Gaza and the West. Consequent on the Nabatean invasion the majority of the Edomites, those who had survived the Judean wars, left and emigrated to the region of Palestine that lies just South of Hebron, and here they founded the state of Idumea to become the ancestors of Herod the Great, the Idumean, and of Antipas his son, the son in law of Aretas. Antipas soon tired of the liaison with the daughter of Aretas as did all the Herods with their spouses, and when he divorced her to marry Herodias she went into the limbo of the other discarded wives.

For some obscure reason Athenodorus, a friend of Strabo, lived for a few years in Petra during the reign of Obodas, the father of Aretas IV: it was information from Athenodorus that enabled Strabo to write a comprehensive account of life as it was in Petra at that time.

According to Strabo a significant number of foreigners were then a part of the general population and he further mentions that, according to Athenodorus, 'they were much given over to litigation amongst themselves, whilst the Nabateans lived peacefully together in sumptuous stone houses conducting their own lucrative affairs'. The Nabateans had a great respect for those who had the expertise for making money, and proved as successful in business as they were themselves; unusual too was the fact that the Nabatean women in society were able to lead a free and unfettered existence, and one that was accompanied by very little protocol. Strabo does point out, however, that an integral part of the social structure revolved around slave labour.

Dhu'l Shara, the Dusares of the Greeks, was the pagan deity of the Nabateans, and was represented by large pyramidal stones to be seen in parts of the valley and especially decorating a monument at the entrance to the Siq; but the main sanctuary of the god was in a large temple in Petra itself, its tumbled remains being known to the Arabs as 'The Kasr el Bint'.

Figure 6: The Forum in Jerash.

Figure 7: The Granite Bowl Jerash Nymphaeum.

An indication that there were Romans in Petra is reflected in an inscription that comes from Seeir: 'Under great King Agrippa, friend of Caesar, Pious friend of the Romans, Apherus the freed man and his son dedicated this'. There is little doubt that the word Seeir in this inscription refers to Petra and the land of Seir, for this was the spelling that was in use in the time of the Edomites.

There could have been a significant number of Jews of the Diaspora in Petra at the time, having migrated there to take advantage of the trade opened up by the caravan routes, though where commerce was concerned the abilities of the Nabateans might have given the Diaspora some stiff opposition. They may well, however, have been included amongst those foreigners mentioned by Strabo. There is in fact a district in Petra, possibly once a suburb, where a number of crosses have been cut into the stones and this is now known as the Moghr Al Nassara which on translation becomes 'The district of the Nazarenes'. This district must once have been a Christian quarter, but the actual sign of the cross could point to the area being later than the immediate Pauline period.

It is not beyond the bounds of possibility that Paul spent his three years in Arabian Petra. It was out of the immediate reach of the Sanhedrin yet in touch by the caravans with Ananias and the church in Damascus. It is also known that Arabians came to the festivals in Jerusalem Acts 11 II: 'Cretans and Arabs- in our own languages we hear them speaking about God's deeds of power'. This being the case it is not unreasonable to assume that Paul had had the opportunities for furthering his missionary work amongst them: the wealth that the trade routes brought into Petra was certainly conducive to making life there pleasant and unfettered. David also appreciated it as a refuge when he fled the wrath of Saul. As to the reason why Paul is so reticent about this period, even to Luke, is another mystery.

That there are no traditions current in Arabia relating to Paul, or records of any missions to the Jews there, could be due to the fact that Petra fell into a decline and final obscurity when the trade routes diverted to Palmyra. Aretas was followed by Malchus II who lost control of Damascus before he died in A.D. 71, to be succeeded by Rabbell II, who died in A.D. 106. On March 22nd A.D. 106 Trajan passed an edict making the whole region the province of Arabia Petraea and then incorporated the old trade routes Into a Royal road from Damascus to Petra. He then moved the provincial Capital from Petra to Bosra and appointed Cornelius Palma the first governor[13].

By the time Diocletian was Emperor the caravans were exclusively using the trade routes to Palmyra, and this brought about the complete isolation of Petra. But by then the volume of traffic had increased to such an extent that a new road had to be built between Palmyra and Damascus; a highway through the desert some three hundred miles long with wells dug at intervals of twenty four miles to water the caravans, and known as the 'Strata Diocletiana'. This spelt the end of any hope of survival for Petra. As a result the region became totally deserted and fell into an oblivion that was broken only by the few wandering tribes of nomads.

For some six hundred years the site of Petra remained unknown to the Western world; its ruins to be discovered by John Burkhardt in 1810, a Swiss and an Arabic scholar who, when on his numerous travels in Arabia heard vague rumours of its existence. His years spent in the

Middle East had given him the opportunity to study and gain an intimate knowledge of the Koran, and this well equipped him, posing as an Arab with an un suspecting guide, to make the hazardous journey on the pretext of sacrificing at the sacred and revered tomb of Aaron on the summit of the Jebel Haroun. This mountain with its precipitous sides overlooks Petra itself and he was thus the first from the West to see and describe the ancient monuments. By this time, however, any records or legends that might have connected Paul with Petra had long since disappeared.

Even in 1939 the journey to Petra was not to be undertaken lightly. Apart from the main towns such as Amman the roads South to Petra, still then very remote and difficult of access, were tracks through the desert. With a friend whose treasured possession was an old Lafayette car, and only he was accustomed to its idiosyncrasies, we set out in the spring of 1939 to make the Journey from Jerusalem to Amman by way of the Allenby Bridge over the Jordan. This and the night in the old Philadelphia Hotel by the ruins of the Roman Theatre presented no problems. Lulled into a false sense of security we soon found the road from Amman a very different matter for it rapidly gave way to a desert with indeterminate tracks that went eventually to a bridge. This was the first hiccup for a flash flood in the wadi, the result of the late heavy rains, had partially demolished it; luckily the wadi by now was dry and a couple of not very energetic Arabs were in the process of rebuilding it. They cheerfully waved and indicated the fact that we should cross the substantial rubble of the river bed to the other side, and here, in the middle, the engine stalled and stubbornly refused to spring into life.

This was a golden opportunity for the two on the bridge to relieve their boredom and down tools; before we could weigh up the situation they were down from the bridge and had the bonnet open. From then on we had no say in the matter. What appeared to be vital parts of the machinery were soon strewn about the Wadi bed, and as the situation appeared to be increasingly desperate, and by now being resigned to the long walk back to Amman, we began to collect our essentials from the car. However, full of smiles they protested that all would soon be rectified, and eventually, after the pieces strewn about had gone back with nothing left over, the engine miraculously fired and we were pushed out of the wadi. They then scrambled back to their work on the bridge and as we left for the next stop at Qatrana they waved us on our way with shouts of 'Allah be with you'. It was a prayer that we hoped would bear fruit.

In an expanse of nothingness Qatraria is an isolated 'Halt' on the old Hedjaz railway that links Damascus to Maan, the track Lawrence of Arabia and his Arabs made a practice of blowing up during the First World War. Just beyond the Halt is another shallow wadi that is usually crossed by a ford, but again the late rains in the hills had made this a torrent of water. It was a barrier that had to be negotiated but once more the engine stalled when trying to cross, necessitating being dragged out with cheerful help by those of the Arab Legion who policed the Halt. However, Allah had made a note of the intercessions of the two on the bridge for a few minutes later the weekly train from Damascus pulled in to take us on to Maan.

Maan had obviously seen better days. A straggling town of one story shops in colours of dirty yellow and white that lay in an oasis of palms, and here we found a taxi, that had also seen better days, with a driver willing to take us on to the Police Post at Elgi. Forbidding in its splendid and romantic isolation on the foot hills of the mountain range behind it, glowing pink and purple in the setting sun it was a large square fort that oozed the very essence of Beau Geste. As the massive doors opened they creaked ominously but we were very hospitably welcomed with tea whilst an escort prepared horses to take us into Petra.

By the time we reached the yawning chasm of the Siq **(Figure 8)** the sun had long since set, and there was little moon to lighten the intense darkness as we entered the narrow pass. On doing so the escort broke into wild shouts calculated to disperse any evil spirits that might be lurking, and then kept up with songs that echoed against the walls as we clattered through the twisting gorge. This towered above till its topmost rim was outlined in the dim light of the stars, and so until the Siq suddenly opened to a view of the facade of the Kasneh, looming out of the gloom of the opposite cliff: the escort now silent but for desultory chatter as we passed the Roman theatre to Nasser's camp, an establishment that looked after the needs of those few travellers who had somehow made the journey.

In the remoteness of Petra the camp was an integral part of the valley's isolation and helped to preserve the atmosphere of a timeless past. A tomb with a trestle bed and a bucket of water did service as a bedroom, whilst a dutiful patron spent much of his time hunting the local gazelle for their steaks to figure on the menu, and when he was lucky they were served in a basic but not uncomfortable rest room. It was the utter silence that shrouded the monuments and hung over the valley that was disturbing; the absence of life broken only by the few scattered tents of the local Bedul clinging tenaciously to life with their ill nourished goats, silently nibbling at the sparse vegetation. Though the crisp detail of the monumental facades cut laboriously into the coloured stripes of the mountain side are now rubbed partially smooth by the elements, they are still the stupendous relics of a forgotten past. In their midst the tomb of Sextus Florentinus remains a battered reminder of the Roman period **(Figure 9)**.These, and the flights of steps to the mountain tops where silent altars stand on lonely terraces their conduits cut in the rock but empty now of the sacrificial blood to Baal, all remnants of an ancient Biblical heritage and an ancient Pagan culture.

But of all the monuments it is the splendour of Pharaohs' Treasury, the Kasneh, glowing pink in the sun that one does not forget **(Figure 10)** and not to be forgotten either is the 'Deir' in its mountain retreat, the massive facade hewn into the golden cliffs that front a spacious court **(Figure 11)**. A narrow stair in the rock climbs steeply to the roof with its topmost pinnacle, and from here wide ranging views look over the mountains and the ragged peaks of Seir **(Figure 12)**. It is a monument that is not far short in height to that of London's St Pauls. These indeed are the remains of a city that epitomise the strange beauty of what was once the capital of Aretas IV, a bustling and highly commercial centre that Paul might well have known, a city that on one occasion was very irreverently described to me as 'The ancient Clapham Junction of the Middle East'.

Some forty years on I again made the Journey to Petra to find the views and the splendour of the monuments undiminished but the silence had gone with the droves of tourists who wandered in and out of the tombs, clambered over the seats of the theatre and lurked behind hidden corners. Amid the ruins the Bedul were still in their tents, but happily for them life was a good deal easier, they were not so destitute and their children better nourished, even the goats were more agile and sprightly. The column of the Kasneh that then lay shattered on the ground those many years back was now happily restored in one piece but mercifully little else.

The tourists of today leave Amman by air conditioned coach to travel the new Royal road to Petra, then to sleep and dine in the comfortable rest house on the site of the former Nabatean Customs Office, or failing that in one of the thirty or more hotels that have mushroomed in the vicinity. Petra is an unforgettable relic of history that has its roots in the Old Testament but is in danger of losing much of its mystery. What used to be the arid waste of Aquaba is now the sophisticated resort of Eliat with more luxury hotels that have all the amenities of the twentieth century. The hot winds that fanned the furnace fires of the ancient copper smelters still blow, but today they compete and lose the battle with air conditioning. The wealth brought in with the tourists today is a different wealth to that which came in with the ships of Solomon and the caravans of Sheba, who was possibly one of the first and most renowned tourists in history.

The number of visits made by Paul to the Apostles in Jerusalem is not at all clear, In Gal 1 17, he confirms that, after his escape from Damascus, he resolved not to go back to Jerusalem but into Arabia for a period of years, to then return to Damascus. In verse 18 he intimates his stay in Arabia being that of three years, and that he then left Damascus to see and stay with Peter in Jerusalem for fifteen days. He is quite specific in the fact that this visit lasted for fifteen days only and it was only Peter and James he was able to see for he states in verse 19, 'But I did not see any other apostle except James the Lord's brother'. At the end of this visit he goes on to record in verse 21 that: 'Then I went into the regions of Syria and Cilicia', which must indicate, though he did not specifically state the fact, that he then returned home to Tarsus.

Luke records a visit in Acts: IX 26 - 31 which, in spite of the fact that it comes directly after Luke's description of Paul's escape from Damascus, verse 25, could relate to a visit of a later date, and one that took place after Paul's description of his visit in Galatians 1 17-21, that there could have been two separate visits is borne out by the fact that in Acts 26: 'Paul assayed to join himself to the disciples; but that they were all afraid of him, and believed not that he was a disciple'. This is the occasion when Barnabas spoke up for Paul who, in order to demonstrate to the Apostles his sincerity, began to preach vehemently the new doctrine in the Jerusalem synagogues, but in such a manner that the Jews rose up in a body and sought to kill him for blasphemy. To defuse the crisis the disciples took him down to Caesarea and shipped him off to Tarsus, making sure that he caught the boat (Verse 30). That Paul bad been somewhat disruptive is echoed in verse 31: 'Meanwhile the church throughout Judaea, Galilee, and Samaria had peace and was built up', but it could also refer to the Political climate in Palestine at that time in as much that the Judean churches were not then being persecuted to any great extent.

Figure 8: The Siq, Petra.

Figure 9: Tomb Facades in the Mountain Sides that Climatic Conditions have Eroded over the Centuries.

Figure 10: The El Khasneh, known as Solomon's Treasury.

Figure 11: The Deir, Petra.

Figure 12: The Mountains of Seir.

The description of this visit in Acts would seem to be one apart from that described by Paul in Galatians. It is in Acts where Luke describes Barnabas speaking up for Paul before the Apostles, and the account gives the impression that there were more of the Apostles at the meeting apart from Peter and James. Furthermore, the duration of Paul's stay in Jerusalem then appears to have been more than that of fifteen days for Luke records Paul preaching in the synagogues as a demonstration of his sincerity. However, it could well be that these two differing accounts, that of Paul and that of Luke, relate to one and the same occasion. If so it is odd that Paul in Galatians omits to make any reference to Barnabas interceding for him, nor does he record his subsequent preaching in the Synagogues.

It is not known when or how Paul and Barnabas became acquainted[14], but in view of the fact that both of them had relatives living in Jerusalem they could well have known each other for a number of years. Not long after the end of the first missionary journey, when Paul and Barnabas were back in Antioch (Galatians 1), they went up to Jerusalem to see the Apostles in an effort to settle the dispute that had arisen over the circumcision of the Gentiles, and here Paul indicates a lapse of fourteen years since his conversion on the Damascus road, generally accepted as being A.D. 39 or 40. This being so his return to Jerusalem to see the Apostles after his three years away in Damascus and Arabia, and subsequently back to Tarsus, would have been around A.D. 42 - 43, which would have been a year or so after Claudius became Emperor on the 24th January A.D. 41 following the death of Caligula.

There is an unspecified gap in time, its duration the scholarly subject of some varying estimates, but one that could amount to some years, between Paul's return to Tarsus and his joining Barnabas in Antioch. Of this period nothing has been recorded, either in Acts or by Paul in his letters, and it is interesting to speculate on how those years were spent.

In the first place there is the question of Paul's family who were dedicated Pharisees, very specifically brought out by Paul in 2 Cor XI 22 when referring to his upbringing: 'Are they Hebrews? So am I. Are they Israelites? So am I. Are they the descendants of Abraham? So am I'. Did they take kindly to Paul's apostasy or did they reject him? Did his sister by any chance join the Church? Later in Jerusalem it was his nephew who was instrumental in bringing the warning to Paul and Claudius Lycias that the Jews were out to kill him. In view of this, the relations between them must have been cordial and not in any way strained. Paul does make a reference to 'my relatives' in Romans XVI 7: 'Greet Andronicus and Junia, my relatives-They were in Christ before I was'. This, however, could be misleading. More than likely it is not a reference to any family relationship, however distant, but an expression denoting they were compatriots.

Again if Paul took his mission to the synagogues of Tarsus how did they react to his teaching? It is far from comprehensible that he would have remained silent; yet there are no hints of him being involved in any unpleasant disputes during this period with the Tarsian Jews. It is possible that he spent some of the time in the founding of the Churches in Syria and Cilicia

[14] Barnabas was one of the first to join the Church. A wealthy Levite he sold his land and gave the money to the Apostles. The respective ages of Paul and Barnabas have not been recorded but it is possible that he knew Paul when he was studying with Gamaliel. The friendship, if there was one, must have lapsed when Barnabas joined the Church and Paul began to persecute it; for Barnabas to come to his help when he was convinced of Paul's change of heart.

that he mentions when he and Silas set out on the second Journey: 'He went through Syria and Cilicia strengthening the churches' (Acts XV 41).

In 2 Cor XI 26-27 Paul mentions the hardships be had to endure when on his travels, some of them incidents that have not been recorded in any detail elsewhere: it could be that some of them relate to this period. What is very apparent is the fact that he had had little if any communication with Barnabas in Jerusalem during this time. It was when Barnabas felt the need for Paul's help in Antioch that the wording in Acts 11 25 & 26. becomes interesting for it is then clear that Barnabas had no idea just where he was to be found and went to Tarsus, no doubt to his home, to find out where he was. 'Then Barnabas went to Tarsus to look for Saul, and when he had found him, he brought him to Antioch'. The passage also suggests that Paul was not at that time to be found in Tarsus and had to be looked for elsewhere.

CHAPTER 2

Antioch and the First Missionary Journey.

During the first centuries A.D. Antioch was one of the three largest cities in the ancient world and could be counted, without any doubt, as one of the most splendid within the bounds of the Roman Empire; for it certainly rivalled the intellectual sophistication of Alexandria and the magnificence of Ephesus that had long reached its architectural perfection in the Temple of the Ephesian Diana. Furthermore the Antioch of the first centuries A.D. could well have been the 'Las Vegas' of the day, for its urban life in beautiful surroundings was more than easy. Rare goods and chattels and other such luxuries were to be found in abundance in the shops and markets, all having been brought in by way of the Arabian trade routes and all testifying to a sophisticated and high standard of living; to say that it was a wealthy and permissive society would be an understatement. No one in their right mind ever wished to leave Antioch.

After the murder of the Emperor Pertinax in Rome in A.D. 193, Percennius Niger, who then commanded the Legions in Syria and was the Senate's preferred candidate to succeed as Emperor, was so besotted and mesmerised with the delights that Antioch had on offer he found he could not bear to tear himself away, and as a result of this dilatory behaviour he lost the position to Septimius Severus, the then governor of Upper Pannonia; for Severus, not letting the grass grow under his feet, marched on Rome with his legions and established himself there as Emperor, in spite of a lukewarm opposition from an apprehensive Senate.

The Antiochenes subsequently felt the wrath of Severus for supporting Niger, who lost his life when confronting Severus on the plains of Issus near Antioch and then, in order to teach the Antiochenes a lesson, he proceeded to demolish a part of the City. However, it seems not to have been too great a disaster for some time later, after the Parthian wars, Severus rested his Legions in Antioch whilst he and his Empress Julia Donna were away on a state visit to Alexandria, a visit made in order to improve relations between Rome and the Egyptians and also to confirm their continued shipments of grain to Italy.

In the days of Paul and Barnabas Antioch covered a far greater expanse than the Antioch of today and would have been much as Severus had found it. The City then spread out from the lower slopes of Mount Silpius to the plains beyond and had the river Orontes flowing through its centre as it does today. The name 'Orontes' has a romantic aura that can bring to the mind the spectacle of a clear sparkling torrent rushing down from the mountains, and so it could well have been in the early centuries A.D., whereas today it is somewhat disappointingly sluggish, muddy in colour and almost brackish.

The main thoroughfare of ancient Antioch extended for some four miles and went the entire length of the City, from one end to the other. It would in fact have been five times the length of Edinburgh's Prince's Street. It had a central course that was wide enough for both carts and chariots to drive abreast, and was flanked on either side by a walk that was protected by a series of colonnades. This was reserved solely for pedestrians and had under the colonnades a variety of shops and boutiques. Many other streets led off at right angles from this main street and these were paved with a marble that glistened white in the strong sun, and here too were situated the Civic buildings, the Agora and the smaller markets, the Temples, the shops, and the fountains; the whole embellished with statues of civic dignitaries, famous philosophers, and the celebrities of past that the Antiochenes wished to honour. All of this was enhanced by Triumphal Arches resplendent with golden adornment, and monuments dedicated by the City Fathers to the Emperors they wished to honour and commemorate.

It was a city of great elegance that had been laid out, more or less, to the precepts of Hippodamus of Miletos, the first individual to formulate the principles of town planning. Ideally it followed the pattern of a gridiron by having a series of buildings arranged in blocks, or insulae, that were separated at regular intervals by intersecting streets; in those days too the air would have been pure and clear, happily free of the atmospheric pollution that bedevils many large cities today.

Beautiful villas that were the domains of the wealthy were situated within the city precincts, and many others were to be found in the suburbs as they spread out over the slopes of Mount Silpius, all of them having the amenities that came with central heating and a sophisticated plumbing; Libanius, a native of Antioch, wrote thus of the water supply:

'In the public baths every stream has the proportion of a river, in the private several the like and the rest not much less, the public fountains flow for ornament since everyone has water within his doors'.

Every section of the City had its own public baths, each striving to outdo the other in its magnificence, and one has only to see those in Pompeii and Herculaneum to imagine how elegant they must have been.

It was a City of substance that pandered to the desires of the very well off. This section of the populace not only included those who had means enough in their retirement to enable them to relax and enjoy an equable climate, but also included those who belonged to Antioch's long standing and very wealthy families of the aristocracy; all of them in contrast to the inevitable and more vulgar nouveaux riches, whose main objective was to indulge in 'one upmanship', something very reminiscent of the present twenty first century.

The scope for pleasure was endless. At night and until the fingers of dawn came over the horizon the whole of the city was brilliantly lit, and here again Libanius writes: 'With us night is distinguished from day only by the difference in the lighting', - this incidentally is the first ever reference to street lighting in any ancient city - and he continues 'diligent hands find no difference and forge on, and he who will sings and dances, so that Hephaestos and Aphrodite here share the night between them'. What could be more descriptive or explicit – 'Las Vegas indeed'![15]

All aspects of society were catered for. The theatres were venues for the theatrical companies that toured the provinces of North Africa, Asia Minor, and elsewhere, together with their extensive props and stage machinery. Here they put on their tragedies, comedies, and

---

[15] H.V. Morton, In the Steps of Saint Paul.

their mimes. Also periodically visiting were groups of performers from other cultures who came to stage displays of their traditional dances, and the companies of musicians who came to give their recitals and concerts, all of them being well patronised. Distinct from all these there was also the large bag of mixed performers who appealed to the more plebeian members of society, the jugglers, the wrestlers, the mimics and the tight rope walkers, not to mention the renowned pugilists who came from Castabala, all of them giving their sundry performances in the streets and market places. How many of us who watch buskers entertaining theatre queues with their antics today, or pass them in the underground stations, realise that they are carrying on an age old tradition that has come down to us from those who performed in the streets of the Roman Empire.

As well as being dedicated to the theatres, and the many other cultural attractions, the citizens of Antioch were also addicted to the races. Their interest in these events was so consuming it became an essential part of their way of life, and this not only in Antioch but notably also in Carthage, and many other large cities of the Empire. The racing stables were national institutions and they fell into two groups. The Blues and The Greens, and many well known jockeys came down to Antioch to take part in the season's meetings, the most renowned and esteemed for their ability being those who came from Laodiciea, a city not unknown to Paul.

The intense rivalry between the two factions and their respective supporters could be very bitter for their intense partisanship spread throughout all strata of society, and occasionally spilled over into civic violence, just as happens today amongst those who support their various football teams. At times this partisanship involved the Emperors, for it was those who came from the stables of the Greens who had the wholehearted goodwill and the active support of both Caligula and Claudius.

In his book 'Ancient Times' Professor Breasted gives an account of the many amenities that the Antiochenes enjoyed through their achievements in technology. They appear, for example, to have developed washing machines that automatically supplied soap and water, and the concierge in some of the villas could open the door by an automatic remote control. The sacred libations for those who worshipped in the Temples could be delivered in a constant quantity from automatic dispensers, and complicated systems of irrigation were developed to give the country an extensive supply of water from the Orontes. Massive water wheels raised water from the river and the like of these can still be seen working today on the Orontes at Hama in Syria. Neither was military science neglected for the loading of stone on to engines of war was accomplished by a series of weights and pulleys.

All this was a part of an everyday existence for the Antiochenes. However, in spite of the fact that the majority of the populace thought of little else but wine, women and song, and took every advantage of the material pleasures of life, associated as they were with a low moral code, the Jewish population of the Diaspora led a more restrained and quiet existence. They were respected in the fact that they did not exhibit so much of that militant and contentious streak that was a characteristic of those of the Diaspora who lived wide spread in other Cities of the Empire. In Antioch, though the two cultures were markedly divided, relations were harmonious enough between the Jewish faction and the Civic authorities for Herod himself to have undertaken and paid for the marble paving that was a feature of many of the city's busy streets. Not only did Herod contribute to the sophistication of Antioch but Caligula also, in as much that during his reign of four years as Emperor he gave the Caligula baths to the city as well as a new aqueduct.

In common with other cities of the Empire Antioch was the home for many religious cults, all tolerated by the Romans as long as they did not have a political bias and it was to this Antioch that Barnabas and Paul came to spread the Gospel. Already in Antioch spreading the Gospel were some of the disciples who had fled Jerusalem after the stoning of Stephen, and these included Lucius of Cyrene, Simeon called Niger and Manaen, who could have been the foster brother of Herod the Tetrach and with him, when children, educated in Rome. These together with Paul and Barnabas were now the prophets and teachers of the Church.

By that time many of the Jews of the Diaspora in Antioch had already absorbed much of the Hellenistic outlook and were prepared to accept the teaching of the Apostolic Church, as did many of the Gentiles, God fearers as they were known, who hovered on the fringes of Judaism but were not prepared to accept the Jewish Law in its entirety. Thus, and in spite of the outrageous permissive society that existed in Antioch, it was these early days in the city that heralded the foundations of the first Christian Church, and it was here that the word Christian was first coined, possibly at first by the more orthodox when referring to them in a derogatory manner.

The Praetorian Guard, following the murder of Caligula in Rome, had by now proclaimed Claudius Emperor, but much against his will, and it was about this time when the great drought, recorded in Acts XI 28. and referred to by Josephus in his History of the Jews, broke out in Palestine. It inflicted a great deal of need and privation for those of the Church in Jerusalem, their difficulties becoming the concern of the Antioch Church, and to alleviate those who were suffering the Church undertook a collection of monies, each member giving what he could afford to a central fund that was to be taken to the Apostles and those of the Jerusalem Church by Paul and Barnabas. One of the jealously guarded prerogatives of the Jews in the Colonial cities of the Empire was their right to collect monies for a yearly donation to the Temple in Jerusalem, and Paul and Barnabas were following this precedent.

Several inscriptions and references are extant from the time of Augustus that relate to this prerogative. One written to Ephesus by Gaius Narbonius Flaccus reads:

'Gaius Narbonius Flaccus, proconsul, to the magistrates of the Ephesians - greetings, Caesar has written to me that the Jews, wherever they may be, are accustomed in accordance with their ancient practice, to gather and contribute money which they send to Jerusalem, it is his wish that they not be prevented from doing this. I have therefore written to you so that you may know that he orders this to be done'.

This letter follows the one from Augustus, who was then known as Octavian, to Narbonius Flaccus, a letter recorded by Josephus that reads, 'Caesar to Narbonius Flaccus, greetings. The Jews, however many there may be, who in accordance with their ancient practice are accustomed to collect sacred money and send to Jerusalem are to do this without hindrance'. Flaccus then sent a copy of this letter to each of the major cities in Asia Minor.

A further letter from Agrippa to Ephesus has also been recorded by Josephus and shows that these monies were often prone and subject to a deal of fiddling, it states:

'Agrippa to the Magistrates, consul and people of the Ephesians, greetings. It is my wish that the Jews of Asia, in accordance with their ancestral custom, exercise the care and custody of the sacred money conveyed to the Temple in Jerusalem, and that those who steal the sacred money of the Jews and flee to asylum be dragged out and handed to the Jews under the law by which Temple robbers are dragged out. I have also written to Silanus, the Praetor that no one should force a Jew to bail on the Sabbath'.

Still a further letter to Cyrene in North Africa was an answer to a complaint from the Jews of that City, in that they had been prevented from forwarding the monies that they had collected to Jerusalem. The pretext being that the Jews had not paid the tax that had been levied by the City administration on these donations. This of course was another local fiddle, and indicative of the pervading ill will that existed between the two large communities in Cyrene, the majority of the populace being purely Greek. On this occasion, however, the Jews won the day and the City fathers had to refund the tax in accordance with the edict of Caesar, if indeed it had ever been paid[16].

Though Barnabas was a native of Cyprus he did have a sister, 'Mary', living in Jerusalem with her son Mark, thus a nephew of Barnabus, and after their arrival in Jerusalem with the donations from the Antioch Church it could well have been that Paul and Barnabas lodged with her, for her house was the accepted meeting place for those of the Church in Jerusalem. It has been suggested that the last supper took place in one of her upper rooms, However, at the time of their arrival in Jerusalem the feelings of the Sadducees and the Pharisees were running high against the Apostolic Church and Herod Agrippa 1st, in order to curry favour with the Jews, had incarcerated Peter and, furthermore, beheaded James the brother of John. It was the custom in Jerusalem for the Apostles and the Church to hold their meetings in secret behind the locked doors of Mary's house which explains why Peter, after his miraculous escape from prison, found it difficult to persuade Rhoda to let him enter. The account in Acts XII is too clear an episode not to have had some basis in truth, or to have been entirely fabricated by Luke, and Peter must obviously have remained in hiding until the death of Herod in A.D. 44. It was the general unrest in Jerusalem at this time, coupled with the fear of Herod's persecutions that must have prompted Paul and Barnabas to take the young Mark with them when they returned to Antioch.

Up to the late nineteen thirties, now many years ago, Antioch was a sleepy Arab town in Syria, and not within the borders of Turkey as it is today. It was then a jumble of narrow streets and houses at the foot of Mount Silpius, and still split into two districts by the Orontes. In some respects the intervening years have seen little change, in spite of the modern suburbs that now spread out beyond the river with their blocks of flats, shops, and luxury hotels. The old roof top

---

[16] See Augustus to Nero, 31 B.C. - A.D.68, David C. Braund.

restaurant that I used to visit has long since vanished and given way to a new complex that makes it difficult to remember exactly where it was, and what had existed there previously.

Thankfully the old town has changed but little, life and business still goes on, very much as it did of old, in the picturesque alleys and squares that are dominated here and there by the minarets of old mosques **(Figures 13 A and 13B)**. Here they lurk behind their battered doors set in the ancient walls of these narrow alleys, shaded as they are with the interlaced canopy of trailing vines. It is only the merchandise in the little shops and booths that reflect the passage of time, for now they are cluttered with the latest transistors, Seiko watches, and every make of calculator.

Simply nothing remains of Roman Antioch and its erstwhile splendour. It is difficult to fathom how it could have been so completely swept away for the few features that remain are the scanty ruins of the aqueduct, parts of the city walls high up on Mount Silpius, and cut into the cliffs not far from the cave that was once the Church of St Peter is the massive head of Charon. At one time the effigy had a golden crown and was a tourist attraction of some antiquity when Paul was in Antioch. The Antiochenes carved it out of the cliff face some two centuries previous to his stay in the city, and this in a laborious effort to placate the gods whom they thought they had offended, and to enlist their protection against the ravages of a plague.

The ancient Church of St Peter in the cliffs of Mount Silpius is reached by threading a devious way through the rambling suburbs of old Antioch to its outskirts. A steep flight of steps leads up the rocky hillside to a gate that gives on to a broad terrace fronting the cliffs **(Figure 14)**. Way back in the past the cave interior was protected by a cream stone facade with windows and a formal entrance and from the terrace there are distant views over low lying Antioch. From here the reflections of the sun on the roofs and minarets can almost, but it does need a little stretch of the imagination, reflect Antioch as it could have been some centuries ago.

On certain days of the week the approach by the narrow road to the steps to the Church is often blocked by a busy tobacco market, the dealers frenetically bidding for the broad brown leaf done up in bales that haphazardly and effectually clutter the street. In the vicinity of the Church there is, more often than not, the ubiquitous Antiochene who will advance in a conspiratorial manner, when he thinks the coast is clear, and proffer in his hand a selection of Roman coins. 'Antika' he says in a hushed and confidential voice as he endeavours to persuade you to buy them as genuine, when one knows only too well they are as spurious as he himself. These vendors are following in the footsteps of an old profession, for many of them were scratching a living in such a manner when Morton visited the Church over fifty years ago.

Behind the facade the cave is lofty and impressive and has a simple altar that stands away from the back wall **(Figure 15)**. In the not so distant past the Church was under the jurisdiction of the Capuchin Fathers, and tradition has it that it was the meeting place for Peter and Paul. One can but wonder if it was here by chance where the argument over Peter's treatment of the Gentiles took place, when Peter came down to Antioch and refused to eat with them, and Barnabas likewise, much to the disgust of Paul.

From a corner in the back of the cave a tunnel leads into the mountain and there being no alternative exit it could have been the escape route should an emergency arise. A tradition that has its origin in lost records of some seventh century manuscripts, at the time then available and used by John of Antioch, state the fact that Paul and Barnabas used to preach in an area that was then known as Signon Street in the district of Epiphania. The site was said to be located in a region that lay somewhere under the cliffs of Mount Silpius: obviously it cannot be pinpointed today, but it is wise to respect old traditions for they often contain more than a grain of truth, and this ancient Church could well go back to the days of Paul and Barnabas.

In the first centuries A.D. Antioch was renowned for the sacred laurel groves that grew in profusion in the nearby sanctuary of Daphne. The groves are now a part of the modern suburb of Harbiye, only a short distance from the city, but it is an area that is still wooded with forest and laurel and with streams that splash over scattered rocks to then rush down the sides of steep ravines to the valleys below. In the Hellenistic and Roman periods it was a district that was greatly revered by the Antiochenes, and renowned through the ancient world for here it was where Daphne was pursued by an over amorous and rampant Apollo. Fast realising that she was losing the race she desperately, and in a last resort, prayed to Venus to help her: on her part it must have been an unwise decision for in no time at all she was turned into a laurel bush. Her endeavour to protect her chastity from the desires of an eager Apollo led her to an end that was probably more than she had bargained for. For a goddess, or whoever, to have come to such a pass rather than let nature take its course, to the Antiochenes and those of the Roman world, was almost incomprehensible.

In the last centuries B.C. and the first centuries A.D. the laurel groves extended over the many acres that were given over to the villas of the wealthy and the Temples dedicated to the unfortunate Daphne. The rites associated with the Temples reflected the many sexual cults that were then prevalent. Syria was renowned for them. Here in the groves the Temples were manned, if that is the right word, by a body of priestess prostitutes who came from far and wide to proffer their services, and not only to the goddess. Wealthy citizens procured these priestesses at a price from the various slave markets of Asia Minor, a notable one being that of Side, and then presented them to the Temples of their choice.

They were known throughout the Empire as the 'Daphnici Mores', and were as notorious as the priestesses who served in the Temple of Venus on the summit of Acro Corinth. They too were renowned throughout the length and breadth of the Roman world and were known as 'The Corinthian Girls', their assets no doubt the topic of many a conversation in the taverns of the Mediterranean harbours.

Tourism has now taken over the Groves of Daphni and in no uncertain fashion. The woods and the views could almost be the same but now the streams, before they reach the falls, are straddled with stepping stones, chairs, and tables where coffee or coca cola is served from numerous little cafes to those who sit astride the waters. However, in many places there is an unfortunate litter of old cans together with small heaps of other detritus, but it could well have been somewhat the same in the days of Paul, for the groves of Daphne were as popular then as they are now.

Figure 13a: Life Today in Old Antioch.

Figure 13b: Life Today in Old Antioch.

Figure 14: Cave Church of St Peter in Antioch.

Figure 15: Interior of the Cave Church of St Peter in Antioch

In the Antioch museum you have only to study the mosaics from the temples and Villas of Daphne, Antiochea, and Seleukia, as well as those from more prosaic institutions, like the one of commendable size that was once the floor of a restaurant, to realise that the efforts of Paul and Barnabas in establishing the first Christian Church in Antioch was of little consequence for the majority of the Antiochenes: they took little notice. Their relaxed and pagan way of life, as vividly demonstrated in these mosaics, continued to prosper for well over two hundred years after the death of Paul. For Picennius Niger to have been loath to have given up the delights of Antioch for Rome, even though it was certain that the Senate would have then made him Emperor, is not to be wondered at **(Figures 16,17,18,19,20)**.

However, in one of the mosaic floors, that could date to the second century, there is a small cross that has not been repeated elsewhere in the design: it is pure speculation as to whether this had, by any chance, any covert Christian significance **(Figure 21)**.

When I came back to the car I had parked by the entrance to the Groves I found that it had been spotlessly cleaned by a couple of youthful entrepreneurs, both armed with cloths and buckets of the clear water from the streams. They were smiling and cheerful and seemed very happy with their remuneration, inflation is as much, or more, of a problem in Turkey as elsewhere.

The itinerary of the first missionary journey, though it is well documented, was not preordained from the beginning but was due to force of circumstance. It began when Paul and Barnabas, accompanied by the young Mark, set sail from Seleukia for the Island of Cyprus. Barnabas was a native of Cyprus and it was only natural that this should be their first objective in spreading the Gospel. Seleukia was the Port for Antioch and in the Roman period was one of the most important in that part of the Mediterranean basin. To reach the bay of Seleukia the road winds its way down from Antioch through the hills and the villages to the coast, a road that did not exist in Morton's day; on his first attempt he had to contend with the winter rains that made the dirt road impassable. In those days it was a fair weather track that gave way in later years to a narrow made up road; now being replaced by a motor way that will undoubtedly have a dire affect on life in the quiet coastal villages.

The bay when reached is extensive, with distant and far ranging views that are dominated to the South by the peak of Mount Cassius and by a promontory at its Northern aspect. Here at the northern aspect are the ruins of Seleukia itself, the ancient site being the village of Teknepinar which is fast accumulating the many trappings of a popular resort. Seleukia is in effect two towns. The larger that was both residential and commercial, being built on the higher slopes of the mountain that overlooked the port whilst the town at the foot of the lower slopes incorporated the harbour with its attendant seafaring installations. The ruins of the upper city cover a vast area and its importance and standing can be judged from the mosaic floors to be seen in the Antioch museum. There are numerous tombs cut into the rocks that are a part of the landscape outside the city precincts, many of them dating to well before the days of Paul and Barnabas: and it is more than likely that the Apostles lodged in upper Seleukia whilst awaiting a suitable boat to take them on to Cyprus.

Little remains of the ancient port: its few scattered ruins have been further obscured by the municipal development that has taken place over the last fifty years or so, and is still progressing. The sea has retreated since Biblical times but even so there are still a great many ashlar blocks that could be the remains of an old mole: for the most part they are tumbled heaps that curve out into the bay and may, or may not, be of Roman origin. However, the one extraordinary feature that has withstood the passage of time is the massive tunnel and conduit that the Emperor Titus cut through the mountain side in A.D. 70, same few years after the death of Paul and a little before the obliteration of Pompeii and Herculaneum.

The whole of this region was subject to sudden and violent storms that, before the construction of this impressive conduit, made the lower town a victim of disastrous flooding, but the conduit was able to combat the situation and the storm water that came down in torrents from the hills was diverted directly into the sea. It was a feat of the first magnitude for certain sections cut through the solid rock are over twenty feet in depth and the whole proved entirely successful **(See Figure 22)**. The entrance to the lower aspect of this conduit is not far from the coastal road and near a modern block of flats, and having found the entrance it is an easy matter to walk up its entire length, its sides reaching to the sky. This then gives way to the tunnel and the whole extends for some fourteen hundred yards. The great majority of the labour that Titus employed on the project came from the many Jews he took as prisoners of war following the sack of Jerusalem in A.D. 70, and in this they were often assisted by mariners and troops from the IVth Syrian Legion. An inscription carved into the rock reads 'Divus Vespasianus et Divus Titus' and this commemorates, and thus corroborates, the date when it was finished.

More inscriptions are to be found in the conduit; some referring to the mariners who were involved in the project whilst others relate to those of the IVth Syrian Legion who also participated in the enterprise. The Emperor Titus was much endeared to and respected by the Maritime community, and this to the extent that they built and dedicated a Temple to him in Ostia Antica, the great port for Rome, where much of it is still intact, even so it is possible that few realise the regard in which he was held by this community.

From here Barnabas, Paul, and the young Mark embarked for Cyprus on the first Missionary Journey, and as there are no records or mention of Paul having had any previous contact with the island this must have been his first visit. They landed at Salamis, a large and busy port that was on one of the major trade routes in that part of the Mediterranean and noted for the export of oil and copper. From the time of Herod the copper mines of Cyprus supplied the greater part of the needs of the ancient world and the island has given its name to the metal for it was then known as 'cyprium', to be shortened in the later centuries to 'cupram'.

Figure 16: Mosaic of a Negro Slave, Antioch.

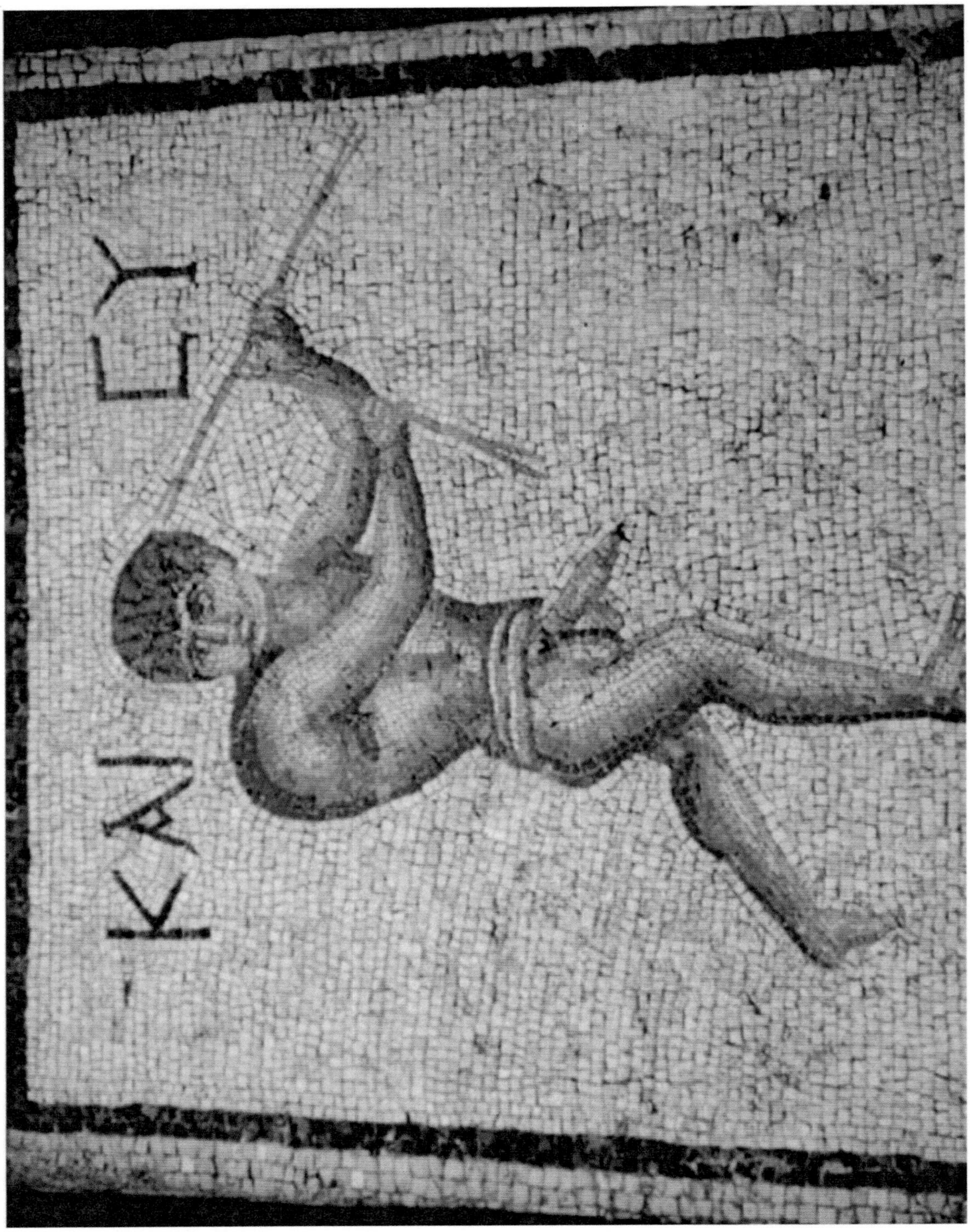

Figure 17: Mosaic of the Happy Hunchback, Antioch.

Figure 18: Orpheus.

Figure 19: Pompeian Couple.

Figure 20: Mosaic of Neptune, Antioch.

Figure 21: Mosaic Floor with the Symbol of a Cross.

Figure 22: A Section of the Conduit cut by Trajan to Divert Storm Water from Flooding Lower Seleucia

The commercial wealth of Cyprus revolved around Salamis and for this reason an inordinate population of Jews had for generations, and well before the Crucifixion, been an integral part of the population. They too had become very wealthy through the export trade, for the Jews of the Diaspora didn't waste their time in cities that had little prospect for good business. Over the years they must have gained a great deal of influence in Salamis for Acts XIII 5 gives an indication as to their numbers, 'When they arrived at Salamis, they proclaimed the word of God in the synagogues of the Jews. And they had John, i.e. John Mark, to assist them'. The ruins of Salamis today, its Agora, its markets and its hippodrome all attest to its extent and erstwhile importance, though one has to use one's imagination to see the extent of its public buildings, its temples and once busy harbour now practically obliterated with sand. One of the major disasters to befall Salamis took place in the reign of Trajan when the very numerous and wealthy Jews of Salamis under the leadership of Artemio rioted to such an extent, as in Cyrene, that they massacred some two hundred and forty thousand of their fellow citizens, the city being largely destroyed in the fracas. Again it was left to Hadrian to expel the remainder of the Jews from the island and partially rectify the damage, the Jews not then ever being allowed to return.

In A.D. 23 Augustus raised the status of Cyprus to that of an imperial province and moved the capital from Salamis to Paphos. It then became the seat of the Roman governor who had the title of Proconsul, and also the headquarters of the Roman garrison. When the Apostles arrived in Paphos from Salamis the governor Sergius Paulus was being somewhat influenced by the Jewish sorcerer Elymas Barjesus. In view of Paul's teaching in Paphos Sergius Paulus decided that they should confront each other before him, a meeting which Elymas had to attend against his fervent protestations. The description of Paul's treatment of Elymas in Acts XIII. 8, 9,10 & 11 is interesting for Paul could have used hypnosis to bring about the Jews' attack of blindness, a condition that appears to have been of a temporary nature, 'You son of the devil, you enemy of all righteousness, full of all deceit and villainy, will you stop making crooked the straight paths of the Lord? And now listen, the hand of the Lord is against you, and you will be blind for a while, unable to see the sun'. It was this denunciation of Elymas by Paul that contributed to the conversion of Paulus to the precepts of the church.

The Cypriots have the tradition of Paul being flogged in Paphos. Nearby the ruins of the Temple to Venus there is a small church with a courtyard that could have been an old Roman market place, and in it are three pillars of which one is supposedly where Paul was tethered and beaten, but this must be taken with a very large grain of salt. Paul's relationship with Sergius Paulus was a cordial one and there is no reason for him to have had Paul beaten, furthermore the relationship was such that it was at this juncture, again supposedly, that Paul changed his name from Saul to Paul. Acts records Paul having been beaten by the Romans on three occasions, but the only one described is that which took place at Philippi.

An inscription on a boundary stone found in the Tiber, dating to the early part of the reign of Claudius, names a Lucius Sergius Paulus as one of the custodians of the river banks. The dating was such that he could be one and the same as the Sergius Paulus of Cyprus whom Paul could have converted to the church. A Lucius Sergius Paulus put up a monument in Pisisdian Antioch to his father who could have been the Proconsul, and a daughter Sergia Paulus became the wife of the legate of Lycia and Pamphilia during the time of Domitian. Other inscriptions in Asia Minor suggest that the Paulus family owned wealthy estates in the district and their important connections with Pisidian Antioch obviously lasted over the years[17].

In view of the above it has been suggested that it was at the instigation of the Governor Paulus that the Apostles should go to Pisidian Antioch on leaving Paphos, and it is possible that they carried with them letters of introduction. Though other reasons have been put forward to account for Paul's decision to take his ministry to Antiochiea, this, the more mundane, would seem to be the most likely even though, according to Acts, it was due to the influence of the Holy Ghost. Acts stipulates this spiritual influence was the reason for the sudden changes in direction made by Paul in his other journeys, when in all probability his decisions were brought about by local circumstance.

To reach Pisidian Antioch, (Antiochiea), meant crossing from Cyprus to Attaleia, today's Antalya, on the Phamphylian coast, the nearest port for the regular shipping, and from here it was but a short distance to Perga situated as it was on the coastal plain and backed by the distant Taurus mountains. However, Strabo has recorded the fact that, in his day, the river Cestrus was navigable some seven miles from the sea to Perga itself with moorings near the Temple of Diana, and it is possible that the Apostles could have used this to their advantage. A hint that this could have been the case is reflected in Act, XIII 13 'Then Paul and his companions set sail from Paphos and came to Perga in Pamphylia'. Though the Cestrus is no longer navigable it still flows through the valley.

In the first century A.D. the road between Attaleia and Perga was well paved for Perga itself was a splendid Greco- Roman city that was one of several to be found along the coast. Sillyon was its nearest neighbour, whilst away up in the mountains lay the more remote and distant Selge. Perga gives the aura of a city of intellectuals and it was in fact the home of the astronomer Appolonius who, in the third century B.C., was the first to come to the conclusion that the moon orbited the earth and that the earth revolved around the sun. It was a city of fine buildings and notable architecture whilst that of Sillyon built on a nearby hill was more austere and very well fortified, so much so that the city had the distinction of being successful in defying Alexander the Great. In view of its position he decided not to waste time by laying siege to it, but passed it by when on his way to subdue Aspendos that lay a little further to the East, and also not far from the coast. Paul makes no mention of Sillyon though a road did link the two cities and, according to local rumour an underground tunnel also exists between them.

To walk through the ruins of Perga is to realize that, in the first centuries A.D. it was a city of great charm and sophistication, clearly demonstrated by the many remnants of sculptured friezes, decorated blocks, and parts of coffered ceilings embossed with the detailed heads of Medusa that are scattered about. Amongst them are the fragments of architectural embellishment that once graced the city's various public and municipal buildings, fragments that are rich in acanthus and geometric decoration whilst others have figures of winged harpies and the replicas of actors' masks of tragedy and humour **(See Figures 23,24 25,26)**.

---

[17] See Pagans and Christians, Robin Lane Fox, also The Book of Acts in its first century setting. Gill and Gempf.

Perga was dedicated to Artemis and Apollo, and a series of marble columns in the street of that name have the figures of these deities sculpted on the drums beneath their capitals; at one time they might have been a part of the famous sanctuary of the Pergan Artemis that, in view of its beauty and splendour, was considered to be one of the wonders of the day.

When the Apostles with Mark arrived in Perga they inevitably must have entered the City through the massive Hellenistic Gate, one that was flanked on either side by large towers, the whole giving on to a spacious courtyard that was horseshoe in shape. The three of them must have passed through this gate on numerous occasions but they did not see the improvements that were wrought upon it in A.D. 120 by Plancia Magna the daughter of Plancius Varius, a past governor of the province of Bithynia. Unusual for a woman in that day and age she attained the highest position in the municipal administration by being appointed the city's chief magistrate. She was also wealthy enough to finance many improvements in Perga's amenities, and these included facing with marble the whole of that part of the Hellenistic Gate that looked on to the central court. To this she added a white marble facade of the Corinthian order, and in the niches of its upper register she placed a number of statues, also in marble, that included those of Plancius Varus and his son C. Plancius Varus. These alterations the Apostles would not have seen nor would they have seen many of the buildings that form much of the ruins that we see today, such as the fourth century gate that was built in front of the Hellenistic one, and the City walls that also date to a later period.

The City was divided into four quarters by two main streets, and of the two the most important was that which began at the Hellenistic Gate, this then went through the centre of the Town to an ornate Nymphaeum built by Hadrian at the foot of the Acropolis Hill. An ornamental conduit carrying water from the Nymphaeum divided this particular street into two broad thoroughfares, each of them some twenty one meters in width, and each of them lined on either side by Ionic colonnades and a tessellated pavement that gave on to a series of shops and boutiques. Each thoroughfare was open to wheeled vehicles that, over the course of many years of traffic, have left deep ruts scored in the paving **(See Figure 27)**.

Such an ornamental conduit dividing the principal street of a city into two wide thoroughfares was a feature that, until quite recently could be seen in one of the main streets of Antalya, and of almost the same dimensions, both sides being associated with their shops and apartments. However, some dignitary from the Municipality has thought fit to have it completely filled in and thus a feature that was quite unique has been destroyed. It was one that could have harked back to antiquity as the Triple Gate of Hadrian also looks out on to this street, Indicating that it could have had its origins in one of the main thoroughfares of ancient Attaleia **(See Figures 28)**.

Figure 23: Example (i) of Marble Decoration that Once Embellished the Public Buildings of Perga.

Figure 24 Example (ii) of Marble Decoration that Once Embellished the Public Buildings of Perga.

Figure 25: Example (iii) of Marble Decoration that once Embellished the Public Buildings of Perga.

Figure 26: Bas Relief of an Actor's Mask and that of a Winged Harpie.

Figure 27: The Main Colonnaded Street of Perga with the Central Water Course fed from the Nymphaeum.

Figure 28: A Similar Water Course in the Main Street of Antalya that has since been Covered Over.

Before entering Perga's main street of columns there is, on the right hand side, the entrance to a large square Agora, and here the doorways and lintels of the shops are very akin and similar to the features and proportions of the Georgian period. In classic style they border the sides of the Agora, and devoid of any decoration they look across tessellated pavements that have black geometric designs to another series of imposing colonnades. These enclose a large area where a round kiosk dominates the centre of the market, a building that could have been either a small Temple or failing that a Macellum, a more mundane meat market. Lying flat on the ground and not far away is a white marble support - the other has disappeared - to what must have been a butcher's slab or counter, for on its flat surface is embossed the bas relief of a cleaver and meat hook **(See Figures 29 and 30)**. This Agora, as it stands today, was not the one that was familiar to the Apostles, for it too was altered in the Fourth Century, when much of Perga was being rebuilt.

The city was not without its municipal baths for there were two such establishments, the most important being that situated only a short distance from the Hellenistic Gate. It was a sophisticated structure that had a series of rooms that were lofty, of generous proportions, and heated by hypocausts. There were also rooms with plunge baths and marble benches alongside the walls to suit the convenience of the bathers. It also had the luxury of a large swimming pool, and in later years the whole complex was approached through a magnificent portal put up by Septimius Severus when he became Emperor. Even taking into account the general sophistication of Perga, there is the impression that these baths could have been more splendid and spacious than the city would have warranted.

The stadium was another of Perga's impressive structures and this could accommodate up to fourteen thousand people. Situated just outside the City walls and not far from the Theatre it remains one of the very few that have survived to the present day. Though it is not in such a good state of preservation as that at Aphrodisias, it leaves little to the imagination for it is possible, even now, to sit on its seats and look across to its tier upon tier, filling them in their ruined isolation with the ghosts of past spectators, and conjure up its once hubbub of antiquity.

It was built on a superstructure of rooms that were mostly given over to shops and boutiques, for some still have on their walls numerous graffiti that perpetuate the names of their past owners, the nature of their trade and their merchandise. Other openings were used for passages through which spectators passed in order to reach their seats in the stadium. As this was not built until the second century it too would have been alien to the Apostles, indeed, had they been able to return to Perga at any time during the mid second century, or later, they would have found the city greatly changed.

The Theatre was built in the Hellenistic period and overlooked the Stadium so that in its original state it would have been familiar to Paul and Barnabus **(See Figure 31)**. Built into the side of a hill it could seat some fifteen thousand people in its auditorium, but in the second century A.D. the structure was improved by the addition of a stage and scaena frons that is rich with the egg and cup decoration that is typical of the period. Its most Important features, however, are the white marble bas reliefs that once decorated the fronts of the stage podium.

They are unique and exceptional for they depict scenes that illustrate the birth and life of Dionysus together with Kestros, the local river god who reclines nonchalantly by a stream.

Here Dionysus is shown being born from the knee of Zeus, and in a further relief being bathed by the Nymphs of Mount Nyssa. The final and most important though has sadly sustained a degree of damage but it was, and still is, an outstanding and inspired comment on life. Here Dionysus drunkenly reclines in a chariot drawn by two panthers that are in the charge of a debauched Satyr, whilst a Maenad with a wreath on her head vigorously shakes a tambourine. The trance-like expression achieved by the sculptor in her vacant eyes, as she gazes into the fathomless distance, sums up an aspect of life as it was at that time, and an aspect that Paul often condemned in his preaching. This plaque was not only a comment on society as it then was but is, in spite of the hundreds of years that have passed, as relevant a comment on much of society as it is today[18] **(See Figure 32)**.

It was here in Perga that the friction between Paul and Mark came to a head, for Mark adamantly refused to continue with the Journey - Acts XIII 13: 'Then Paul and his companions set sail from Paphos and came to Perga in Pamphylia. John, however, left them and returned to Jerusalem' and he forthwith made his way back home to leave Paul and Barnabas to set out for Pisidian Antioch. The relationship between Barnabas and Mark was certainly a close and cordial one, which leads one to suspect that Mark's decision to abandon the journey could very well have been due to a severe clash of personality between him and Paul.

Being a young man and hardly past his youth it is conceivable that Mark found their experiences in Cyprus emotionally exhausting, in view of the fact that Paul's general attitude could be overbearing and his dissemination of the Gospel brooked little argument; for it is very apparent from Acts that the initiative and organisation of the journey had by now passed from Barnabas to Paul. Some theologians have suggested that Mark might not have agreed with many of Paul's dogmatic views, but whatever the cause of Mark's desertion it rankled with Paul over many years. Perga was one of the few Cities where his missionary activities did not bring about their expulsion by an irate Jewish community, and this could have been due to the fact that such a community, if indeed there was one, had little significance or influence in the City, moreover the main objective then was Pisidian Antioch.

The road to Pisidian Antioch that Paul and Barnabas took when leaving Perga is one that is open to conjecture. Maps that illustrate the route of the first journey invariably show it going to the North of Perga and thence to the Southern tip of Lake Egridir; then to skirt the Eastern aspect of the Lake before reaching their destination. H. Metzger favours this route (**See Map**). In spite of the fact that a road did exist here in the Roman period its exact course is not known, but it is thought to have followed the valley of the Aksu River. A road crossing the mountains would have been difficult and also to be taken into consideration was the almost certain hazard of an attack from the Pisidian bandits.

---

[18] For the ruins of Perga see Ekrem Acurgal, Ancient Civilizations and ruins of Turkey.

Figure 29: The Agora with Shop Fronts that are Reminiscent of the Georgian Period.

Figure 30: Relief of a Cleaver and Meat Hook on the Plinth of a Butcher's Counter.

Figure 31: The Hellenistic Theatre.

Figure 32: Marble Bas Relief of Dionysus in his Chariot in the Theatre at Perga.

On one occasion when leaving Pisidian Antioch for Antalya I took the road that, after leaving Lake Egridir, goes by Ispata and the rose fields to then pass the nearby important site of Sagalassos. By twists and turns it descends through the mountains giving on the way the most splendid views over deep green and wooded valleys, to pass finally the turning to Termessos before dropping down to Antalya in the Pamphylian plain. The Apostles would not have used this road.

My reason for going to Antalya was to see Ibrahim Buyukbenli, an old friend and mentor who had been with me on many previous and memorable journeys. I have rested on a stool by a cobbler's booth, some four feet wide and five feet deep, sipping tea amongst a pile of dilapidated footwear that the cobbler had spread abroad across the pavement, waiting for him to finish stitching the flapping sole of Ibrahim's shoe. In Konya he once suddenly vanished into a shop in the street of the jewellers, one that glittered with gold, for a small cabouchon ruby that had caught his eye, a present for his sister; and in Syrian Antioch he quickly cured my ailing stomach with one of his very obscure potions.

Over an evening meal we discussed the route that the Apostles might have taken from Perga, and it was then that he mentioned the Perga Sillyon road. Today this is a minor road that goes from Perga to Lake Egridir through the villages of Sillyon, Candir, Gebiz and thence to Ayvali and Aksu that is near to the southernmost aspect of the lake. Ibrahim told me that this used to be an age old track that shepherds used when driving their flocks to the pastures by the lake; it was one that climbed directly up through the Aksu Valley until it reached Egridir. He told me his father often took him that way to the lake when a boy, and on one of these journeys, not long before they reached the lake, he so fell that he broke his leg very badly. It was an accident that has left him with a permanent disability for complications set in when they got back to Antalya; so much so that it necessitated a journey to Istanbul for treatment. Communications then in Turkey were often not as easy as they were in the first centuries A.D, under the Pax Romana for the only way then to reach Istanbul from Antalya was by boat. 'What if he dies on the way?' said his father to the physician, 'he will if he doesn't', was the instant reply.

We once discussed the question of reincarnation. He had just recounted a peculiar case that had occurred recently in a village near Syrian Antioch, one that appeared to have had some such inexplicable features. In the course of conversation, and with his tongue in his cheek, Ibrahim remarked on his hopes that Allah would see fit to grant him a better body when next time round. The track that Ibrahim knew as a boy could well have been the course of an ancient route that is thought to have gone north from Perga to the Lake. If so it is very doubtful as to whether it was paved, even though there are still the remnants of a portion of paved road near Selge that was situated a little to the East in the mountains.

Many of the old Pisidian towns were organised as small city states and had, to a certain degree, been influenced by the Hellenistic culture. Many were governed by the Elders or City Fathers, and their word was usually heeded, however, the populace could overturn their rulings if their feelings to the contrary were strong enough, and on one historic occasion this happened to be the case in Termessos.

The Pisidians themselves were not over friendly and where outsiders were concerned were apt to be truculent, and those who inhabited the fastnesses of Termessos in the mountains often made periodic forays from their remoteness to pillage the nearby coastal towns of Pamphylia, especially that of Phaeselis. All of them guarded their little patches very jealously and it was for this reason that the Roman occupation in Pisidia was not at all popular, for the Roman presence in the region had to be more than adequate to keep the peace and put down banditry from the mountain tribes. Thus there were more cities concentrated in the Pisidian district that had the status of Colonia than elsewhere in Anatolia; and cities having such a status had also a permanent garrison of troops who could be called upon to deal at once with any uprisings or disturbances that could endanger Roman interests in the area.

In effect the Apostles appear to have had the choice of two routes; the shorter one that went through the Aksu Valley to Lystra. The other, a more circuitous route, was that of the great Sebaste that was paved its entire length and was about twelve feet in width. This road connected Perga and Antiochiea and passed through the cities of Cremna and Comama on the way to Antiochiea. These cities had Colonia status, as did Antiochiea and Iconium on the Sebaste, in that they held garrisons of troops from the Legions for protection. There were several milestones on the road confirming that the road had been built by Caesar Augustus in 6 B.C.[19] By choosing to use the Via Sebaste the Apostles had the advantages of safety and the security of the Colonia cities and also that of making use of any traffic which happened to be going their way. Though it was thought originally that the lower part of the road must have connected the Pisidian towns with Pamphylia and the coast there was no direct evidence of this until 1989 **(See Map)**.

Dame Freya Stark, when on one of her journeys through Pamphylia, was the first to record and photograph the remains of a paved Roman road she found near the town of Dosmealti, a town that lies at the foot of the Taurus Mountains and only a few kilometres from Antalya. In her book on 'The Campaigns of Alexander the Great in Asia Minor' she described the road that had a number of ancient sarcophagi in its vicinity, together with the ruins of cisterns, shrines and churches, and what also could have been the remains of inns; all testifying to the fact that it had had a long and continuous use as a highway and that its origins belonged to the Hellenistic period.

---

[19] The fact that Comama was one of the Roman colonies on the great Via Sebaste has been confirmed by an inscription found there that dates to 6 B.C. It states ' Imperator Caesar Augustus, son of god, Pontifex Maximus, consul 11 times, designate for a twelfth, imperator 15 times, in his 18th year of tribunician power, built the Via Sebaste under the supervision of Cornutus Aquila, his propraetorian legate. This ties up with the inscription on the milestone found at Dosmealty by David French— to be described later in the text— and confirms that it was Augustus who built the road in 6 B.C.

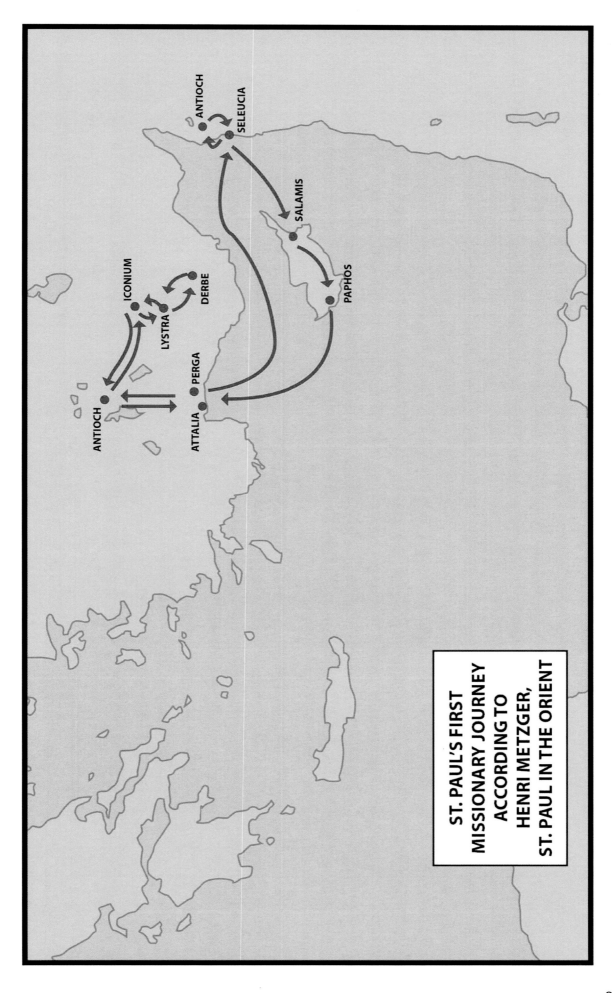

ST. PAUL'S FIRST
MISSIONARY JOURNEY
ACCORDING TO
HENRI METZGER,
ST. PAUL IN THE ORIENT

Figure 33: Remains of the Aqueduct that Brought Water to Pisidian Antioch.

Dr David French, in the course of his research into the Roman roads of Asia Minor, decided to investigate what he told me when I met him in Ankara he liked to call 'The Freya Stark part of the Sebaste'. Not long previously he had again read her book, and in the light of what she had recorded went to the site to discover that, in spite of the many years that had passed by, it was just as she had seen it. It followed the easiest route for a paved road from the Pamphylian plains to pass through the Taurus Mountains to the Pisidian uplands. Here beside an ancient wall and a gate, that marks the top of the rocky defile of the pass, he found in situ what she did not record, one of its original milestones.

The inscribed text dates it to 6 B.C., the period when Augustus was Emperor and it reads 'The Emperor Caesar Augustus, son of Julius Caesar now immortal, chief priest, consul for the 11th time, designated to be consul for the 12th time, acclaimed as triumphant commander for the 15th time, holder of the tribunician power for the 12th time, made the Via Sebaste under the supervision of Cornutus Aquila, the Emperor's legate with the rank of Praetor.

Perga was the Metropolis of Pamphylia and prestigious enough for the Via Sebaste to have gone from there to today's Dosmealti and thence through The Taurus to Colonia Comama and Colonia Cremna. The road would then have gone on to Antiochea. This important discovery of the lower extent of the Via Sebaste and the fact that it began at Perga could indicate that, of the two alternatives and in spite of it being a longer route, the Via Sebaste was the road that the Apostles might surely have taken, and by that time it would have been some fifty years old; on their eventual return from Derbe they would have come directly to Perga, where they spent some time preaching the gospel, before going on to Antalya for the boat to Syrian Antioch.

Pisidian Antioch, or Antiocheia, was also a Colonia; a city that sprawled across a raised plateau that extended from the North to the West on the foot hills of the Sultan Dagh Mountains, and from the city itself there were extensive views over the plains of Anthius to the South. To be seen in the distance, from the vast acreage of its magnificent site, is a short length of aqueduct that lies alongside the old road, all that remains of the extensive system that brought water from a tunnel in the Western hills to the town. The thread of its ashlar blocks can glow in the sun, bright against the blue shadows that sweep across the hills and change constantly as the clouds drift over the sky, or become etched dark in the patches of light that shift and play over that distant expanse **(See Figure 33)**.

From the military and strategic points of view Antiocheia was the most important City of Colonia status in Pisidia, for it lay at the junction of five roads, one being the highway of the Via Sebaste. It was also the Capital of the Pisidian district of the Roman Province of Galatia, a district that was constantly threatened by the Pisidian tribes that lived in the nearby ranges of the Sultan Dagh; to cross over them from Yalvac to Arkseray is to appreciate their difficult terrain, and the formidable barrier that they must have presented.

Today the road leaves the foothills where the bright yellow gold of the earth shouts back at the sun, and when leaving the villages, climbs out of the valleys to wind up and around the peaks that are devoid of any greenery, but still glow from the ochre coloured earth. Obviously it would have been very difficult country for the legions to police, and it was doubtless for this reason that the Pisidian Antioch of Selecus Nicator, founded to commemorate his father Antiochus, was elevated by Augustus to the status of Colonia to then become the home of 7th Augustan Legion.

Veterans of the Alauda Legion, who were known from their regimental badge as the 'Larks'[20], were also settled in the City and could he called upon if a crisis arose, and though Pisidian Antioch was administered in the first place on democratic Hellenistic principles, when raised to the status of a Colonia the city became subject to Roman law and order. Being a garrison town with its endless facilities for trade it had, apart from those citizens of Greek extraction, a synagogue with an influential and thriving Jewish community, no doubt one of the reasons for the Apostles' journey. The veterans together with their supporting military personnel lived in their own establishments away from the town, for at one stage in history a bitter quarrel broke out between the garrison and the townsfolk, and this was not resolved until the military command cut the aqueduct, thus depriving the recalcitrant citizens of their water supply.

Again it is disappointing that so little of Pisidian Antioch has survived the centuries for the city was once so much a part of the life of Paul and his ministry. There are the meagre remains of the baths, and a theatre that is now but a grassy bowl in the side of the hill; well after the time of the Apostles this had a road built across its stage. There are also the foundations and fragments of stonework from two Basilicas of the Byzantine period, the site of the finest being on a slight rise and one that must have been a building of some considerable size. An inscription in the remains of its mosaic floor names 'Optimus' who, from A. D. 375-381, was Bishop of Pisidian Antioch. This, however, has been covered again with earth to ensure its preservation.

A colonnaded street of some dignity that had shops and was known as the Tiberia Platea led to the Temple of Augustus on the Platea Augusta. Though the remains are scanty, as is so often the case, there is still enough left to indicate just how splendid this region of the City must have looked. From the street an impressive flight of twelve steps gave onto a Triple Arch that was dedicated in A.D .50 to Claudius, it would thus very probably have been in the process of construction during the visit of Paul and Barnabas. It formed a boundary of the Temple precinct where the Temple itself was raised on a high podium to be approached by a second rise of steps. Hewn from the solid rock of the hill that backed the Temple precinct was a crescent shaped wall of some height that once was part of an esplanade that had a colonnade on two levels, the top in the Ionic and the lower in the Doric order, and this formed a back drop to the precinct **(See Figure 34)**.

Heaped together and lying around are the many tumbled drums that made up the Temple's fluted columns whilst nearby are the various marble sections from the frieze of the Triumphal Arch. It must have been the impressive focal point of the City's architecture. However, it is the decoration of the Triple Arch and the Temple that are of the utmost interest,

---

[20] H. V. Morton, In the Steps of Saint Paul. These must have been veterans from the Vth Alaudae, one of four legions that Tiberias had stationed in Lower Germany under Aulis Caecina. Veterans of the seventh legion who had served with Augustus at Philippi, and also in the Perusine War, had also made their home in Pisidian Antioch together with auxiliaries locally recruited in Asia Minor. Mitchell, Anatolia. The four legions deployed in the Middle East were the III Gallica,; VI Ferrata; the X Fretensis that was stationed in barracks near the Jaffa Gate in Jerusalem; and the XII Fulminata.

for amongst the fine carvings of bulls' heads ornamented with exotic wreaths there are the figures of a Triton and a Winged Nike, both commemorating the victory of Augustus at the naval battle of Actium and the final defeat of Antony and Cleopatra. For such a reference to have found a place on such a monument to Augustus, in a city situated as it was in the foothills of the Pisidian mountains, points to the degree of Antiocheia's importance. Furthermore parts of a copy of the text of the 'Index Res Gestae' of Augustus have been found in the excavations, a more complete copy of the text being engraved on the walls of the Temple to Augustus in Ankara, the only other copy in Greek was discovered in Apollonia in Phrygia.

Included in the decoration of the Arch is Capricorn, the birth sign of Augustus whilst another figure in the decoration refers to the conquest of the local Pisidian tribes; but on one fragment that is unique is the large carving of a poppy seed pod, for this must denote the cultivation of the poppy in this region being a flourishing industry during the last centuries B.C and the first centuries A.D. **(See Figures 35 and 36)**. Opium must have been a drug as common in use then as it is now; and what is more remarkable is the fact that the road to Yalvac going through the local country villages has on its either side, at the right time of the year, vast fields spectacularly white and purple with these poppies in full bloom. I stopped to photograph them **(See Figure 37)**. The fact that the cultivation of the poppy as an industry has persisted here since the early Roman period makes one realise even more that little has altered, in spite of the centuries that have passed and the cities that have crumbled.

Apart from the Temple to Augustus another of importance dedicated to the Pagan god Men was located, together with its associated buildings for its priests and acolytes, on the Karakuyu Hill some way out of the city. This predated the Roman occupation by many years and, according to Strabo, its priesthood was prominent amongst the local socialites and owned considerable tracts of land around Antiochiea itself. The Temple had a throne for a god and troughs for the rituals of purification. It was a cult that probably had its origins in Northern Galatia for it is very likely that the Temple to Augustus in Ankara now occupies the site of the one that was originally dedicated to Men. This was another aspect of the Pagan cults that were in opposition to Paul's Apostolic mission.

Luke gives a graphic description of the reception that both Paul and Barnabas had on arriving in Pisidian Antioch, where initially they had some marked success with their Mission in the synagogue that had present its full complement of Jews, Proselytes, and Jewesses, 'the honurable women' behind the purdah lattice. However Acts records in XIII 44, 45, 'The next Sabbath almost the whole city gathered to hear the word of the Lord' - this must have included the Gentiles of the city also – 'but when the Jews saw the crowds they were filled with jealousy'. It was only when the Jewish community realised that the teaching of the Apostles was endangering their preserves that they acted. The city being a Roman colony, and Paul being a Roman citizen, it was difficult for the Jews to take direct action. They then appealed to the magistrates, but being devious they accused the Apostles of preaching insidious blasphemy and in so doing quietly stirred up the many devout and honurable wives of those who wielded influence in the city, together with many of the other proselytes whose lives revolved around the Synagogue. Strabo has mentioned the power that women in society exercised over men when it came to religious dogma at that time, and it was this outright rejection of Paul and Barnabas by the Jewish community that precipitated their enforced departure. But it was the acceptance of the Apostles' teaching by many of the Gentiles that prompted Paul's historic utterance in verse 46 'it was necessary that the word of God should be spoken first to you. Since you reject it and judge yourselves to be unworthy of eternal life, we are now turning to the Gentiles'.

Pisidian Antioch is also connected with the conversion of St. Thecla, as narrated in the Acts of Paul and Thecla. They are thought to have been written by a church proselyte in the late second century A.D. and are, for the most part, considered to be legendary. If the legend has any basis in fact, it is strange that Paul, who is quick to mention other converts by name, does not mention her in any of his writings. It is more than likely that a Thecla did exist, for nearly all legends have a kernel of truth.

In brief the story recounts how Paul left Pisidian Antioch for Iconium, some sixty miles distant, by the Via Sebaste, and met up with Onesiphorus who had come out from Iconium to meet him and to proffer his hospitality; it is noticeable here that there is no mention of the presence of Barnabas on the expedition. Next door to the house of Onesiphorus was that of Thecla who, when at her window one day overheard Paul and Onesiphorus discoursing on the subject of charity in the adjacent garden, and was so impressed with what she heard that she became a dedicated convert to the Church. This did not go down at all well with Thamyris, her Greek lover, whom by now she had begun to shun and do her utmost to avoid and he, being more than distraught, appealed to the authorities who promptly had Paul imprisoned.

On hearing the news of the imprisonment Thecla went down one night to the prison with a bribe for the jailer to let her join Paul, whereupon he converted her to the faith. When she was found with Paul in the cell the next morning she was condemned by the city magistrates to be burnt forthwith, this to be an example to the women of Iconium, for Iconiun at that time was not subject to Roman Law and administration. The magistrates took this course of action in order to demonstrate to the women of Iconium the fate they must expect, should they too indulge in such rash behaviour, and Paul was given a sound beating before being expelled from the City.

Divine intervention saved Thecla when fierce rain storms immediately put out the fires around her, whereupon she escaped and went in search of Paul to eventually find him in an old rock cut tomb outside the city limits, hiding there with Onesiphorus and his son and, remarkably enough, a number of these tombs are still to be seen in the countryside a little to the South of Konya.

The narrative continues with Paul and Thecla returning together to Pisidian Antioch, just at the time when the city was in the throes of preparing for a festival, and here Thecla is noticed by the high priest Alexander who, taking a sudden fancy to her, immediately left his procession to accost her. Thecla, having none of it, assaulted him in no uncertain fashion by knocking the wreath from his head, something that was the most significant part of his insignia as a high priest and thereby committing gross sacrilege. In retribution she was condemned to death by facing wild beasts in the arena, and to await her fate she was put into the care of Tryphena, the Queen of Pontus and a woman of some sixty years.

Figure 34: The Site of the Temple to Augustus at Pisidian Antioch.

Figure 35: Part of a Marble Frieze from the Proplyon that gave onto the Temple of Augustus showing the Relief of the Poppy Head.

Figure 36: Detail of the Poppy Head.

Figure 37: A Field of Opium Poppies.

Her appearance in the amphitheatre with a resulting bloody death was calculated to give the climax to the festivities, and add the final touch to a closing spectacle.

She was said to have appeared naked but for a loin cloth in the arena, thus appalling those spectators of the Greek population who were, unlike the Romans, not so appreciative of these scenes of cruelty. However, she was spared the fate of being torn apart by the protection of a sympathetic lioness, whereupon the other beasts in the arena promptly went to sleep. Having surmounted all the efforts to destroy her she had finally proved her point and was released, and when clothed she again left Pisidian Antioch in search of Paul. It is recorded that she finally found him in Myra where she greeted him thus: 'I have received the washing o Paul, for He that hath worked together with thee in the Gospel hath worked with me in my baptising'. It is asserted that she then returned to Iconium as a missionary.

There are many inconsistencies in the story. The later version having Paul and Thecla going to Pisidian Antioch together is due to an inaccurate translation of an earlier version, and there are no records of Paul having met her in Myra, The only contact that Paul had with Myra, as far as the New Testament is concerned, was when he was there with Julius the centurion, waiting for a grain ship to take them on to Rome. But it is possible that there is a smidgeon of truth somewhere, for whoever was responsible for the account was well acquainted with the spectacles and procedures that took place in the Roman amphitheatres, occasions that were very popular with those who inhabited the Cities of the early centuries A.D.

Thecla is said to have ended an ascetic life in Silifke at the advanced age of some ninety years; high up on a hill overlooking the old town of Silifke are the ruins of a large basilica that is dedicated to St Thecla and dates to the fifth century. Here there is a tomb that may or may not be that of the Saint, for there is another legend that puts her tomb in a cave above a convent dedicated to her in the village of Maloula that lies in the mountains nearby the Damascus Aleppo road; the pass above the convent being known as that of St Theckla. Though it is now considered that many of the stories relating to St Thecla are more legendary than factual the possibility is that a Thecla did exist; one who obtained the sanctity of Sainthood and was revered enough to have had a Basilica erected and dedicated to her memory.

Silifke is the site of the Romano Greek city of Seleukia on the river Calycadnus, and from here a direct road went through Claudiopolis, another Colonia, to Labranda, today's Karaman near ancient Derbe, and thence through the plains to Konya. The nearness of this basilica to Konya, ancient Iconium, and the supposed home of Thecla must be of some historical significance, and it is in the river Calycadnus where Frederick Barborossa was drowned in 1190, thus bringing about the dispersion of the German Knights who participated in the Third Crusade.

After their arrival in Iconium, by taking the Via Sebaste from Antiocheia, both Paul and Barnabus preached in the Synagogue where they again had some initial success, not only with some of the Jews but also with the Gentiles. But the fervent preaching of Paul again caused such dissension and animosity amongst the Jews, and various other sections of the populace, that the Apostles deemed it wise to leave hurriedly before the magistrates of Iconium could take action on the complaints that were being lodged against them. Paul's uncompromising zeal in the Synagogues was such that it divided the city for the greater part into two hotly opposed factions, those Jews and Gentiles who accepted the Gospel, and those who were so vehemently against the Apostle's teaching that they prompted the Elders to side with them in hatching a plot to stone and kill them (Acts 14 1-6).

According to Sir William Ramsay the administration of Iconium was in the hands of Greek Magistrates, and though in its other aspects it was Roman it did not have the stability of a Roman Governor, thus it was easier for the passions of the populace to be fermented and aroused to the extent that they could take matters into their own hands. In such circumstances Paul as a Roman citizen could not claim the protection of Roman law, thus Paul and Barnabas did the sensible thing and fled the last twenty miles or so down the Via Sebaste to Lystra, that lay to the South in the Konya plain.

The Iconium of the Romans, which in a fit of egotism the Emperor Claudius renamed Claudiconium, lies almost in its entirety beneath the mosques, the public buildings of the Ottoman period, and the souks of the later Capital of the Seljuk Sultans, to reach the peak of its prosperity in the twelfth century under the Sultan Ala et Tin. On two occasions the city was threatened by the Crusaders, especially those of the force that was led by the Emperor Barbarossa in 1190, but in spite of a battle that was fought against the Seljucks beneath the city walls, little damage was inflicted on the town.

Today Konya can be regarded as the Canterbury of Turkey and is renowned for the Mosque of the 'Whirling Dervishes', founded in the XIIIth century by the mystic poet Jelal-ed din who was born in 1207. Kemal Ataturk disbanded the Dervishes when he came to power and the mosque became a national museum. It still contains the revered tomb of the poet and has also many other interesting relics that include rare mosque lamps of Arab glass, musical instruments, Korans and original books of verse by the Persian poet Heifitz.

Sir William Ramsay also makes interesting observations in 'The Cities of St Paul' where he suggests that the Dervish movement could have been influenced by Christianity. He points out that blue was then the sacred colour and not green, as it is today in the Islamic culture and wine was not debarred but drunk as a matter of course. The whirling dance to the haunting music of the flutes was an essential part of the Dervish culture, and could have had its origin in the early rituals that the Phrygians observed in the cult of Cybele.

The Mevlana has a solitary minaret and an emerald green cupola that rises in a conspicuous way above the ancient walls of its enclosure, and in the compound are the cells of its former young students and dancers. Their old cedar wood doors look out to a paved court that is splashed with bright colour from the many beds of roses, and a nearby fountain of white marble, that once did service for those who washed before prayers, lies in the shade of a canopy supported on slender columns. It's one of the loveliest of Turkey's monuments, but unhappily the old shops and buildings that once looked out over the square have now given way to a disastrous shopping precinct that has an integral car park in its basement, the whole continually swears at the adjacent Selemiye Camii in its Ottoman splendour for such is progress. It is all a far cry from the world of Paul and Barnabas.

The present road to Lystra crosses the vast Konya plains that are bounded on the far South by the blue haze of the Taurus ranges, and a little to the West by the peaks of St. Theckla and St Phillip. The site of ancient Lystra is not far from the small and picturesque village of Hatunsaray and though not a great distance from Iconium it lay in, what at that time, was the district of Lyaconia. Though the city had the status of a Colonia with Roman administration it also had a mixed population that were, for the greater part, the indigenous Lycaonians who were fluent mainly in their own tongue; the remainder being Greek together with a significant number of Jews of the Diaspora.

When setting out to drive from Konya to Lystra I found that it was more than easy to lose the way amongst the spread out and complicated muddle of its suburbs. Many kind directions were proffered that were, more often than not, erroneous and suggested a right turn here and a left turn there, and then to follow one's nose till confusion was absolute. After a number of lengthy detours I eventually hit on the narrow road that led across the plain to Hatunsaray, but even then I fared far better than Morton who first attempted the journey in 1935, for in those days there was no road at all. His efforts to reach Lystra were foiled by the winter rains that swept the Konya plains and bogged his car down in a sea of mud.

The site lies about a mile from the village of Hatunsaray and here I was fortunate enough to find the local blacksmith who was only too eager to drop his work for the diversion of taking me there. On my way to the village I had unwittingly driven through the site and its few remains, for much of the fabric of its monuments and buildings are now a part of the structure of the seven arched bridge that crosses the stream before the village is reached. Not only have the stones of Lystra been used in the fabric of the bridge they are also to be found in the walls of farm sheds and housing in the district of Hatunsaray itself, and often with inscriptions.

The greater part of the City once spread over a steep hill that is bordered on one side by the stream that now flows partly into a cistern, known locally as the Sultan's Pool, before it disappears under the bridge. It runs through a lightly wooded valley that is obviously a favourite place for picnics, and from the top of the hill, still a part of the site, the landscape spreads away over slightly rolling country. The whole area was covered with the golden stubble from the harvest, as many other sites are at this time of the year, and as we climbed the hill through the stiff yellow stalks it was difficult to visualise that this was once the site of a busy city with its streets, temples, baths and public buildings. All that can be seen on the ground are the marble remnants and the bits of potsherd that the foot kicks up; all but for one lonely object that still remains to indicate the erstwhile splendour of Lystra, a stained marble capitol that lies tumbled on its side in the stubble **(See Figure 38)**. There is something very poignant in its isolation when you gaze over the expanse of the surrounding country and down to the stream. This must certainly be the capital that Morton records having seen in 1935, when on a later journey, 'The capital of a massive marble column projecting from the earth'.

Figure 38: A Capitol Lying Amongst the Corn Stubble at Lystra. All that is left in situ of the ancient city.

I was looking for the altar that was first described in 1885 by Professor Sterret. There was not a sign of it as we thoroughly scoured the site and the blacksmith, who knew the site well, could not recall having seen it. I later learnt that it was somewhere in the Konya Museum, but this must have happened after Morton visited Lystra in 1935 for he then took a photograph of it standing in situ. Miraculously it was the one and only monument left, before its removal, to confirm that this was indeed the site of ancient Lystra, for its inscription when translated runs: 'Gemina Lustra, the Fortunate, being a Julian colony, dedicated to Augustus Caesar as a god: the altar being decreed by the Urban Council'. Lustra was the Roman spelling for the Greek Lystra, and it is also a confirmation that the city had the status of Colonia, like that of Pisidian Antioch.

Paul and Barnabas would have arrived in the City around A.D. 47 and it seems that the visit was not predetermined but one of necessity for, having to leave Iconium for their own safety, they had little choice but to follow the Via Sebaste, still paved, the twenty odd miles or so to Lystra. It was the nearest place of refuge and the last town on the Imperial road and here they continued their missionary work. Paul's healing of the crippled man at Lystra demonstrates the simple pagan outlook of the majority of the Lycaonian citizens, for they at once assumed Paul and Barnabas to be the earthly incarnations of the gods Jupiter and Hermes. A significant phrase in Acts XIV 12 describes Paul being called Mercurius by the Lycaonians because he was chief speaker, a remark that seems to substantiate Paul having taken over the drive and direction of the mission. It also suggests how his uncompromising exhortations in the synagogues were the prime cause of the violence that erupted against him from the Jews of the Diaspora, for Barnabas does not appear to have attracted so much abuse. Jupiter was obviously the deity that the Lycaonians most revered and was the equivalent, more or less, of a patron saint, for it was the chief priest of the temple of Jupiter who endeavoured to honour the Apostles with a Pagan festival and Pagan sacrifices. An odd feature regarding the Temple is noted in Acts XII 13 for it appears to have been located without the City walls, an unusual situation.

The fact that Lystra did have citizens of Greek extraction is confirmed in the fact that Timothy, who was born there to become one of Paul's most loved and trusted followers, had a Greek father and a Jewish mother. It was not solely the Jews of Lystra, however, who were responsible for turning the feelings of the citizens against the two Apostles, but the Jews who had followed them down the paved Via Sebaste from Iconium and Pisidian Antioch, specifically to stir up the populace against them. For the Jews of these two cities to make a point of going to Lystra with such hostility and expressly for this purpose, and taking the advantage of a paved road, must cast a light on Paul's character and demonstrates again his lack of tact and outspoken approach when expounding the Gospel, a technique that inevitably offended the sensibilities and the rigid views of the wide spread Jewish Diaspora.

There are many references to Timothy in the letters of Paul. In Romans Paul describes him as his fellow worker, and he later sends him to Corinth asking that they receive him well. He is Paul's trusted agent to the Thessalonians and the Philippians, and he finally becomes Bishop in Ephesus. The saddest references are in Paul's final letter to Timothy from Rome in which he recalls the persecutions he and Barnabas endured in Pisidian Antioch, Iconium, and Lystra whilst on this first journey - Tim. 3-11 - and in verse 5 he nostalgically mentions Timothy's Grandmother Lois and his Mother Eunice. The very fact that the references are so personal makes it certain that Paul visited Lystra and stayed with the family when on his second and third missionary journeys, and that the Church of Lystra could have had its origins and was centred in their house. Although Paul omits to make any reference to the Jews of Pisidian Antioch, or Iconium, when on his second and third journeys it is certain from his last letter to Timothy that he never forgot the treatment they handed out to him when on this first journey with Barnabas. The carved capital that lies in the stubble is the one tangible thing remaining in situ that links the past with the acres of corn that yearly cover Lystra today.

I spent more than two hours walking over the site with the blacksmith before returning to the car parked under the trees by the stream. It was early afternoon and in the cool shade by the stream a family from the village were having a picnic. The glaring heat from the sun overhead was beating back from the yellow stubble and we were thirsty, so I asked my companion to come with me to the village cafe for some tea, but he insisted that we return to the coolness of his forge where I was seated on a low stool. He then disappeared for a few moments to return with a can of goat's milk, ice cold, and two tin cups.

In no time at all we were joined by the men of the village for word had got about, and a visitor from afar was not a common occurrence. In spite of the language difficulties there was a lot of cordiality and laughter as I prepared to take photographs of the blacksmith by the plough he was repairing when he offered to show me the site; and after ritually exchanging our addresses, I set out for Derbe. Paul and Barnabas did the same thing the day after the Jews had stoned and left him for dead outside the City walls. Barnabas appears to have escaped such treatment, and not to have attracted the enmity that fell to the lot of Paul (Acts 14, 19).

It is quite some fifty miles over the Konya plains from Lystra to Derbe, a region that can be bitterly cold in winter and stinking hot in summer. It must have been a far from pleasant journey for the two Apostles whatever the season for there is little cover and the paved road of the Via Sebaste ended at Lystra. In summer the midday heat that rebounds across the plain from the distant blue haze of the Taurus Mountains would have turned the track to a sea of dust, and the bleak winter storms a sea of mud. The mind can boggle at the mechanics of the Apostles' journey for they had little choice but to make it. They were forced south to Lystra by the Jews of Iconium, and when forced to leave Lystra there was little option but to go on to Derbe, the last available refuge before the mountains, for an immediate return to Iconium in the face of the Jewish opposition would have been out of the question. The fact that the paved road ended at Lystra was the deterrent preventing the Jews from Antiocheia and Iconium following them.

Today the narrow metalled road from Lystra passes through an expanse of country that, in June, can be bright on either side with the deep bronze of ripening corn, the lighter yellow of the barley and the even lighter tracts of land where the crops have been harvested. In summer its verges are vivid with a small but deep blue borage, patches of dwarf pink hollyhock, yellow daisies fighting with the deeper yellow of an achillea, clumps of rose coloured tares and a ground cover of small pink columbines that keep their cups close to the earth as they turn them to the sun. But much of this lavish vegetation disappears when the road joins the main highway.

Derbe is not marked on the maps of today and Morton, who visited the site in 1936, recorded the City being situated on the Gudelisin hill that is near the range of the Kara Dagh, or Black Mountains; he was then following the directions of Sir William Ramsay. This attribution has since proved incorrect for the true site of Derbe is situated on a high bill in the shape of a huge boil that rises isolated from the surrounding flat plain **(See Figure 39)**. The authenticity of the site, that brooks no argument, has been confirmed by the discovery of an inscribed tablet that is now preserved in the Karaman Museum, a nearby town that was the ancient Laranda **(See Figure 40)**.

The site is further to the West of the Gudelisin hill and in its relationship to Lystra has far more credibility. Derbe and nearby Laranda, were the last towns on the Konya plain before the road descended through the Taurus Mountains to Claudiopolis, today's Mut, on the way to Seleukia, today's Silifke.

Derbe not being marked on the map, and not knowing its exact location I sought the advice of the Director of the Karaman museum, who at once suggested that his Deputy Director, Ahmet Uner[21], should drive me the ten kilometres to the site. We passed through several remote and straggling villages before reaching the hill that rose suddenly out of a plain that was backed by the Kara Dagh Mountains. Again what artefacts that have survived, apart from the inscription, are now in the Museum and amongst them is one that could have been the remnant of a winged Nike. Nature has again taken over and completely obliterated an ancient and once flourishing City.

Climbing the mound we passed a deep pit covered with plastic bags, "recent illicit excavation" said Ahmet "They come at night with metal detectors to dig up antiquities, and the site is so isolated we cannot protect it without constant supervision, unfortunately there are no funds available as yet for that, nor for any systematic investigation".

My mind went back to Acts XIV 20-21: 'and the next day he departed with Barnabas to Derbe, and they preached the Gospel to that City and they taught many'. This passage is also revealing for, apart from Perga, this was the site of one of the few cities where the Apostles were made welcome by the citizens who did not in the end forcibly eject them.

Though there is nothing whatsoever left on the site it gives the impression that Derbe was more of a parochial town than Lystra. Not being a Colonia its population must have been considerably smaller than that of Lystra and given over more to agriculture than commerce. However, it is possible that there was a degree of Roman influence for it was the last city in the Eastern aspect of the district and for this reason it has been suggested that customs were levied here on goods that passed through to the West. The reception given to the Apostles by the citizens of Derbe was cordial and hospitable, and this also leads to the suspicion that prospects for trade in Derbe were, for the Jews, not worth much consideration. If there was a Jewish community it must have been insignificant; for the Jews who came down from Iconium

---

[21] I am more than appreciative of the hospitality and unstinting help that I had over two years from the Directors and staff of the Karaman Museum.

to hound the Apostles from Lystra obviously thought it not worth the effort and time to pursue them further.

In Acts XX 4 Luke refers to a Gaius of Derbe, one of his many converts in the city and one who joined him in his ministry. Though it is not specifically stated, Gaius could have joined up with Paul and Silas when they visited Derbe on their second missionary journey. In conjunction with Sopater of Beroea, Aristarchus, Secundus, Timothy and others, this Gaius is specifically mentioned in Acts XX 4, when they left Greece with Paul and returned to Asia Minor on the final stage of the third missionary journey. He must therefore have found his way to Greece at some time or other, and more than likely in the company of Paul. Today the hill is as remote and bare as if nothing of any historic importance had ever been associated with it or ever taken place there.

On the way back to Karaman Ahmet suggested that we stop off in one of the villages, through which we had previously passed, to visit the family of one of the Museum staff who looked after their local affairs, so we stopped by an old low stone built homestead on the outskirts of the village to be greeted by the family, a son of some twenty years with his father and mother. Having taken off our shoes at the threshold we were led into a cool and comfortable sitting room to be entertained with the local chat from father and son, whilst his mother prepared the tea. Away in the kitchen she busily baked the large flat rounds of unleavened bread, sliced up cucumbers and tomatoes and boiled numerous eggs. When all was ready it was brought in with glasses of tea for her hospitality to be dispensed by her son, which he did with a slight humility and the charm of an inherent dignity. His mother, who had one of the most benign and contented faces, later appeared in the traditional and voluminous Turkish dress to see that all was as it should be. She ran her household with a calm and poise, together with a quiet and efficient capability that was a salutary lesson, and an indication of what many of us in the West have lost in the scramble for unlimited wealth, and an ever increasing standard of living.

After putting on our shoes at the threshold we bade farewell, and following the custom of the West I put out my hand to her, but considering it not fit to touch any male but those of the family, she smiled warmly, slightly inclined her head and gave me her salaams. I finally returned to the one and only hotel that was not nearly so salubrious, and was in fact more than extremely basic. When I had previously asked for a room there was only one available for, surprisingly enough, all the others were occupied. The one I was shown had four beds of a somewhat doubtful cleanliness, the plumbing being decidedly antiquated. It failed to work and it was obvious that nothing had come from the hot water system for years, but there was nothing else available in the town and there was little for it but to take it. However, in order to avoid being invaded by three other unknowns who might have been seeking accommodation in the late evening, I ensured my privacy by buying the right to the other three beds, and then firmly locked the shaky door. As the tariff for each bed worked out to the equivalent of one pound and fifty pence sterling, the deal was more than worthwhile, especially as I was awakened suddenly with a jerk at midnight from a furious and prolonged banging and rattling of the locked door, but that I ignored.

Figure 39: The Site of Ancient Derbe.

Figure 40: The Inscription found by the Director of the Karaman Museum, the Ancient Laranda, and now in the Museum confirming that this was once the site of the Ancient Derbe.

The following year I made a point of going to see Ahmet again in Karaman, but when he heard that I contemplated spending the night once more in the hotel he insisted that I should stay with him and his family in his flat. This offer I gratefully accepted and we later went to the region of the Bin Bir Kelisi near the village of Maden Sehir, the valley of a thousand churches that lie under the bleak Kara Dagh Mountains. Here in the plain and the foothills are the ruins of two Byzantine towns, and spread about in the country are the vestiges of chapels, apses, and naves that were once a part of the many Byzantine churches and monasteries that flourished here in the ninth and tenth centuries. We later took the car over the coarse rubble of a winding steep track to the village of Degli that is situated beneath one of the summits of the Kara Dagh range and from here, in its complete isolation, there are the most splendid views over a landscape that spreads away into the dim distance below. Here again the village is clustered amongst the remains of more churches and chapels, the smallest and best preserved being built on a small escarpment that looks out over a precipitous drop to the plain below. It is small enough to be the sanctuary of a single hermit **(See Figure 41)** whilst others have been converted into cow byres and various farm structures, the largest of them now doing service as the Mosque.

Over the years the village population has dwindled to some thirty individuals that make up some seven families, and their essential water is brought daily by the village donkey from a spring some way distant by another peak. I asked Ahmet how they fared in the winter and he replied:

'It is very hard, especially in the extremes of the winter, but none of them would leave here to live in the valley. When they have to they walk to Maden Sehir and then make the long climb back, and this they do on average about twice a year'.

A youth of about eighteen, having the ruddy and fresh complexion that reflected his outdoor life, showed us the ruins and proudly the Mosque, and when we were about to leave I told Ahmet I would like to give him something as a token of our visit. "No more than two thousand lira" said Ahmet, which, at the then rate of exchange, was the equivalent of sixty pence. He was horrified at the thought of taking anything for what be considered his duty in showing us hospitality, until I gently insisted and put it into the pocket of his shirt. Little though it was it would be helpful when he did the trek down to Maden Sehir.

Before returning to Karaman we visited another of the Museum's staff who lived in one of the villages not far from Maden Sehir, and kept an eye on the archaeological sites in the surrounding district. In the course of conversation it turned out that he had spent more than twenty years of his working life on the railways in Holland, before deciding to retire and go back to the village of his birth. I asked him if he missed the amenities that had been a part of his life in Holland, but obviously not, he was a happy man.

From Karaman the road goes south to the mountains before dropping down through the pine covered hills to Alahan and its final descent to Mut. At Alahan another rubble track ascends through the pine woods to the Byzantine monastery, of the same name, that is situated just below another peak. Its position is even more spectacular than that of the village on the Kara Dagh and here again the views range over vast and open tracts of country that spread out below like a contour map. Much of this splendid basilica is still intact and more than enough of the fine detail that was carved in the stonework is left to demonstrate what was once the elegance and fine proportions of the monastery buildings. Here a thriving community committed themselves to the Church and lived out their time in peace and tranquillity and in surroundings that did much to lift the spirit **(See Figure 42)**.

The ruins of other chapels and churches are to be found in the district and some of them still have the remnants of fresco decoration. All of them must have been founded in these remote districts for the tranquillity of their surroundings - a condition that was certainly conducive to a life of religious contemplation, and undoubtedly also in the fact that the site of Derbe with its Pauline associations was not far distant.

The decision of Paul and Barnabas to return to Attaleia by way of Lystra, Iconium, and Pisidia was a courageous one. They could have taken the shorter route from Alahan as it goes down through the mountains to Mut, Roman Claudiopolis, and then on to today's Silifke and the coast, but it was their desire (Acts XIV 22, 26) to strengthen those who had joined the church on this missionary journey that prompted them to return the same way, even though it could have been fraught with further animosity from the Jews nevertheless; they must have been somewhat circumspect on their return journey, for Luke makes no record of any subsequent violence being directed towards them when on their way back to Attaleia.

Figure 41: One of the Remote Chapels of the Bin Bir Kilise on the Summit of the Kara Dag Mountains.

Figure 42: Ruins of the Basilica of the Monastery of Alahan.

CHAPTER 3

The Second Missionary Journey.

Shortly after the end of the first missionary journey, when Paul and Barnabas were back in Antioch, a dispute arose in the Antioch Church regarding those Gentiles who had accepted the Gospel and then decided to join the Church. The acrimonious dispute centred around the necessity for them to submit to the rite of circumcision as a matter of course and Paul was of the opinion that, as far as he was concerned, the Gentiles were not obliged to be circumcised as a pre-requisite for their acceptance of the Gospel. But, as has been said, the state of circumcision, together with the strict observance of the Torah and the compulsory keeping of the dietary laws, were the essential parts of Jewish ritual.

Circumcision for the Hellenised Jews, 'The Grecians', who had accepted the Gospel was not a problem, they had already been circumcised; but for the Gentiles it was a stumbling block for they regarded the condition as an utterly deplorable mutilation and quite unwarranted in the circumstances. Paul was quick to realise that any insistence on the rite, as a condition to be observed when joining the Church, was counterproductive; and he also realised the fundamental truth that, in the eyes of God, the act of circumcision was immaterial and not to be considered a guarantee of salvation; a precept that the Jews would never acknowledge or recognise.

In view of the violent disputes that constantly arose in Antioch over the Gentiles with their dislike, and complete rejection, of circumcision, Paul and Barnabas decided to go to Jerusalem in the hope that they might be able to resolve the issue, and to thrash out with the Apostles, and the Jerusalem Church, the question as to the actual necessity for the Gentiles to submit to the rite. Acts XV describes the arguments in Jerusalem as being long and bitter, especially on the part of those Pharisees who had seen fit to join the Church for, having already been circumcised, they had nothing more to lose. However, it was eventually agreed by all concerned that the Gentiles had no need to submit to the rite when accepting the Gospel, and letters to that effect were taken back to the Antioch Church by Silas, Paul, and Barnabas.

However, not long after their return from Jerusalem Peter, for some undisclosed reason came down from Jerusalem to see them, possibly the circumcision of the Gentiles was still a question, and in the course of his stay fraternised and ate with those Gentiles who had joined the Church. Normally it was the rigid custom of the Jews not to have any social intercourse with the Gentiles; sometime previously when in Joppa Peter had baptised the centurion Cornelius in nearby Caesarea, and then been subject to severe criticism from the Apostles for his action - Acts XI 1 - 3:

'Now the Apostles and the believers who were in Judea heard that the Gentiles had also accepted the word of God. So when Peter went up to Jerusalem the circumcised believers criticised him saying why do you go to the uncircumcised men and eat with them'?

Not long after Peter's arrival in Antioch a heated confrontation began when a delegation, possibly from James, also came down to the Antioch church and then refused to eat with the Gentile converted, and this to the extent that Peter, and then Barnabas, also ceased their fraternisation with the Gentiles and took their meals with those from Jerusalem. This was something that Paul could not tolerate and he furiously accused them of hypocrisy, the degree of his extreme annoyance is pithily summed up in Galatians 2 & 11:

'But when Cephas came to Antioch I opposed him to his face, because he stood self condemned: for until certain people came from James, he used to eat with the Gentiles. But after they came he drew back and kept separate for fear of the circumcision faction. And the other Jews joined him in this hypocrisy, so that even Barnabas was led astray'.

It was the beginning of a distinct rift and coolness between them and one that seems to have lasted over the years, for Paul makes little reference to Peter In his subsequent letters.

Paul gives a more complete version of this visit to Jerusalem in Galatians 2, where he mentions that Titus, a Gentile from Antioch and one of his later trusted companions, went with them on this occasion. Titus, of Greek extraction, refused to be circumcised when accepting the Gospel and Paul expresses in Galatians 2, 3-6 his indignation at the false believers who secretly spied on them in an effort to force Titus to conform to the Law. It is possible that Paul took Titus to Jerusalem to demonstrate to the Apostles the fact that a dedicated Gentile need not of necessity be circumcised.

To the Jews the importance of circumcision was instrumental in their efforts to inflict the rite on the Gentile converts, and this became almost the equivalent of a running sore with Paul, for he brings up the subject time and again in his letters. In Romans 2. 25-26 he points out to the Jews that the act of circumcision does not guarantee their salvation, nor in any way does it form an amnesty for their transgressions, either major or minor, that many of them might habitually make against the Law, and that the Gentiles who sincerely and truly accept the Gospels and abide by the Law are far more likely to achieve salvation, in spite of their retaining their natural foreskins.

In Romans 3. 1. Paul pursues the subject further: 'Then what advantage has the Jew? Or what is the value of circumcision'? And he further dwells on the uselessness of the rite in Galatians 6, 15 where he says to the Jewish faction: 'For neither circumcision nor uncircumcision is anything; but a new creation is everything! as for those who follow this rule - peace be upon them', and this he reaffirms very forcibly in 1. Corinthians VII 19: 'Circumcision is nothing, and uncircumcision is nothing, but obeying the commandments of God is everything. Let each of you remain in the condition in which you were called'. This continued attack by Paul on the necessity of being circumcised to attain salvation, a cherished aspect of the Jewish religion and culture, must have been a major factor in fostering the hatred that the great majority of the Jews felt for him. However, the winning of this argument was a watershed; Paul's inspired stance against the endeavours of the Jews to enforce their rite on the Gentiles has certainly spared the males of the Christian Church today from having to, willy-nilly, undergo the rite of circumcision as a religious necessity, it now being a matter of choice.

The reluctance of the Apostles to recognise or accept Paul as truly one of them was the great disappointment that remained with him throughout the years of his mission. One can see the Apostles' point of view. Up to the Crucifixion they had all been the close companions of Jesus and were continuing with his work, and here was Paul their one time ardent persecutor, on his own admission, now asking to be equally accepted as one of them. His resentment and bitterness is constantly being reflected in his letters, and at times is very marked.

In most of his epistles he begins by describing himself as an 'Apostle of Jesus Christ by the will of God', but his feelings are clearly evident In 1 Corinthians IX 11 - 29 where he asks, 'Am I not free? Have I not seen Jesus Christ our Lord? If I am not an Apostle to others, at least I am to you; for you are the seal of my Apostleship in the Lord', and he then goes on to say in his defence 'Do we not have the right to be accompanied by a believing wife, as do the other Apostles and the brothers of the Lord and Cephas'. Again in 1 Corinthians XV 9, where his non acceptance still rankles he says to those in Jerusalem, 'For I am the least of the Apostles unfit to be called an Apostle, because I persecuted the Church of God'. His most acid outburst, however, must be that directed at Peter in 2. Corinthians 11, 5 - 6 where he says: 'I think that I am not in the least inferior to these Super- Apostles. I may be untrained in speech, but not in knowledge; certainly in every way and in all things we have made this evident to you'.

This lack of acceptance by the Apostles from the outset could have helped to stimulate the drive and energy that lay behind and helped sustain him during the various privations that he encountered whilst on his missionary journeys; but in some respects a slightly masochistic streak does seem to come to the fore in his personality, as shown in 2 Corinthians 11 23 - 30, where he appears to exult in his long list of misfortunes, especially in verse 30: 'If I must boast, I will boast of the things that show my weakness'.

It is generally accepted that the second missionary journey began in A. D. 50, possibly at sometime in March when the rigours of winter had passed, and all indications point to it having lasted for some three years or more. Paul's mode of travel has been subject to a deal of speculation. For the most part it would seem to have been on foot, or possibly by donkey where and when available, and this would have limited the daily distance covered. Travelling overland was usually undertaken between March and early November for only the most intrepid, or those obliged to make essential journeys on business matters, would risk making journeys during the Winter months, especially when mountain passes such as that through the Cilician Gates of the Taurus had to be negotiated[22].

There was also the question of the overnight stops. If no convenient shelter was available at the end of the day the night would have had to be spent at the mercy of the elements. It is possible that Paul is referring to such occasions in 2 Cor 11, 27, 'in toil and hardship, through many a sleepless night, hungry and thirsty, often without food, cold and naked. And besides other things, I am under daily pressure because of my anxiety for all the churches'.

---

[22] Travel generally ceased from November 11 to March 10 except for those who were classed as professional travellers. Ramsay in his book, Roads, records the fact that Cicero crossed the Taurus by the Cilician Gates in Nov 51 B.C. Antigonus tried to cross in the winter by the same route in 314 B.C. and as a result lost a large number of his troops in the snow. The question arises as to whether Paul travelled only in the open season. In I Cor 16 he mentions spending the winter with them, "perhaps I will stay with you awhile, or even spend the winter." However, his remarks as quoted in 2 Cor. 11 27, do suggest that he did on occasion undertake journeys during the winter months. See The Book of Acts, Gill and Gempf for further discussion.

Accommodation would have been available In the villages and towns where travellers could have relied on a degree of hospitality, and this was certainly forthcoming in the Christian houses that Paul would have encountered on his journeys[23].

When the project of a second missionary Journey was discussed Barnabas was adamant that Mark should go with them, and this led to a heated situation between the two Apostles. According to Luke 'the disagreement became so sharp that they parted company'. The fact that Paul flatly refused to take Mark on the journey was enough to cause a permanent split in their relationship; Barnabas then setting out for Cyprus and taking Mark with him. Paul makes little mention of Barnabas In his subsequent letters and is only reconciled to Mark when both of them are in Rome during the time of Paul's detention in his hired house. Mark at some time must have left Cyprus but there is no record of Barnabas having done so; his tomb being near Salamis it is possible that he did not.

Silas stayed on in Antioch until he and Paul set out on the second journey. Initially they went north from Antioch to pass through the Kizil Dag Mountains by the Syrian Gates and then, more than likely, turn down to Arsuz on the coast that was once the old Roman town of Prosopolis. Traces of this road are, or were, still extant, and they would then have followed it along the coast to Alexandretta, Mopsuestia, Adana and Tarsus. Just North of the mountains another road went across the Plains of Issus, where Alexander routed Darius and the Persians, to Nicopolis where it then turned West to Tarsus, but this route would have had little advantage being well out of the way and, apart from Nicopolis, there were few if any other towns on the road.

Acts XV 41 indicates they went through Syria and Cilicia confirming the churches, but no towns are specifically mentioned. These were probably founded by Paul in the years between him leaving Jerusalem and joining Barnabas in Antioch. The boundary of the Province of Cilicia began near Syrian Antioch and encompassed an area that was backed by the Taurus Mountains. The part of the Province that lay due West of Tarsus included the port of Pompeopolis and the coast as far West as Corycos; a region that was governed by Cicero around 50 B.C. Neither does Paul specifically mention Tarsus by name even though they must have stayed there, for Tarsus was the last city on the road before it passed through the Cilician Gates; the only way through the Taurus Mountains into central Anatolia. A section of this road with its fine broad slabs of paving stone can be seen today near the town of Pozanti, some thirteen kilometres North of Tarsus and just beyond the Taurus. At a junction a little beyond Pozanti the road branched into two forks, one going westwards to Laranda (Karaman), Ancient Derbe, Lystra, and Iconium, whilst the other went north to Ancyra, today's Ankara.

An alternative route would have been the coastal one by boat from Selucia, the port for Syrian Antioch, to Silifke on the South coast, and then by road through the town of Pompeopolis, today's Mut, before the climb through the Taurus Mountains to Derbe. The

---

[23] An alternative route would have been the coastal one by boat from Pompeiopolis to Seleukia, today's Silifke on the Kalykadnos, and then by road from today's Mut through the Taurus to Derbe, today's Karaman. This however would have been a dangerous route through the mountains. The route through the Cilician Gates could have been nearer and more acceptable during the open season.

route through the Taurus would have been hazardous through possible banditry. That through the Cilicean Gates would have been more acceptable during the open season.

Luke gives few details of the second journey in Acts XVI but, meagre though they are, they do confirm that Paul with Silas, visited Derbe, Lystra, and Iconium and in that order. Though Pisidian Antioch has not been mentioned they must have passed through the city on this first part of the journey. Thus, after having passed through the Cilician Gates, the road to the West from the junction must undoubtedly have been the route they used. Paul's first and obvious objective on this second Journey was to revisit those who had joined the Churches they had founded when he and Barnabas were on the first journey, but it is not clear as to whether Gaius left Derbe with them on this occasion or not, for Paul does mention a Gaius of Derbe as being with him at a later date in Corinth. He is specific though in the fact that Timothy joined them at Lystra and was with them for the rest of the journey.

Timothy had a Greek father and a Jewish mother, and it would seem that the family had some standing; not only were they well thought of in Lystra but also in Iconium. In view of the fact that Timothy was partly of Jewish stock it is apparent that Paul went to some lengths to avoid any confrontation with the Jews of Iconium, as he had previously done, for he took the step to personally circumcise Timothy. In spite of his decided views on the necessity of the rite as far as the Gentiles were concerned Paul must, on this occasion, have circumcised Timothy as a sop to the sensibilities of the Jews of Iconium, and it has also been suggested that the rite itself could have taken place in Iconium and not Lystra. It is noticeable that Paul on this second journey, and on his third, did not indulge in any controversial activities as far as the Jews and the Roman administration were concerned in Lystra, Iconium or Antiocheia.

After leaving Pisidian Antioch (Antiocheia) it was Paul's intention to take the Gospel to Ephesus and the cities in the Roman province of Asia, and to this effect with Silas, Timothy, and possibly Gaius of Derbe, they would have left the City Westwards by the Via Sebaste and gone through the rolling hills to Appolonia. At Appolonia they would have left the Via Sebaste to then take the road to Apamea, that was almost certainly paved, and one that went on directly to Ephesus through the Meander Valley. This formed a part of the highway that went from Ephesus to the Euphrates, and it was also a link with many of the other cities that the Greeks had established long before the Roman occupation: their peoples would have been a great potential for Paul in the furtherance of his evangelical mission having as they did a Hellenistic background.

Another road from Antiocheia went North before turning West on to Pessinus (**See Map - Henri Metzger**), but this would have been an unlikely choice for it was unpaved; moreover it would have been a difficult and dangerous journey through mountainous regions where travellers were very susceptible to attack from the Pisidian tribes and, furthermore, it was not on the direct road to Asia and Ephesus. Travelling the road today from Yalvac to Bagkonak and then through the mountains to Aksehir gives an indication of the difficulties that might have befallen those who ventured this way in the first century A.D. It is very exposed and bare of trees and in parts where the bright yellow ochre of the earth shouts back at the sun there is little vegetation.

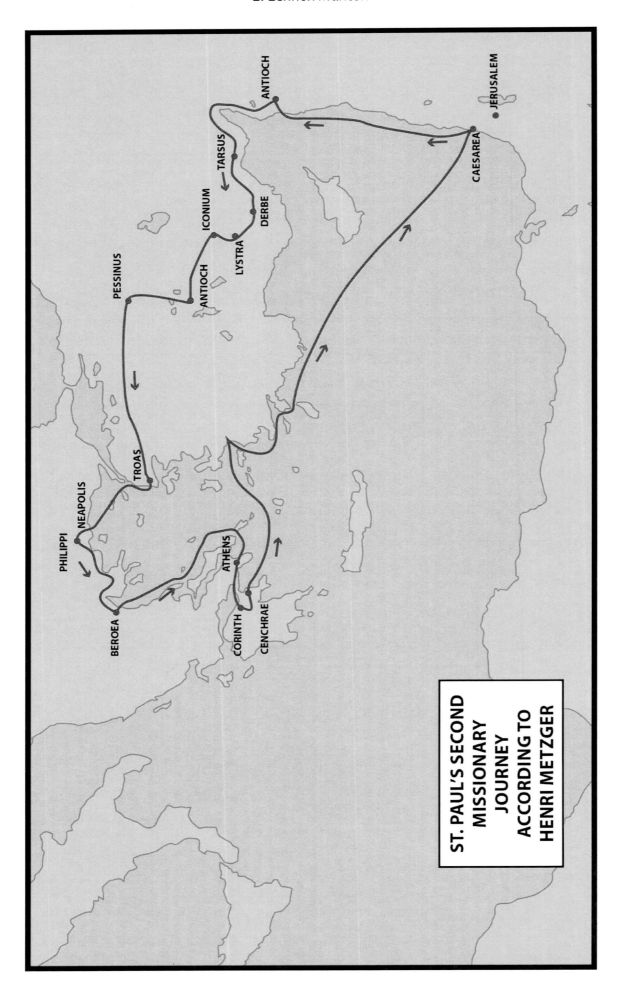

ST. PAUL'S SECOND MISSIONARY JOURNEY ACCORDING TO HENRI METZGER

However, there is a school of thought that postulates the Apostle, together with his companions, having taken this route into Northern Galatia with the possible object of visiting Ancyra, would then return through Mysia to Alexander Troas. However it has been pointed out by Professor Mitchell that the distance from Pisidian Antioch to Ancyra is 312 kilometres and from Ancyra to Troas 771 kilometres, in all a detour of 1083 kilometres which does not in the circumstances seem practical. I have myself driven from Pisidian Antioch to Ankara by way of Philomelium, and thence from Ankara through Gordium to ancient Dorylaeum (today's Eskisehir); to do this section of the journey on foot, or with whatever limited transport, such as a donkey, that could have been at Paul's disposal would have been a very daunting task. On balance it seems very unlikely that they went into Northern Galatia to visit Ancyra.

Luke records in Acts XVI 6, 'They went through the region of Phrygia and Galatia, having been forbidden by the Holy Spirit to speak the word in Asia'. This part of Phrygia would have been an ethnic district, like Lyaconia, that was incorporated into Southern Galatia when the Romans extended the Province Southwards, thus in the days of Paul the Province of Galatia extended from a part of Pontus known as Pontus Galatica to Pamphylia in the South. The cities of Appolonia and Apamea, that lay more to the West, were thus in the Phrygian district of the Province of Galatia. In 800 B.C. Phrygia was ruled by the wealthy Midas family of the Kings of Gordium, the city being destroyed by the Galatian Tribes from today's Toulouse as they passed through in the Third Century B.C. Strabo described Gordium being a small village in Roman times. The ruins lie west of Ankara and it was there where the chariot of Midas stood in the Temple of Zeus, the yoke and shaft being tied by the Gordian knot. The city, however, was destroyed by Galatian tribes from Toulouse as they passed through in the third century B.C. The ruins of the city can be seen lying west of Ankara. The ethnic district of Phrygia became district of some size having Loadiciea on the River Lycus, its metropolis.

However, their different peoples were all referred to as Galatians; the citizens of Appolonia being thus described in an extant inscription of the first century A.D. It is the course of their journey from Apamea that gives rise to a deal of speculation, and it could be in Apamea where Paul took the decision not to proceed further into Asia, as he had originally intended, but to turn to the North, and possibly not at the behest of the Holy Ghost.

There could have been a more mundane reason for his sudden change of itinerary. Ephesus was the centre for the Roman administration of Asia and the seat of the governor of the province It must not be forgotten that Claudius was now Emperor in Rome and for some time had had a great deal of trouble where the Jews were concerned, particularly in Rome itself. Their repeated squabbling together with their periodic rioting in pursuance of what they considered to be 'their rights' had so angered Claudius that in A.D. 49 he finally passed an edict that had them evicted from Rome. It has been suggested that the trouble arose through dissensions between the Christian Jews and the more Orthodox, Aquila and Priscilla being amongst those who went to Corinth whilst others sought refuge with the Diaspora in various other parts of the Empire. This influx of the deported seeking refuge in these cities could well have strained their relations with the local Roman administration; they do not appear to have been popular in Philippi[24].

Paul's traumatic encounters with the Jews and the authorities in the cities of Antiocheia, Iconium, and Lystra, situations that had practically involved their entire populations, must have given him a reputation for being the cause of serious municipal disruption, a reputation that must have spread to the neighbouring provinces and not have helped his cause. Rioting in any city was apt to give it a bad name and such situations when they arose were severely dealt with by the Roman administration, a case in point being a celebrated one that took place in Pompeii during the games in the Theatre with the rival town of Nuceria. Numerous people lost their lives and Nero banned further such occasions for a period of ten years.

In Apamea it is possible that Paul came to the conclusion that the Roman presence in Asia was more formidable than he had previously thought; the unfortunate experiences he had undergone when on the first journey could have made him wish to avoid, if he could, any possible confrontation with Roman officialdom; in no way a coward he might have considered that discretion was the better part of valour. Thus they turned Northwards towards Bithynia, and at this juncture nothing specific is known of their movements until they reached Alexander Troas; one can only surmise as to the possibilities, for Luke has dismissed the whole of this part of the journey in three short verses, Acts. XVI 6, 7, 8.

Their most likely route from Apamea, in the region of today's Dinar, would have been to Prymnessus, Armorium, and Pessinus, along a road that might not have been paved but passed through pleasant country where travelling was reasonable, Pessinus was in the district of Northern Galatia and from here the road went on to Germa, another of the cities that Augustus raised to the status of Colonia.

Northern Galatia was once a part of the Hittite Empire before it fell under Persian administration, and Paul would have found its peoples of a somewhat different cultural background when compared with those of the Aegean region. In the distant past some migratory tribes of the Gaulish Tectosages left the district of Toulouse to settle in the region of Ancyra whilst the Tolistogolgi took over the district around Pessinus.[25]

After a series of defeats in their battles with Attalus, the King of Pergamum, they formed a Galatian confederacy in the North Eastern part of the country which eventually became a part of the Roman Empire. Augustus eventually annexed the whole region and then made Ancyra, today's Ankara, the Metropolis of Northern Galatia and the centre for the cult of Rome and Augustus. But in spite of the advent of Rome the roads in this region remained unpaved until one was built by Titus in A.D.80, long after the time of Paul.

[24] Josephus records an early edict of Claudius that confirms the Jewish rights throughout the Empire, 'King Agrippa and Herod, my dearest friends, have asked me to allow the Jews of the whole Roman Empire to keep the same rights as the Jews of Alexandria. I most gladly agreed --It is therefore proper that the Jews of all the world under our sway keep their ancestral customs without hindrance. --- It is my wish that the magistrates of the cities and colonies, both inside and outside Italy, have this edict of mine inscribed and set up for not less than thirty days in a place where it can easily be read from the ground.' It seems that Claudius eventually lost all patience with them in Rome, in spite of his earlier edict!

[25] The latter part of an inscription found in Ancyra reads as follows - 'In the governorship of Fronto, Metrodorus, son of Menemachus and the natural son of Dorylaus, gave a public feast. ... son of Seleucus, gave a public feast and provided oil for four months. Pylamenes, son of King Amyntas, gave a public feast for the three tribes and at Ancyra sacrificed a hetacombe and presented spectacles and a procession; likewise a bull fight and bull-fighters and 50 pairs of gladiators. He provided oil for the three tribes for the whole year and presented a wild beast fight. The three tribes here, the root stock of the Galatians were the Tolistobolgi, Tectosages and the Trocini.

Pessinus was originally a Phrygian Temple State and a part of the original confederacy but the Temple cult that had been in the hands of Phrygian eunuch priests known as the Galli, was now governed by a body of five Phrygian and five Galatian eunuch priests who came under the control of the chief priest, another eunuch known as the Archigallos. The cult centred round a sacred black stone that was known as the Baitylos, possibly a meteorite for it was supposed to have fallen from the sky. It was thus considered to be the embodiment of the goddess and as such was kept in the Temple sanctuary[26]. The cult was not unlike that of Emesa, today's Homs in Syria, which also centred around a similar stone that was kept in the Temple sanctuary, but here the high priest Bassianus had a daughter called Julia Domna who, in the third century A.D. became the second wife of the Emperor Septimius Severus. The custom that must have most endeared the cult of Emesa to its adherents was that which obliged every girl, on becoming nubile, to kneel before the sacred stone in a completely naked state, and to remain there until some male just happened to pass by, look in, and ritually deflower her.

Another somewhat similar cult was practised in the city of Hierapolis that lay East of Antioch. Here in the large forecourt of the Temple stood two phallic pillars that were scaled by young men during the spring festivals. At this time the forecourt was the scene of wild orgiastic ceremonies where the obscenities not only included the priestesses but also the eunuchs, to the extent that many young males in their frenetic fervour to honour the goddess joined the ranks of the Galli by self emasculation, then donating their severed parts in a presentation casket to the goddess. One such casket suitably decorated with scenes of the cult is now in the Fitzwilliam Museum in Cambridge. These pillars were the origin of those that were used in the Christian period by the Stylites, the pillar Ascetics of whom St Simeon was the first and the most renowned. He lived on a pillar near Antioch that reached a height of some forty cubits and this, till his death in A.D.459, was a popular and constant tourist attraction for the curious, not to mention the pilgrim hordes.

The cult that was peculiar to Pessinus had many of these features but was also linked to that of Cybele, known also as the Magna Mater and roughly the equivalent of Aphrodite. Over the years the priests of Pessinus managed to accumulate very great wealth and they reached the peak of their influence around 204 B.C. A great body of lesser eunuch priests, flautists, trumpeters and girls with tambourines, took part in the Temple rituals, the whole becoming so famous that the cult spread to Rome. The Senate considered the stone so sacred, and to have such powers of protection, they had it brought from Pessinus to lodge on the Palatine Hill where they hoped it would save Rome from the advance of Hannibal.

From thence on the Eunuch priests with their conical Phrygian hats and their tambourines were a common sight as mendicants in the streets of Rome and their great festival, that also took place in April and lasted for some six days, centred round the Temple on the Palatine hill. However, over the years the cult lost much of its meaning though the April festival was still

---

[26] As the cult stone of Pessinus had fallen from the sky it was considered by all to be supernatural, and the symbol of the Magna Mater Cybele that had the power of protection over the people against any impending disasters. When the fall of Rome was threatened by Hannibal during the Second Punic War the Senate had the stone brought from Pessinus in the belief that it had the power to protect them. Appian writes ' As certain direful prodigies sent by Jupiter had appeared in Rome, the decemviri who consulted the Sibylline books said that something would fall from heaven at Pessinus in Phrygia (where the Mother of the Gods is worshipped by the Phrygians), which ought to be brought to Rome. Not long after, the news came that it had fallen, and the image of the Goddess was brought to Rome, and still to this day they keep holy to the Mother of the gods the day on which it arrived'. (Appian, The Hannibalic War). Livy recounts a similar story.

observed, and its echoes are still apparent in the custom of erecting Maypoles on Mayday. By the third and fourth centuries A.D. it was a common custom in Rome to employ eunuchs as domestics, a habit that could have had its origin with the eunuch priests of Pessinus.

The Romans must have returned the sacred stone to Pessinus when Hannibal was defeated and the threat to the Capital was over, for a new Temple was built in Pessinus during the first part of the first century A.D. In common with the many other Temples in Anatolia it faced to the West, but in this case it had columns with capitols of the Ionic order that matched the Ionic porticoes of the new Agora. Paul must have seen these comparatively new buildings when he and his companions visited Pessinus; to them the cult of Magna Mater, still very much in evidence with its eunuch priests and Archigallos, must have been very offensive.

The Greek influence and culture was not nearly so evident in Northern Galatia. For the most part the indigenous population had not forsaken the ancient deities that included the mother goddess Cybele and the Phrygian Sabazios who was later equated by the Greeks with Dionysus. The popular god Men, the moon god of Asia Minor was still worshipped as the protector of families, guarding them against illness and misfortune, and his statues always show him dressed In the Phrygian manner and wearing the traditional Phrygian cap, In spite of the advent of Rome and the cult of Augustus firmly established in Ancyra the Phrygians and the Galatians still retained their loyalty towards their more primeval pantheon of deities, a factor that could have provoked a more immediate challenge to Paul's mission: it was the same cult that had flourished and been a part of life in Pisidian Antioch for many years before the visit of Paul and Barnabas.

Some have regarded Paul's letter to the Galatians to have been his first, written about A.D. 49. and addressed to the peoples of Northern Galatia, 'The Northern Galatian Theory', but others suggest it was written when he was in Macedonia around A.D. 52 - 55 and then sent to the Churches in the cities of Pisidian Antioch, Iconium, Lystra, and Derbe, Cities that were situated in the Southernmost aspect of the Province, for, as has already been pointed out, these cities in the time of Paul were considered to be Galatian, and Paul, in his letters, has not made any specific reference to any named city in Northern Galatia, nor are there any references to them as such in Acts.

If they went to Pessinus it is likely that they made little headway with the Galli, and they would then have gone on to Germa, a Colonia that would have had some Jews of the Diaspora and been on the way to Dorylaeum, today's Eskisehir, and Bithynia. If they did not visit Pessinus they could have taken the road that went directly from Amorium to Dorylaeum. Dorylaeum was near the Bithynian border and Luke records in Acts 16, 7: 'When they had come opposite Mysia, they attempted to go into Bithynia, but the spirit of Jesus did not allow them'. Bithynia was also a large Roman Province having Nicomedia, its capital or metropolis, situated at the Eastern tip of the Sea of Marmaris, and having its Northern boundaries bordering on the Black Sea. Nicea and Nicomedia would have been Paul's immediate objectives for Dorylaeum in the district of Mysia was on the direct road to these cities in Bithynia. It could be in Dorylaeum where Paul decided once again to change course and go westwards to Alexander Troas.

Bithynia was also a Province of some considerable importance with a significant Roman administration. Trajan, when Emperor, sent the younger Pliny to Nicomedia as governor and amongst his letters to the Emperor there is one seeking advice as to what line he should take with the Christians. The reply from Trajan was almost brusque; he was told not to actively seek them out but if, when discovered, they did not recant their beliefs and pour the libations that were due to the cult of the Emperor, they were to be brought before the courts.

When Paul reached the borders of Bithynia it is possible that he found the Roman presence there more marked than he had expected, and once more thought it unwise to take the Gospel into a situation where there was again the risk of a serious confrontation with the administration. After leaving Pisidian Antioch the changes in the course of their intended journey must have been due to the force of local circumstance, and it is intriguing to speculate as to just what the circumstances were to have brought about these changes of direction.

Paul's intention of taking the Gospel into Bithynia having being thwarted, there was little other choice but to go through Mysia to Alexandra Troas, a major port on the Aegean coast. He could not go north into Bithynia nor could he go south into the Province of Roman Asia Minor. His only choice, if he did not wish to abort the whole mission and return to Antioch by the way be came, was to go due west to the coast and Troas.

Troas has often been confused with neighbouring Troy, a city that had nothing to do with Paul's journeys for it lay in a plain to the North, and being well away from the sea had no harbour facilities. Troas was a large city that derived its name from Alexander the Great and had been raised to the status of a Colonia by the Emperor Augustus. It had city walls that extended for some two miles and a population near on an hundred thousand, and was also considered to be a major port in the Roman world, Augustus designated it the 'Colonia Augusta Troas', when he raised its status so that its administration was Roman when Paul and his companions arrived in Troas.

The maritime importance and the prosperity enjoyed by Troas was due to the large harbour built in the Hellenistic period, and this in spite of the fact that the movement of shipping depended entirely on the prevailing winds; by sea it was the essential and crucial link with Neapolis, the port for Philippi in Macedonia. The great Via Egnatia went from Neapolis to Dyrrachium, today's Durrazzo on the Adriatic, and this was the main highway used by the Imperial post from the provinces in Asia to Rome. But today all this has gone, the extensive site of one time Troas is now mostly wooded with Vallonea oak trees, descendants of those that could well have been there in the days of Paul, the acorns now being gathered to be used for dye, and amongst them are the vestiges of its ancient city walls and the ruins of the Hadrianic baths. The remains of the harbour can still be seen and this together with the rest of the fabric of the city was built in granite obtained from the nearby quarries.

Again nothing is known of the route that Paul and his companions might have taken from Dorylaeum to the coast. Paved roads that went West through Mysia to the coast may have existed but, if they did, no records of them exist today, nor have any remnants of them so far been discovered. A road that was paved around 1 B.C. is known to have existed in the Troad in the time of Paul. This followed the coast from Adramyttium through Alexandra Troas to

Lampsacus, and quite possibly it extended as a paved road to Cyzicus in the Propontis. Some have suggested that Paul took this coastal road from Cyzicus but in reality it appears unlikely. To reach Cyzicus and the paved highway meant a long cross country journey skirting the borders of Bithynia North West from Dorylaeum. The important city of Prusa, today's Bursa, lay on this route, but for Paul to have broken his journey here would have been out of the question for Prusa lay within the borders of Bithynia.

Obviously one cannot determine the exact route taken by Paul and his companions but it is interesting to look at the alternatives. If he and his party did not opt for the coastal route they must firstly have left Dorylaeum for Cotiaeum, today's Kutahya, a town that still carries on the tradition of the famous Iznik ceramics. Dr French has suggested that they could have gone from Kutahya to Aizanoi, today's Cavdarhisar, where the city's impressive temple to Zeus still stands, one of the best preserved in Turkey today. Here engraved on the walls of the Macellum, a round building that was once the meat market, is the entire text of an edict formulated by Diocletian to combat the rampant inflation then afflicting the Empire. It was nothing less than a comprehensive prices and incomes policy that had to be rigidly adhered to. From Cavdarhisar they could then have followed the valley of the Macestus river to Hadrianutherae.

However, there is now a good road that goes North West from Kutahya to Tavsanli, Dursunbey, and Balikesir, a road that is far more direct and could well have followed an earlier track. Dursunbey must have been near the site of ancient Hadrianeia and Balikesir near that of Hadrianutherai and communications, whether by roads or tracks, must have existed between these important cities.

From Hadrianutherae there were several options. They could have gone on to Adramittium, another port largely given over to local shipping, and thence to Assos before taking the paved road to Troas some thirty two kilometres distant. Alternatively, after leaving Hadrianutherae they could have struck off along paths that went through the mountains to the towns of Argiza, Policlina, and Scepsis before dropping down to Troas and these towns were so situated that a day's journey would have covered the distance between each of them. A little West of Balikesir there is a road that goes North to the region of Argiza, and there are still tracks and dirt roads that connect with Policlina and Scepsis, a city that in the time of Paul was well known for the school of philosophy that was founded by Pyhrron and his pupil Timon, their adherents disbelieving everything and known as the 'Sceptics'.

Paul's arrival in Troas marked a significant event in his life, for it was the beginning of a long association with the City and his relationship with Luke. It is from this point that the 'we' passages begin in Acts XVI 10. From here on descriptions of incidents in Paul's journeys and related situations appear to have been recorded by a third person, who at that time was accompanying him, and used the 'we' as if describing an eye witness account of the events in question. From Paul's references to Luke, after their meeting at Troas and subsequently till his martyrdom in Rome, it would seem that it was Luke who was with him for much of the time and responsible for what appear to be first hand and accurate eye witness accounts.

Scholars have debated the origin and source of these passages and questioned if they were the entire work of Luke. However, they do contain information that is historically correct and the timing given for covering the distances of some of the journeys appear to agree with map references. It is significant too that Luke in his Gospel 1, 1 - 4 says to Theophilus: 'Since many have undertaken to set down an orderly account of the events that have been fulfilled among us, just as they were handed on to us by those who from the beginning were eyewitnesses and servants I too decided after investigating everything carefully from the very first, to write an orderly account to you'. By and large it would seem that the descriptions of situations in which Paul found himself when Luke was with him could be an accurate record.

According to Eusebius Luke, the 'beloved physician (Col IV 14) came from Antioch, but he could well have been of Macedonian stock from Philippi, a city of Colonia status where Latin was spoken and the administration Roman. Some consider him to have been a student when he met Paul, possibly aged between 23 and 25, but it is far more reasonable to assume that he was already then a qualified physician and working in Troas. Luke was a Gentile and some are of the opinion that he was influenced by the faith healers of the school of Aretaeus of Cappadocia. Be that as it may it is more likely that he studied medicine and graduated from the Aesculepium at Pergamum, one that was much nearer to Philippi than Epidaurus in the Pelopenese, and as equally renowned. Its many facilities included an extensive medical library, the ruins of which can still be seen, and a course of treatment that was centred around the large Temple of Aesculapius and included a degree of auto suggestion and possible hypnosis. Its reputation carried on well into the second and third centuries for Pausanias, who was born in Lydia in the second century A.D., was one of its later graduates: before be set out on his travels through the length and breadth of Greece. When on these journeys he wrote his 'Baedecker', a work that extended into ten volumes and one that has given valuable information regarding the ancient world[27].

Galen, the great physician and anatomist, was born in Pergamum in A.D. 130, and in due course became one of the Institution's great teachers, to finally end his life at the age of 70 years as the personal physician and confidante of the Emperor Marcus Aurelius. The journey from Neapolis to Troas and thence to Pergamum would have been far less difficult than the journey from Macedonia to the medical school at Epidaurus, and their respective reputations were about equal.

Troas too had its own small Aesculepium associated with Smintheus, the local god of healing, a cult associated with that of Apollo. This was associated with hot thermal springs in the city suburbs to the South and were a part of the Aesculepium facilities, the whole no doubt being used as a Spa; the hot springs are still there, not far from a salt works that once flourished in the mid nineteenth century. The question arises as to whether Luke was the, or one of the, medical practitioners associated with this establishment when Paul, Silas, and Timothy arrived in the City.

---

[27] There has been some recent speculation as to whether Luke was in fact a qualified Physician, in spite of Paul's description of him in Col, IV, 14. However, Paul was not in the habit of making erroneous statements, and until proved to the contrary, it should be assumed that Luke did in fact have a medical training.

The mixed population of Troas must have been receptive of Paul's teaching for there is evidence that the church he founded had a considerable following, and one that congregated in the House of Carpus (Acts XX 7-12) it is also not too much to assume that Carpus was a native of Troas. Though his occupation has not been recorded he must have been well to do, and Paul obviously used his house as a base to have left his cloak, his books and his parchments there, 11 Timothy IV 13. Moreover, it is also not too much to assume that Carpus and Luke bad been friends for some time before Paul and his companions arrived in the city. Thus one must not discount the possibility that the man from Macedonia, who figured in Paul's vision, was none other than Luke, for Acts gives the distinct Impression that Luke was well acquainted with Macedonia and Philippi. The first 'we' that occurs in Acts XVI 10 could well indicate it was Luke's suggestion that they should all go to Neapolis and Philippi to spread the Gospel. Having arrived at Alexandra Troas there was little else that Paul and his companions could do but go into Macedonia and Greece if they did not again wish to abort their mission and return directly to Antioch.

That they chose to make the journey by sea is born out in Acts XVI 11 where Luke records the fact that they broke their journey for the night at Samothrace before setting out the next day for Neapolis. This seems to be the first time an accurate and detailed account of a journey undertaken by Paul appears in Acts and is indicative that Luke was with them to record it, for it was but a day's sailing with fair winds from Troas to Samothrace and Samothrace was equidistant between Troas and Neapolis. On another occasion Luke records the sailing time from Philippi to Troas being that of five days with adverse head winds, what could be another accurate observation.

Neapolis was not a big harbour. Its small town was clustered around the base of a rocky hill to rise up in terrace upon terrace to the summit where a temple, that reflected on a smaller scale the Parthenon in Athens, housed the Venus of Neapolis, the treasure of the Neapolise.

The sea is now well back from the old quay, but a plaque that supposedly marks the spot where Paul first put foot on European soil can be seen in the pavement at the rear of the Church of St Nicholas of Patara. From here the ancient Via Egnatia ascends and crosses Mount Symbolum to the plains of Philippi, where it traverses the length of the city Forum.

The remains of Philippi, which also had the status of a Colonia, are quite extensive but in view of the fact that the city lacked a Synagogue the Jewish population could have been minimal. The prospects for trade in Philippi might not have been attractive enough to encourage the Jewish entrepreneurs, in spite of the fact that Philippi was a Colonia and must have had a military garrison. On the other hand, however, it does appear to have been a fact that the indigenous Philippians were not at all well disposed to those of the Diaspora. Owing to the lack of a Synagogue Paul mentions that they prayed by the river where he met and converted Lydia, a proselyte from Thyatira, a city and a district that was connected with the luxury trade of purple dye and dyeing; there are inscriptions from Thyatira that refer to the city's 'guild of dyers'[28]. The purple trade was generally the prerogative of men who had to have ample resources and they were often elected town councillors; thus the purple trade must have been operative in Philippi itself and Lydia must have had ample means for her to become involved. After having been baptised by Paul, possibly on

---

[28] Paul records in Acts. XVI. 15. that he baptised Lydia and her household which must indicate that she was the owner of a somewhat substantial property and after her baptism invited Paul and Silas to lodge with her. There has been some speculation as to whether Lydia was a widow who had inherited the property, or owned it in her own right, or was she a divorcee? There is also the possibility that she could have been a freedwoman associated with the imperial household and hence her connection with the purple trade. Whatever her circumstances she was obviously a woman of some status in Philippi whose house was a possible meeting place for the Christian community. For further discussion see 'Acts and the House Church'. The Book of Acts in its Greco- Roman setting.

the river bank where they all met on the Sabbath, the church in Philippi was centred in her house, thus establishing the first Christian church outside Asia Minor.

Though there were few Jews in Philippi to object to Paul's ministry, he even so managed to fall foul of the authorities by curing a half witted girl of oracular speech and for this both he and Silas were summarily beaten and imprisoned for depriving her owners of their livelihood. Their aggrieved indictment before the magistrates is recorded in Acts XVI 20: 'These men are disturbing our city; they are Jews and are advocating customs that are not lawful for us Romans to adopt or observe'. This anti Semitic feeling, that the magistrates must also have had, could have been a reflection of Roman feeling towards the Jews after their recent expulsion from Rome by Claudius. It is also clear that Paul and Silas were regarded as the equivalent of vagrants and as such did not have a fair hearing, the owners of the slave girl could have been citizens of some standing in Philippi to have gained the degree of support that they obviously had from their compatriots. The magistrates having concluded that the Apostles were responsible for the civic disturbance decreed that they should be stripped and soundly beaten, the most severe penalty for the offence and then thrown into the innermost cell of the prison and put in stocks. Treatment meted out to the lowest of felons. It was the timely earthquake that night that altered the situation. It was then that the jailor, who had more than heaped indignity on them, was converted and took them to his house to feed and dress their wounds.[29]

Acts XVI 36-37 describes the circumstances of their imprisonment and from the wording of verse 37 it would appear that Silas too had Roman citizenship: 'they have beaten us in public, uncondemned, men who are Roman citizens, and have thrown us into prison; and now they are going to discharge us in secret. Certainly not! Let them come and take us out themselves'. The Apostles had been publicly humiliated and were now intent on exacting a degree of humiliation on the Magistrates themselves. After abstracting a due and humble apology for the infringement of their Roman citizenship they, apart from Luke, went on to Amphipolis, Appolonia and Thessalonica; Luke possibly deciding that it was not practicable for him to go on further being obliged to return to his work in Troas. Throughout the years the Church in Philippi remained very loyal to Paul, for they were one of the few to send him by Epaphroditus their gifts of money at the time of his final imprisonment in Rome.

Acts XVII 2 records Paul remaining in Thessalonica for three Sabbaths and taking the opportunity to preach in the Synagogue, but the Jews who repudiated his teaching once again stirred up the rabble of the town and laid before the magistrates complaints accusing him of treason, a charge that they knew could not be ignored. Not only were Paul, Timothy, and Silas involved, but Jason and many other converts were detained by the magistrates. In order to secure their release, Paul, Silas, and Timothy, having remained in hiding during the fracas, then left quietly by night to travel the forty odd miles to Beroea, the Verria of today. It would seem that

---

[29] The owners of the slave girl were Romans, Acts. XVI. 21. and as such could have been veterans of the legions who had settled in Philippi with their pensions and allocation of land. It was the normal practice to settle veterans of the legions out of Italy, especially Rome, and many were sent to Timgad in North Africa. As such they would have had some social status in Philippi and been heeded by the Magistrates. The fact that a synagogue did not exist in Philippi suggests that the Jews were not welcome there. Paul and Silas were strangers having no social status and were therefore classed as vagrants in view of the charges brought against them. They were thus humiliated by being stripped and beaten to the extent that the flesh was cut, Acts 16 33, and then thrown into prison where they were held overnight in the innermost cell, Acts 16 24, and their feet held in stocks. These were the ultimate acts of humiliation meted out to felons and debtors. A question thus arises, why did Paul and Silas not declare their Roman Citizenship in the first place and avoid the Magistrates inflicting such an action? However, Paul was not now in Asia Minor and it is possible that he had no documents with him to prove his Roman citizenship. He and Silas may not have wished to run the risk of lengthy legal wrangling to determine their status with the possible waiting for a visit from the provincial governor to adjudicate. They could also have been apprehensive over a possible associated lack of funds had this been the case. However the final declaration of their status resolved the situation. See Rapske, Paul in Roman Custody.

Jason was also a person of some wealth who had offered hospitality to Paul and one had who suffered at the hands of the rabble. When they came to his house to detain Paul with Timothy and Silas, they had already left for Beroea.

In Beroea the pattern was again repeated, for in spite of being favourably received by the Greek citizens and the Jews of Beroea, who oddly enough always remained well disposed towards him in the synagogue, but it was, however, the Jews of Thessalonica that made a point of going down to Beroea to stir up more trouble against him. Leaving Silas and Timothy he once more had to make a hurried departure to the coast to find a boat for Athens. It is again evident that Paul's personality and his approach in spreading the Gospel was unacceptable to many of the Jews of the Diaspora, and the cause of their violent reactions that upset the administration of the city concerned.

Paul would have seen classical Athens in its splendour, dominated by the Acropolis with the Erectheion and the Parthenon, the sad ruins of which we see today. The centre for public life in Athens was the Agora where business and politics were discussed. Around the Agora were the temples of the various cults, and in the Agora itself the Temple of Ares. The entrance to the Agora was situated between the Stoa Poikile and the Stoa Basileios and Paul, when entering the Agora, would have noted these cults being reflected in the numerous statues that were concentrated about this area; some of them decidedly pornographic such as that of Hermes with an erect phallus. Paul makes reference to these in Acts 17, 16: 'he was deeply distressed to see the city full of idols'. So he argued in the synagogue with the Jews and the devout persons, and also in the market place every day with those who happened to be there; some of them dismissing his rhetoric 'to the extent that some said "what does this babbler want to say". However his discussions with the Epicurean and Stoic philosophers would have been received with more interest and are thought to have taken place in the region of the Stoa Poikile (Acts 17, 18).

Paul's speech to the Aerophagos is recorded in Acts 17, 22-30. This was the body of the City administration and the Athens court that some suggest met in the Stoa Basileios of the Agora. Paul's discussions in the Agora led them to have him preach before them but the actual site where it took place is not certain. The name Aeropagos can also refer to the Ares Hill that overlooks the Acropolis, and it seems in all probability that it was here on the summit where the meetings of the Aerophagos council took place. Legend has it that it was here where the original trial of Mars took place, hence its other name 'The Mars Hill'.

During subsequent trials the Judges are said to have sat in the open air on benches hewn out of the rock, and on a platform that was reached by a flight of steps that came up from the Agora. There is a description of the site in Wordsworth's Athens and Attica:

'Sixteen stone steps, cut in the rock at its south-east angle, lead up to the hill of the Aeropagos from the valley of the Agora, which seems to be the point of the hill on which the council of the Aerophagus sat. On a level area Immediately above the steps is a bench excavated in the limestone rock that forms three sides of a quadrangle to face the south, whilst on the east and west side there is a raised block. The bench complex could have been for the tribunal and Pausanias, who described this complex, thought the blocks were those assigned to the accuser and the accused'.

Pausanias also described a temple to Mars being then on the brow of the hill and a sanctuary of the Furies being in a rocky cleft below the seats of the judges. This could have been the scene where Paul fervently addressed the Aeropagos bringing into his discussion the altar to 'The unknown god', and succeeding in converting, amongst others, Dionysius the Aeropagite, and a woman named Damaris (Acts 17, 34).

In spite of the ruined state of Corinth there is much of it that would have been familiar to Paul. The remains of the Temples, the Agoras, the Odeon, the Theatre, with its views to the mountains and the far off snowy peak of Parnassus, are still in situ. The few columns to remain standing are those of the Temple to Apollo. Sadly the elegant porticoes that ran the length of the South side of the Agora and once formed the boundary of the Temple precinct and the market are not, though their course is still discernible. It was a city of noise and bustle, of statues, fountains and open squares, the whole dominated by a triumphal arch that had on its topmost aspect the sun god Helios with Phaeton, his son, driving golden chariots drawn by prancing horses. This Arch situated at the South Eastern aspect of the Agora gave on to the broad Lechaeum road that terminated in flights of steps going down to the great harbour, steps that Paul must have trod on many an occasion.

To the East and at the foot of the Arch stood the beautiful fountain of Peirene. Built originally in the sixth century B.C. it was considerably altered in Roman times to have a series of six arches with Doric columns that supported an architrave carrying a further series of Ionic columns; not only that, it was even more enhanced by another colonnade that was extended to enclose a large forecourt. This was another of the splendid monuments of Corinth that would have been familiar to Paul. Water from two springs was channelled into reservoirs concealed behind the facade before being allowed to feed the fountain by flowing gently into six basins, one within each arch. From there it spilled into a large rectangular pool let into the forecourt. Like all fountains this was a focal point where the elderly and otherwise of ancient Corinth were apt to browse in the heat of the day. The fountain also did service as an oracle. Those requiring an answer to a problem would throw a coin into the pool to have it answered by a sepulchral voice from behind the waters. Excavations have uncovered a priest's hole situated behind the cascade from whence the inspired deliberations of the gods were delivered **(See Figure 43)**.

It is generally conceded that Paul stayed in Corinth between the years A.D. 50-52, although Metzger is of the opinion that he left Corinth in the autumn of 51 to then return to Jerusalem, together with Silas and Timothy, after the two of them had left Beroea where they had remained for a time after his enforced departure. This would have coincided with the latter part of the reign of the Emperor Claudius who, not so long previously, had evicted the Jews from Rome; an act that had enforced Aquila, a Jew from Pontus in Northern Bithynia and Priscilla, whose family was possibly of Roman stock, to migrate to Corinth as refugees in order to make a new life for themselves by setting up their tent making business **(See Map)**.

Corinth had a population that comprised all nationalities, their efforts being directed into the sole objective of making money, and in such an environment there was, ipso facto, a large colony of the Jewish Diaspora. It was a fertile ground that presented endless possibilities for Paul's mission for the populace In general was prone to the worship of the pagan deities, and not the least that of Venus in her Temple high up on Acro Corinth from whence the City and the country spread out and beyond like a vast open map.

This was the Temple to Venus, famous throughout the Mediterranean and the Roman world, where the priestesses who performed the numerous Temple duties were known as the 'Corinthian Girls'. They numbered nigh on a thousand, and their sacred rites extended to any male who cared to visit them. They were originally thought to have been priestess prostitutes though this interpretation is now in dispute. However, for them to have been known as 'The Corinthian Girls' throughout this part of the Mediterranean leaves them open to some degree of speculation as to their activities.

Corinth was one of the most important commercial cities of the ancient world for it lay at the centre of the trade routes between the East and West, and for this reason was one of the busiest ports in the Mediterranean where the harbour was constantly crammed with the shipping that continually plied the Mediterranean basin. There were numerous taverns in the area that catered for the maritime trade, and here no doubt the Corinthian Girls would often have been a topic of conversation. The harbour being open to such a diverse maritime trade the repairs to torn sails and awnings must have formed a good part of the work that came the way of Aquila and Priscilla, in which Paul assisted when he Joined them.

Apart from the Temple to Venus on Acro-Corinth the city was also renowned for industries that included the manufacture of fine bronze castings and a beautiful pottery known as "Corinthian Ware" that was one of their world wide exports. The site of the potteries with their kilns and clay beds have been excavated, and in the process many old pot shards and moulds have been found together with various other waste products. Though the actual site of the synagogue has not as yet been discovered it is the opinion of some that it was located in this area. If so it was in this area where Paul first directed his teaching to the Jewish communities in the Synagogues, until they rose up against him; in Corinth it was no exception for, apart from Crispus their leader[30], they all repudiated his Apostolic mission with such force and animosity that Paul once again turned to the Gentiles (Acts XVIII 6).

His followers in Corinth came from all walks of life and he names many of them including Tertius, who recorded his letter to the Romans, Quartus, Fortunatus, and others such as Titius Justus, and Erastus who possibly held the post of aedile and was treasurer to the Corinthian municipality, and as such would have had some wealth. An inscription on a slab of pavement has been found in Corinth that reads 'Erastus pro aedile (at)es (ua)p(ecunIaI) stravit, - in return for his aedileship Erastus laid (the pavement) at his own expense'. This could well be the Erastus known to Paul and mentioned in Romans l6:23.

---

[30] Crispus was one of some social importance and standing in Corinth being one of the Synagogue rulers and responsible for organising much of the organisation of the Synagogue activities, as in Acts. 13. 15. He was also a public benefactor to various municipal projects. Acts. 18. 8 records Paul's baptism of Crispus together with his household. His conversion would have given Paul's mission some impetus and Crispus, being wealthy, would have had a large house where the Church could congregate, as they must have done at times in the house of Aquila and Priscilla. Their house was used for gatherings of the Christian community in Ephesus and later in Rome following their return from Ephesus.

Figure 43: The Periene Fountain at Corinth.

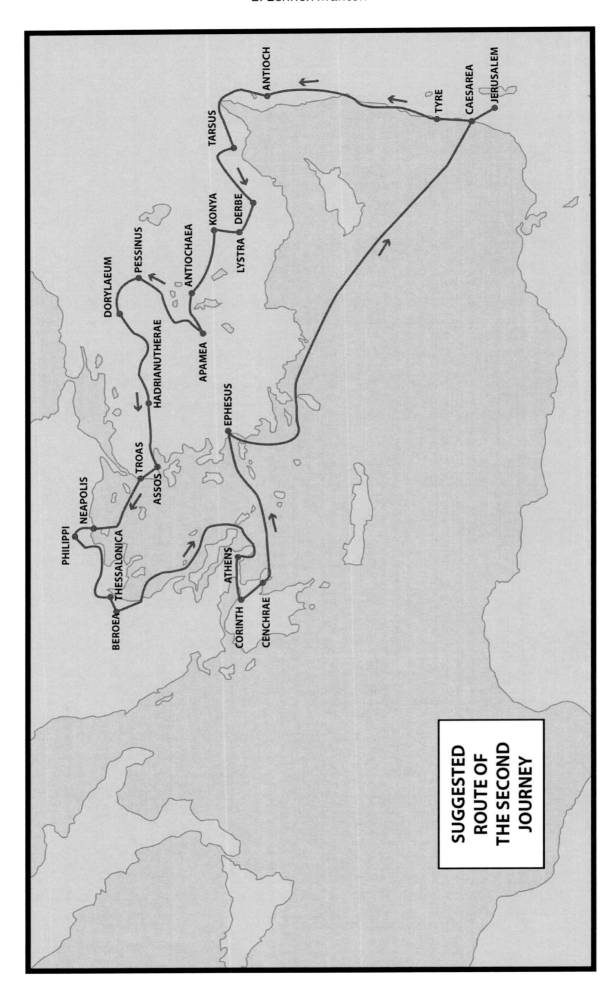

SUGGESTED
ROUTE OF
THE SECOND
JOURNEY

There was also Titius Justus who, according to Morton, was a member of the wealthy Titii family of potters[31]. This too is not beyond the bounds of possibility for he was a man of some considerable means and it was in his house where the Christian Church would foregather. Amongst them would have been those other converts who had joined the church, such as Jason, Lucius Sosipator and Crispus, the one who vacated his post as the leader of the Synagogue in order to join them.

In A.D. 27, Corinth became the Capital of the Roman Province of Archaia and the seat of the Proconsul, and from Acts it is known that Claudius appointed Gallio to this prestigious post in May A. D. 51 or 52. This date seems to be confirmed by an inscription found in Delphi where Claudius mentions his friend Lucius Junius Gallo having been appointed proconsul of Achaia, and is dated to the first half of A.D. 52 and it is possible that he took office in A.D. 51. It is possible then that Paul arrived In Corinth early on in A.D. 50. Gallio was born in Cordoba in Spain, and took his name from one of the intimates of his father, a Junius Gallio whose brothers were Lucius Annaeus Senneca, the philosopher and writer who complained so bitterly about his quality of life when living next to the municipal baths, and Annaeus Mela whose son was Lucan, the poet.

All those who knew Gallio spoke well of him, of his amiability, his lack of any spite, and the fairness that be showed in all of his dealings. His arrival in Corinth was the signal for the Jews to put before him the usual list of trumped up charges in which they accused Paul of having acted contrary to the Roman Law that protected the Jewish Creed. The Jews had long been waiting for such an opportunity and they took full advantage of it, but Gallio, in view of their behaviour in Rome, must have been well aware of their tactics for he immediately dismissed the charges and prepared to have the court cleared. It was the ideal opportunity for the Gentiles to take the matter into their own hands and before Sothenes, the leader of the Synagogue, could leave the precincts of the court they seized him and gave him a sound thrashing. This episode could have occurred at the Bema, a large flat stone dais situated at the furthermost end of the Agora, for it is thought that petitions and complaints, and all other municipal matters that needed discussion, were brought before the proconsul at this point. It speaks much for Gallio in letting them get on with it, he having realised that the motives that had instigated the Jews into bringing the charges were rooted in religious dogma and vindictiveness.

Paul's letters to the Thessalonians were written from Corinth, possibly around A.D. 52, but it is questionable if his letter to the Romans was written and sent during this period. Following

---

[31] Titius Justus owned and lived in a large house next to the Synagogue the ruins of which have not as yet been discovered, but it is thought to have been near the potteries owned by the Titii family, thus all three establishments could have been in the same area. He could have been one of the God - fearers Acts.18. 7; whom Paul converted and his house large enough to be a venue where those of the Church could assemble for meetings after Paul had been debarred by the Jews from preaching in the Synagogue. Paul mentions in 1. Cor. 1. 16. the fact that he baptised Gaius as well as Crispus. Quite possibly this Gaius was in fact Titius Justus, his full name being Gaius Titius Justus. An inscription found on a standing stele in Aphrodisias relates to the Diaspora and God-fearers. The text listed both Jews and non Jews, the non Jews being listed to show their inferior status, but nevertheless respected and wealthy members of society who were in business in Aphrodisias and contributed to charitable institutions for the relief of the poor and wanting, such as a community soup kitchen and the distribution of free hot food, almost a modern 'meals on wheels'? Also listed were nine members of the city council. Though this inscription dates from the third century A.D. its provisions could well have been operative in Corinth in the first century A.D. and Titius Justus well known to the Jewish community for his munificence. Apart from Titius Justus Paul also mentions his baptism of Stephanas and his household, another wealthy benefactor of Corinth. Crispus, Stephanus and Gaius Titius Justus were three of the very affluent citizens of Corinth. For more information on the Aphrodisias inscription see Reynolds and Tannenbaum, *Jews and God fearers at Aphrodisias.*

the riot of the silversmiths in Ephesus, when Paul was on his third journey, he left Ephesus for Macedonia and his final visit to Corinth. It was his intention then to spend the winter months in Corinth before going on to Jerusalem and there is the possibility that his letter to the Romans was sent at some time during these months. However, near the end of the Epistle he sends his warm greetings to those of the Church in Rome naming amongst others Andronicus, Amplias, Urbane, Herodion a kinsmen, Narcissus, and Rufus and his mother: as they were all still resident in Rome and had not been amongst the Jews deported they could have been Gentiles. The Gospel of St Mark XV 21 records 'and they compel one Simon a Cyrenian who passed by, coming out of the country, the father of Alexander and Rufus, to bear the cross'. Could this Rufus and his mother have been the son and widow of Simon of Cyrene? It is an intriguing thought.

However, Paul also sends his greetings in verse 3 to Priscilla and Aquila and the church in their house. From this it is obvious that they had returned to Rome, possibly not long after Paul's final departure from Ephesus. His reference: 'Who have for my life laid down their own necks; unto whom I not only give thanks, but also all the churches of the Gentiles'. Frustratingly it has not been recorded when, where, and in what circumstances they risked their necks for the welfare of Paul. The household of Aristobulus is also mentioned. He was possibly the great grandson of Herod the Great who was made the governor of Lesser Armenia in A.D. 55 by Nero. Tacitus mentions the fact as does Josephus. Also named amongst those sending their salutations to Rome in Acts XVI 21 are Lucius, Jason, and Sosipator. Lucius originally came from Cyrene and taught in the church at Antioch (Acts XIII 1). Jason came from Thessalonica and was involved in the fracas that precipitated Paul's escape by night to Beroea. As a result Jason was subsequently badly treated by the populace and brought before the magistrates. Sosipater came from Beroea and, together with Aristacchus, Secundus, Gaius of Derbe, Timothy, Tychicus and Trophimus, accompanied Paul when he left Corinth for Macedonia and Asia (Acts XX 4).

That the Apostolic Church had been established in Rome for some time before the arrival of Paul in Corinth, makes one wonder if it could have been the work of Peter. If so Peter must have gone to Rome at some time following the quarrel with Paul in Antioch over the circumcision of the Gentiles, and after the beginning of Paul's second missionary journey with Silas.

It was Phoebe, the deaconess of the church at Cenchrea[32], a small Port that lay South of Corinth in a bay that was almost surrounded by mountains, whom Paul entrusted to take his letter to the Romans, and it was from here that Paul, after a stay of some eighteen months in Corinth, together with Aquila and Priscilla caught a boat that took them the short passage to Ephesus. Cenchrea was some nine miles distant from Corinth, seventy Roman stadia, and has been described by Pausanias as going through avenues of pine trees and past many tombs, amongst them that of the Cynic Diogenes. The road obviously went through the Necropolis district of Corinth.

---

[32] Phoebe must have been a woman of some means and one who could well have owned her own house where those of the Church could meet, and where she provided hospitality for those in need, and this apart from her position as a deaconess. (Klauck, Hausgemeinde and Hauskirche).

His short stay in Ephesus must have included a Sabbath for his preaching in the Synagogue was well received by the Ephesian Jews. His reception was such that it could have dispelled any of his previous doubts about taking the Gospel into Asia and must have been one of the deciding factors to influence the course of his third journey; that and the fact that Aquila and Priscilla were now in Ephesus to spread the gospel whilst establishing their new business venture in new surroundings.

Quite why they left Corinth with Paul is unclear, unless it was his intention for them to establish a foothold for the Church in Ephesus. They must have been in Corinth for some three years or more following their eviction from Rome, and business in Corinth must have been good for, apart from tents, there was plenty of scope for their work in the repair of sails for the harbour shipping and the making of various awnings for the periodic festivals. The Church in Corinth was now flourishing and many new converts had joined by the time they left with Paul for Ephesus, and it is also apparent that Timothy and Silas remained behind to continue the work.

Following the departure of Paul the subsequent behaviour of many of those of the Church in Corinth proved disappointing and more attuned to the lax way of life there, not a few of them reverting to their old pagan habits and succumbing to the city's immorality and round of pleasure, a situation that provoked Paul's first letter of disapproval to the Corinthians. During the years he spent in Ephesus, when on his third journey, it is thought that he might at some time have gone back to Corinth for a short period, but even if he had it was his last visit following the riot of Demetrius that left him depressed. He then saw the extent of the problems that faced the Church from the teachings of false prophets, and his second letter to the Corinthians castigating them and exhorting them to mend their ways was thought to have been written from Macedonia. Paul's most arduous and lengthy journeys were those that he made throughout Asia Minor, but Corinth must have proved a major challenge for his missionary work.

In Acts XVIII 20,21,22 Luke sums up the last part of Paul's journey from Ephesus to Jerusalem: 'When they asked him to stay longer he declined; but on taking leave of them he said, "I will return to you if God wills". Then he set sail from Ephesus. When he had landed at Caesarea he went up to Jerusalem and greeted the Church and then went down to Antioch'. He could have lodged with Philip the Evangelist in Caesarea before making his way to Jerusalem, and when in Jerusalem he could have stayed with his sister. How Paul returned to Antioch is questionable. He could have returned overland through Tyre and Sidon then along the coast through Berytus, Byblos, Tripolis in the Lebanon and Tartous before finally reaching Antioch; a long and arduous journey. However the route of choice could well have been by coastal vessel from Caesarea Maritima to Seleukia.

CHAPTER 4

The Third Missionary Journey

Paul's decision to go on a Third Missionary Journey must have been taken in view of the unusually warm reception he had had from the Jews in the Synagogue at Ephesus when, at the end of his second journey, he stayed there for a short while before going on to Jerusalem. Acts 18 22, relates when he had landed at Caesarea he went up to Jerusalem and greeted the Church, and then went down to Antioch. It would seem that be started out on this third journey from Antioch alone, for he makes no mention of anyone having been with him, nor does he give details of any events that might have occurred during, what turned out to be, his last visit to Antioch.

Barnabas and Mark were certainly not there and there are no indications as to where they were, or as to what they were doing. Barnabas could have been in Cyprus on another mission, and by that time it is possible that Mark was with Peter in Rome, for Peter then was no longer the head of the Church in Jerusalem. By the time Paul and Barnabas had reached Antioch at the end of their first missionary journey James, the brother of Jesus, had already taken over the leadership of the Church and it was then that Paul and Barnabas went up to Jerusalem with the sole intention of discussing with the Apostles the vexed question of the circumcision of the Gentiles; it is quite clear that Peter was present on that occasion: but could have left Jerusalem for Rome at a later date.

Some authorities are of the opinion that James became head of the Church almost immediately after the Crucifixion had taken place, but there is little recorded in Acts to confirm this contention. The Nag Hammadi Scrolls that appear to relate to the Gospel of St Thomas and were discovered in Egypt, seem to confirm that it was James the Righteous, not Peter, who was the first to lead the disciples after the Crucifixion. Eusebius also records James as being the first elected leader of the Jerusalem Church, but it is strange that James, who does not specifically figure in any of the recorded activities of Jesus and the Apostles prior to the Crucifixion should, directly after that event, become the head of the Church instead of Peter. However, it would appear from Acts. 1. 13 - 26, that Peter did have the initial authority and it was he who took the lead when the eleven remaining Apostles came together in an upper room to elect a twelfth Apostle in place of Judas Iscariot. It is obvious that James was not at this meeting, nor does he seem to have been involved with the Apostles in other instances recorded in Acts. (II. 3, 7 - 41, III. 1 - 26. and V. 28 - 33) that appear to confirm Peter's initial authority.

The rift that occurred between them when Peter came down from Jerusalem to see Paul in Antioch appears to have been a gulf that was never completely overcome and was due to Peter having declined to take his meals with the Gentiles who had joined the Church, and possibly too over the question of their circumcision, and this could explain Paul's subsequent silence where Peter is concerned, for he makes very few references to him in his later letters.

In view of the fact that Paul went on this third journey alone, as has been pointed out, and as there is no mention of any companions having been with him it makes one wonder why he again decided to go by road to Tarsus, if in fact he did so. It would have been a much longer and more exhausting journey than that by a local boat plying the coast from Seleukia to Tarsus, which had its harbour facilities in the Rhegma Lake by the river Cydnus.

It is more than likely that Paul spent the winter months in Antioch before setting out on his third journey, quite possibly in the Spring of A.D. 54, for the weather by then would have been more suitable for travelling. To have undertaken long distances by road in winter, and especially through the Cilician Gates, was to be avoided unless absolutely necessary, and in Acts XVIII. 23. Paul does indicate that he spent some considerable time in Antioch before setting out for Ephesus[33].

He records the fact that he visited again the Churches of Galatia and Phrygia when on the way and in that order, but did he include in his itinerary a visit to Ancyra in Northern Galatia? Henri Metzger in his 'Routes de St Paul' is of the opinion that he did. Having passed through the Cilician Gates his route, according to Metzger, was westwards to Derbe, Lystra, Iconium, and then North to Ancyra, and on leaving Ancyra his road to Ephesus would have taken him through the towns of Gordium, Germa, Ipsos, and Sardis (**See Map showing Metzger's route**).

Grollenburg is somewhat of the same mind but in his opinion Paul, after passing through the Cilician Gates, went directly North from Tarsus to pass through Cappadocia and the city of Archelais to Ancyra. After Ancyra the suggested route to Ephesus was through Germa and Apamea and by following this road Paul could well have passed through Colossae and Laodiceia. For Paul to have visited Ancyra before going on to Ephesus would have meant a considerable detour, and could well be questionable, for it is very apparent from Acts XVIII 20. 21 that his main objective was to take the Gospel to the Jews at Ephesus. To have chosen a circuitous route would have greatly increased his travelling time and, furthermore, by following the itinerary of Grollenburg Paul would not have gone through the cities of Derbe, Lystra, Iconium and Pisidian Antioch, a condition that does not appear to fit in with Acts XVIII 23 (**See Map showing Grollenberg's Route**).

The main highway that left Pisidian Antioch at the northern aspect of lake Egridir was the great Via Sebaste that went on to Appolonia, and there it would have joined another road that went to Ephesus through the cities of Apamea, Colossae, Laodicea, and Trailles, the site of today's Aydin. It has been suggested that Paul endeavoured to avoid the main roads whenever possible, but this road would have had distinct advantages as it was the easiest route to Ephesus, his main objective, and as he was travelling alone there would have been less of a hazard of falling foul of bandits and being robbed.

Acts XIX 1 states that whilst Apollos was in Corinth, Paul passed through the interior regions and came to Ephesus where he found some disciples. This seems to be indicative of the fact that Paul took the direct route to Ephesus when leaving Pisidian Antioch, but the authorised version of the New Testament mentions Paul having passed through the upper

---

[33] It is not reasonable to think that Paul, travelling alone, would have undertaken this journey during the winter months, the closed season for travel either overland or by sea. As has already been discussed winter travel was undertaken by those who had no other option but to do so. In this case Paul would have surely waited until the spring before setting out.

'coasts'; a phrase that some have considered could point to the possibility that Paul, when on this journey, could have visited the Bithynian district before arriving in Ephesus. But to have made a detour of such an extent, when Ephesus was his main objective would not have been very logical and it is significant that Paul, when on this third journey, makes no references whatever to Bithynia, but does in detail where Ephesus is concerned. There was, however, a short branch road that went from Laodicea to nearby Hierapolis and then directly on to Sardis a city that had an important synagogue and a large Jewish population. Paul omits all details of his third journey but it is certain from Acts XVIII 23 that he must have gone to Pisidian Antioch. From there he could have taken the direct road that went to Colossae before going on to Laodicea, then to Hierapolis, and finally through Sardis to Ephesus, a route that would have fulfilled the description of the 'upper coasts', and that of the 'New Revised Version' that translates

'Paul passed through the Interior regions'. From Sardis there were many alternative ways of reaching Ephesus through the local towns, not the least being that of Smyrna (**See Map Showing Suggested Route**).

The exact extent and location of the boundaries of the Asian Provinces in the first century A.D. are conjectural, though in their approximation they are correct. When the Romans enlarged the Province of Northern Galatia by extending it to the South, the districts of Pisidian Antioch and Iconium came within its compass. Whilst further to the west in the Province of Asia the cities of Laodicea, Colossae, and Hierapolis were in the district of Phrygia.

The present town of Denizli is within easy reach of these three ancient cities, Colossae some sixteen kilometres from Denizli to the west, and Hierapolis on an escarpment overlooking Laodicea in the distant haze of the plain below some sixteen kilometres to the North. All three of them figure prominently in the letters of Paul and all three of them are of some one hundred and sixty kilometres only from Ephesus. These three cities lie in distance on the road just approximately half way between Ephesus and Pisidian Antioch. Colossae was thus ideally situated for a break in Paul's journey from Pisidian Antioch to Ephesus and easy for him to visit Hierapolis and Laodicea where the Church was situated in the house of Nymphas. Laodicea occupied an extensive flat site above the river Lycos, and had far reaching open views to the Taurus and Olympus mountains. Of the Phrygian towns it was the most influential being the Metropolis of the district and the seat of the Governor.

Early in 50 B.C. Appius Claudius retired from this prestigious appointment, but in so doing he left such complete chaos in the judiciary and the district administration that it fell to the lot of Cicero to restore order in the city and further good relations in the surrounding district; in order to complete this task he was compelled to live for some months in Laodicea before going on to Tarsus as Governor of Cilicia. In A.D.129, some eighty years later, the Emperor Hadrian and his wife made a state tour of Asia Minor and this included an official visit to the city where they had a very warm welcome from the Laodiceans who, to commemorate the event, later raised a Triumphal Arch in a suitably prominent part of the town.

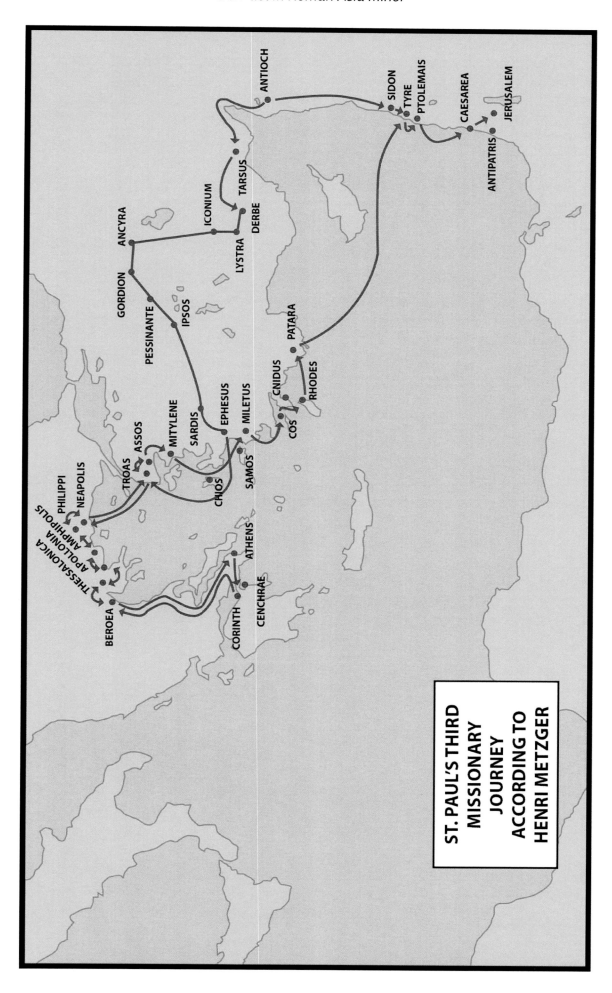

ST. PAUL'S THIRD
MISSIONARY
JOURNEY
ACCORDING TO
HENRI METZGER

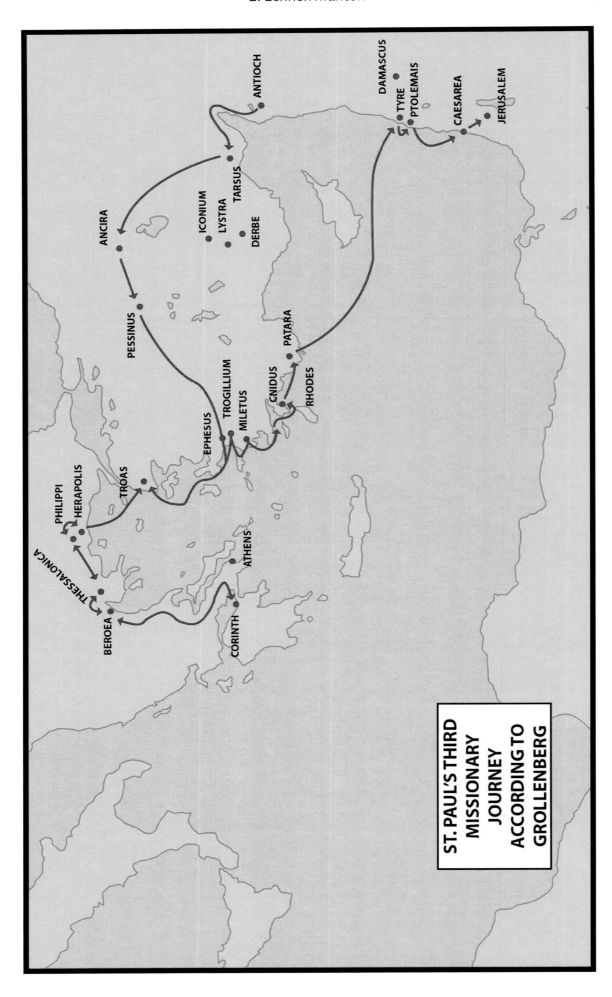

ST. PAUL'S THIRD
MISSIONARY
JOURNEY
ACCORDING TO
GROLLENBERG

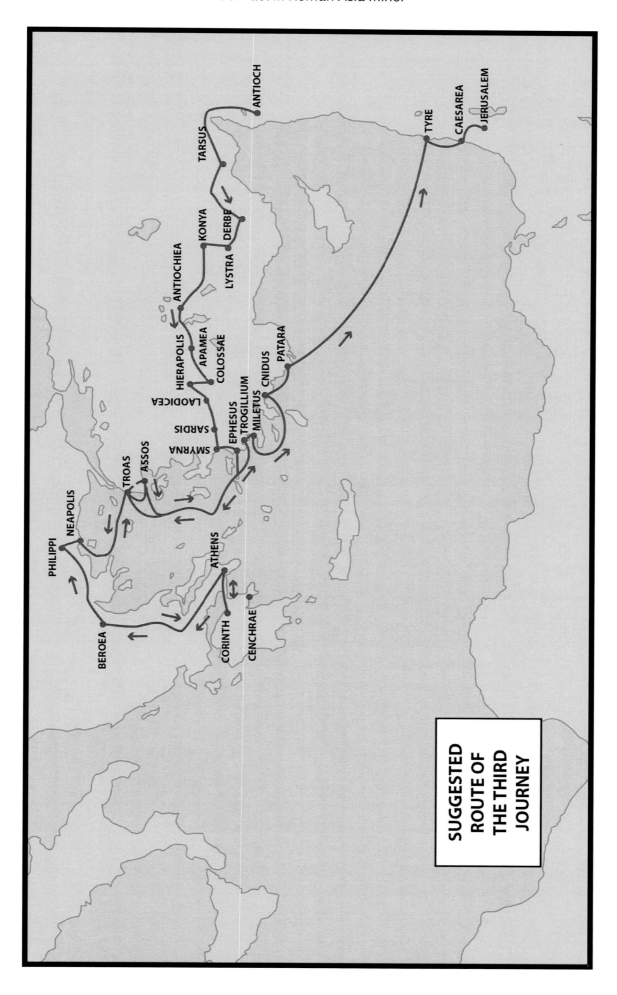

SUGGESTED ROUTE OF THE THIRD JOURNEY

As has been noted, the city was held in high esteem for its horses and jockeys, many of them regularly taking part in the annual races at Antioch where they were welcomed for their expertise, and their ability in giving a certain lustre to the events. But apart from this facet of their heritage the Laodiceans were also renowned for their flocks of black sheep, a breed that was unique to the district and not to be found elsewhere in Asia Minor. The cloth they manufactured from the wool was remarkable for its fine texture and softness, and was of such a quality that it soon became known throughout the Roman world as Laodikeian. The tunics and cloaks made locally from this cloth were equally as famous and prized and were known as 'Trimita'. In the course of time they were so much sought after that Laodicea itself was often referred to as Trimitoria.

Diocletian became Emperor some two hundred years after the death of Paul and it was during that period when the financial stability of the Empire was afflicted by rampant inflation. In an endeavour to rectify the situation he passed an edict that debased the currency by withdrawing its silver content, an edict that was in effect a prices and incomes policy. This edict can be seen engraved in its entirety on the walls of the Macellum in the Agora at Aizanoi, today's Cavdarhisar. In it Diocletian laid down the charges applicable for all commodities and the incomes allowed for all trades and professions, such as carpenters, librarians, assistant librarians and so on: each son of a family having to follow in his father's footsteps. Failing to do so or to follow another occupation was punishable by the death penalty. The Laodikean cloth figured in the list of commodities listed in this edict, where its cost per length was categorically laid down. This woollen industry flourished in the days of Paul, as it had been over many decades in the past and it continued over the ensuing centuries; there is little doubt that it made the cloth merchants and those who dealt in the wool of Laodicea very prosperous and some extremely wealthy.

In Paul's second letter to Timothy, one that he could have dictated when he was incarcerated in chains in the Mamertine prison in Rome, he asked 'When you come bring the cloak that I left with Carpus at Troas, also the books and above all the parchments' (11 Timothy IV. 13). Even though it is thought that this letter is not entirely the work of Paul, it does nevertheless have a decided feeling of authenticity, for much of its content must have derived from an original source. One can go even further and speculate that Paul, when on his way to Ephesus, visited Laodicea and bought the cloak to eventually leave it with Carpus at Troas. These garments being so valued by their fortunate owners there is little wonder that Paul was anxious to have it back, his circumstances being what they were in the Mamertine prison at that time.

It has been suggested that the cloak was made from a goat hair cloth that was known as Cilicium and woven in Tarsus. But even allowing for the fact that various qualities could have been produced the product must generally have been coarser in texture as it was primarily used in the manufacture of tents. Thus a garment made from the famous Laodicean would have been much more desirable and something to cherish.

However, H.V. Morton was of the opinion that the cloak could have been a Kepenikler, a garment impervious to wind and water and one that was then used by shepherds to give them adequate protection in the fields against the Anatolian winters. The material has a very firm texture and is stiff enough to prevent it from being folded in any way, this enables the garment to stand upright and without support when not being worn. Remarkably the present day shepherds still use these Kepeniklers and I was fortunate enough to find a small factory in Konya where they are still being made, and was shown the whole process of their manufacture from the production of the compressed felt-like material to the stiff finished article; however the very nature of their awkwardness would have made such a garment very impractical for the needs of Paul.

The fact that he not only left his cloak at the house of Carpus, but also his books and asks Timothy to bring them with him too must raise another question, for it suggests that he left Troas in such a hurry that he had scant time in which to collect his things. If at the end of his two years detention in Rome Paul had in fact won his appeal, and been released by Nero, he could have regained his freedom and returned to see Carpus and Timothy in Troas before going on to Colossae to stay with Philemon. He intimates his intention of making such a visit in the letter he wrote whilst waiting to be brought before Caesar, 'One thing more - prepare a guest room for me, for I am hoping through your prayers to be restored to you' (Phil. 22). That he could have made the journey to Colossae and Laodicea at some time after his first trial and acquittal in Rome is borne out by the fact that his first letter to Timothy in Ephesus was written from Laodicea - Tim 1. 3. Here Paul infers that he has made Timothy the Bishop in Ephesus so it must have been written at some time after Paul's acquittal.

After having visited Philemon at Colossae it is speculation that a natural course of events would have been his return to the house of Carpus in Troas; to possibly be arrested there by the agents of Nero and then taken back to the Palatine Prison in Rome to await a second trial. An explanation for a sudden departure from Troas could have rested on the vagaries of the weather. The movement of shipping from the Troas harbour depended entirely on the prevailing winds so as soon as conditions were favourable all haste was made to round up and embark all those who were due to sail with the vessel. When the winds did suddenly become favourable Paul would have had little consideration and been forced to embark in a hurry.

One disadvantage for the Laodiceans was the state of their water. It was generally more tepid than cold and this was due to a series of hot springs that are still to be found on the escarpment not far from Hierapolis and also by the city Itself. Here the waters spill over the cliff to leave a frozen cascade of calcium deposit, spectacular in its extent and its brilliant whiteness, this has given the region the name of the 'Cotton Castle.' **(See Figure 44)**. Pollution in the past turned some of the whiteness to a dirty brown but this has since been controlled with the beneficial result of a returning brilliance. It is a spectacle that has turned the extensive ruins of Hierapolis into the modern resort of Pammukale.

The whole area in the past must have had volcanic origins. The steaming springs to be found near the ruins of the ancient city have been a feature of the landscape since well before the Romans, who were not slow in adapting them to their own use as a Spa. It was this activity that affected the Laodicean water, and it was so well known that St. John mentions the phenomenon in Revelation III. 14 - 17. Over the passing years the Laodiceans had become so wrapped up in their wealth and their lax and laid back attitude towards the Church that John, in his exasperation, likened them to their water. 'I know your works, you are neither cold nor hot. I wish that you were either cold or hot. So, because you are luke warm, and neither cold nor hot. I am about to spit you out of my mouth'. Laodicea was one of the seven churches of Asia and not the only one to suffer his wrath, for the back sliding habits and the ever increasing licentiousness of those of Ephesus, Pergamum, Smyrna, Sardis, Thyatira and Philadelphia were also to feel the lash of his tongue.

Strabo has recorded the existence of another celebrated temple to the Pagan god Men, one that was situated on the road to Carura some twenty kilometres distant from Laodicea and here in the vicinity, according to Strabo, was a medical school that could have had some significance. Galen, when teaching at the Aesculapium in Pergamum, described two compound remedies that originated and were solely the product of Laodicea. One made from spikenard was used in a treatment for the ears and the other, described by Aristotle as a Phrygian powder, was a specific that was used for the eyes. It came from a local Phrygian stone and could be applied as an ointment or salve. In his diatribe against the Laodiceans John says in Revelation III. 18:

'Therefore I counsel you to buy from me gold refined by fire so that you may be rich; and white robes to clothe you and to keep the shame of your nakedness from being seen; and salve to anoint your eyes that you may see. I reprove and discipline those whom I love, be earnest therefore and repent'.

This suggests that the peoples of Laodicea could have been subject to a specific eye disease that was cured or abated by their remedy, and that this remedy was efficacious is very evident for it was used elsewhere in the Empire by the second century A.D. and its production ceased to be the sole prerogative of the Laodiceans. Exactly in what way this disease manifested itself is not known, though it must at the time have been a common complaint, much as Trachoma was throughout the Middle East until the advent of the antibiotic Achromycin. If left untreated Trachoma usually ended in blindness and it has been suggested that it was this complaint that was the cause of Paul's eye trouble. That Paul did suffer periodically from some eye complaint could be hinted at in Galatians IV. 15 - 'What has become of the good will you felt, for I testify that had it been possible you would have torn out your eyes and given them to me'.

However, Trachoma was not likely to have been the cause of his trouble for the complaint was a difficult one to cure before the discovery of antibiotics. Although Paul did complain on occasion about his sight and is thought to have dictated some of his later epistles, there is no indication whatsoever that his eyesight was such that he was verging on being totally blind.

The Egyptians of the early dynasties were often, as they are today amongst the Fellaheen, the victims of Trachoma. A treatment prescribed in the medical Papyri of the time took the form of a salve, which made from the powdered dung of the sacred Ibis suspended in a honey base and was smeared on the eyelids. Present day analysis has shown the dung to contain a significant content of Achromycin, which speaks much for the medical knowledge of the ancient Egyptians. Who knows what the active principle was in the Phrygian powder and by chance did Paul ever make use of it.

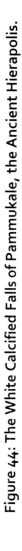

Figure 44: The White Calcified Falls of Pammukale, the Ancient Hierapolis.

On one occasion the Turkish Government was generous enough to arrange a journey for me to Edessa in Eastern Turkey, which began at Smyrna airport where I was greeted by Seref Unal who had been with me on a previous occasion, and by Nijat who drove the car. Both of them made the weeks that we had together a more than memorable event, and on the way east we visited the sites of Laodicea, Hierapolis, and Colossae. Although Laodicea is extensive nothing substantial remains of a City that many centuries ago was classed as the Metropolis of Phrygia, its prosperity in the main being due to the fact that it lay at the intersection of the trade routes from the Euphrates to the West and from the South Coast of Asia Minor to Sardis.

Laodicea was founded by Antiochus II in honour of his wife whose name it commemorates, and so it had a Hellenistic culture before the advent of the Romans. In Paul's day the city had a significant Roman garrison and a large population of the Jewish Diaspora. The few blocks of masonry, all that is left of its past splendour, are avoided by the local farmers when growing their yearly crops of wheat and barley across the site, and during the month of June it is covered with stiff golden stubble from the recent harvest. A mass of pot shards and marble chippings litter the ground at the base of the stubble, and here and there are the scattered pieces of elaborately carved friezes and other architectural remnants. Sadly the greater part of the city fabric was taken and used as hard core when the railway that runs between Smyrna and Dinar was under construction, and there is no doubt that much of Lystra and Derbe suffered the same fate.

Scooped out of the side of a large hill is the massive bowl of the Hellenistic Theatre looking out and down to the river Lycos the remains of its stone seating partly covered with the harvest stubble **(See Figure 45)**. Not far away is the bowl of a smaller Odeon that was an addition to the city's amenities in the later Roman period. The only monuments to relieve the barren site are the scanty remains of the Nymphaeum, once an imposing structure that dominated the junction of the two main streets. Its large central basin faced onto the street and the whole structure was then ornate with marble reliefs depicting the Legend of Ganymede and that of Theseus and the Minotaur **(See Figure 46)**.The scanty remains of the baths dedicated to Hadrian and his wife Sabrina are the heaps of ashlar blocks spread about the area, a complex that must have been built on the site of a previous establishment at some time after A.D. 117.

Paul would not have seen these embellishments to the City for the Nymphaeum was built between A.D. 211 – 217, when Caracalla was Emperor, nor would he have seen the Stadium for this was built around A.D. 71, a few years before the sack of Jerusalem by Titus in A.D. 76 and the destruction of Pompeii by Vesuvius in A.D. 79.

The members of the Church in Laodicea met in the house of Nymphas. In his letter to the Colossians Paul sent him their greetings and his own salutations, together with those from Epaphras, a native of Colossae who happened to be with him in Rome at the time.

Figure 45: Ruins of the Great Theatre at Laodicea.

Figure 46: All that Remains of the Nymphaeum that once lay at the Junction of the two Main Streets of Laodicea.

It is very apparent that many of the Christians who were a part of the population in Laodicea during the early part of the first century A.D. were subject to constant harassment from the Jewish faction, and not only from them but also from the few Jews who, even though they had accepted the new teaching, still regarded their Gentile counterparts to be less than worthy of any consideration: this due to their persistence in not keeping the dietary restrictions and their adamant refusal to submit to ritual circumcision.

In contrast to Laodicea and in spite of the passing centuries a great deal of Hierapolis has survived. Here too there was a large Jewish population and here in A.D. 80, some fifteen years after the death of Paul, the Apostle Philip was martyred. He was not the Evangelist Philip who converted the chief Eunuch of the Ethiopian Queen and who then with his dedicated virgin daughters lived for some years in Caesarea Maritima where he entertained Paul, Luke and possibly Aristarchus (See Acts, 21, 8), this at the time when they were on their way from Greece with the Pentecostal donations that had been collected for the Jerusalem Church.

No one knows when the Apostle Philip left Jerusalem to spread the Gospel in Hierapolis. The traditions that he did so are late and confused, but even so are such that a Martyrium was built and dedicated to him on the slopes of the hills behind Hierapolis, a shrine that inevitably became a focus for the pilgrims who made the journey in the high hopes of a miracle cure for their various ailments. It must have been the 'Lourdes' of the day, but the body of St Philip does not rest there for it is thought to lie in Santi Apostoli in Rome **(See Figure 47)**.

The main street of Hierapolis went the length of the city and stretched from the South Gate at one end to the Arch of Domitian at the other, an Arch that was erected by Julius Frontinus when proconsul for Asia in A.D. 82 - 83. The street had colonnades on either side, some still standing, and then went North of the Arch to an extensive Necropolis beyond the city limits where there are still a considerable number of well-preserved tombs dating from the Hellenistic and early Christian periods.

The theatre is exceptional and much of it in a very good state of preservation. It is unusually rich in sculptured friezes and has a number of panels decorating the Scaena frons that show dancers in a bas relief, but much of this magnificence is later than the Pauline period. Nearby are the ruins of an important temple that dealt in oracles and was dedicated to Apollo. A college of priests maintained the Temple and in their spare time interpreted the apparent wisdom of the god. The whole complex revolved around a grotto containing a sacred spring of water, that was very far from fresh and maintained a temperature of some 95 degrees that gave off a noxious vapour considered to be lethal. No doubt carefully calculated doses of this vapour stupefied the priests and heightened their supernatural powers. It was a phenomenon that was the hub of the Temple activities and enhanced its reputation by attracting the curious of the ancient world, as it does so today.

About the time when Epaphras was concerned with the Church in Hierapolis an unknown slave boy was leading a disenchanted existence in the city, an underprivileged life that was destined in due course to become one of fame and wealth. His name was Epictetus, one of the great Stoic Philosophers, and one can but wonder if as a slave boy in Hierapolis he ever saw Epaphras or Paul.

Figure 47: The Martyrium of the Apostle Phillip who died in A.D. 80 at Hierapolis.

It has long been maintained by many authorities that Paul did not at any time visit Colossae, but this would appear to have little credibility for the direct road from Pisidian Antioch to Ephesus went through Appolonia, Apameia and Colossae. Colossae itself was just about equidistant from Pisidian Antioch and Ephesus making it ideal for a break in Paul's journey. However, the main reason for the argument lies in Paul's letter to the Colossians. This was written and sent from Rome by Tychicus at the same time as his personal letter to Philemon taken by Onesimus to Colossae. In it he exhorts his 'Saints' to be wary and not led astray by false doctrines - verbal sabotage on the part of those Jews who disliked the Gentile converts for not conforming to the tenets of the Jewish traditions. This he puts very strongly in Colossians II. 4, 8, 11, 16 & 18, whilst he further exhorts them in Colossians III to follow a better way of life. However, he does express his concern in Colossians II, 1, for those of the Churches in Colossae and Laodicea by saying 'for I want you to know how much I am struggling for you, and for those known to her for some time and held her in high regard, and where but in Colossae'. The intimacy that Paul expresses in the opening phrases of the letter could not have been brought about as the result of hearsay, or by any casual meetings away from Colossae, which in the case of Apphia would not have been likely.

The question of Onesimus is also intriguing. The letters give the impression of a young man of possibly some twenty years or so, a slave who could very well have been acquired from the notorious slave markets in the port of Side on the Pamphylian coast. Here again it is generally accepted that he stole Philemon's money to go to Rome where, quite by accident he met Paul, and having met Paul was duly converted to become a dedicated Christian. Onesimus is then sent back to Colossae with a letter to Philemon, in which it is recommended and urged by Paul to treat Onesimus as a brother in Christ, to regard him in the future as more than a servant and not to treat him as a runaway slave.

Paul had nothing against slavery as such. Throughout the Roman Empire it was an inherent way of life and an institution that went on well into the 4th century A.D. Many well-known personalities, such as Epictitus began their careers as slaves, and on gaining their freedom could amass great wealth and become very influential. What Paul does underline is the way in which slaves should be treated, and in this respect be writes in Colossians III. 22:

'Slaves, obey your earthly masters in everything, not only while being watched and in order to please them, but whole heartedly, fearing the Lord. Whatever your task put yourselves into it, as done for the Lord and not your master'.

And in Colossians IV 1: 'Masters treat your slaves justly and fairly, for you know that you also have a Master in heaven'.

Was Paul by chance here having a gentle condemnation of Philemon for not treating Onesimus as he should have done, for in Colossians IV. 9 he makes it clear that Onesimus is now a beloved brother and "one of you" and it is Onesimus and Tychicus who take these letters back to Colossae. Slaves were at the bottom of the pile of the accepted social status and even if a slave embraced the Christian Church this social structure was an accepted part of life as far as Paul and the Church were concerned. Slavery was essential for the smooth running of the Empire, be it in the households of the wealthy or in any other menial work. To Paul social status was irrelevant as long as a Christian slave followed the Church and worked conscientiously, and it was not incumbent on the Church to organise the freedom of a Christian slave.

There seems to have been a fundamental clash of personalities between Onesimus and Philemon, and being a slave it was one that Onesimus could not resolve, for in his letter to Philemon Paul describes him as being in the past 'formerly useless to you'. This attitude on the part of Onesimus was one that could have stemmed from a deep seated grievance that Paul was able to resolve and make him, as he writes in his letter 'indeed useful'. The grievance could have had something to do with the Church in Philemon's house which Onesimus may have wished to join, but being a slave was given little encouragement in spite of the fact that many slaves were Christians[34].

Onesimus must have known Epaphras, a native of Colossae, and must too have been aware of the fact that Epaphras was then in Rome with Paul, as too were Aristarchus, Mark, Luke and Demas. Epaphras was a pillar of the Churches in Laodicea, Hierapolis and Colossae, and together with Philemon, could well have been one of their founder members. In the past Onesimus could then have seen and spoken to Paul when carrying out his duties in Philemon's household and knowing, as he must have done from the general conversation, that Paul and Epaphras were now in Rome, went there specifically to see him for advice, taking enough of Philemon's money to help him on his way.

If Onesimus had wished to escape from his household duties merely to enjoy the city flesh pots why go to Rome, when it would have been far easier for him to have gone to Antioch where, if Antioch lived up to anything like its scandalous reputation, there were equal and even far better attractions on offer. Furthermore, the chances of being recognised in Antioch would have been very remote whereas in Rome, just to be on the loose, he could have run into Epaphras and trouble. Onesimus having left in these circumstances there is the suspicion that Philemon knew exactly where he had gone and for what reason, for little effort appears to have been made to apprehend him, knowing that a master had complete jurisdiction over a slave to the point of life and death.

It ought not to have been a difficult matter for Philemon to have caught up with Onesimus before he reached Ephesus, and even if he had not done so there was the chance of apprehending him before he left by boat for Rome. On the other hand Onesimus could have been aware of this hazard and so decided to make his way to Rome from the port of Troas and then take advantage of the Via Egnatia. Whichever course be took he could possibly then have had to wait for a suitable boat, and had Philemon been at all determined there would have been a good prospect of detaining Onesimus before he left Asia Minor.

In the first part of his letter to Philemon Paul 'butters' him up, having understood the reason why Onesimus came to see him in Rome, 'Perhaps this is the reason he was separated from you for a while, so that you might have him back forever, no longer as a slave but more than a slave, a beloved brother, especially to me but how much more to you'. Paul then undertakes to repay the sum that Onesimus 'borrowed' but adds as an afterthought, 'I Paul am

---

[34] Since Onesimus is Greek for 'useful' Paul is making a pun. Many Christian slaves were to be found working in the Imperial households.

writing this with my own hand; I will repay it. I say nothing about your owing me even your own self'. Here Paul puts it artfully to Philemon that he should consider how much he is indebted to Paul, but not from any monetary point of view. This slight degree of moral blackmail on the part of Paul denotes a far from casual relationship with Philemon's household and is strongly indicative of the fact that Paul was no stranger to Colossae and the district.

Little further is known of Onesimus after his return to Colossae with the letter from Paul, nor has anything been recorded of the welcome that he might have had from Philemon, but in view of the letter, there is little reason to think that it was other than cordial. In later years it is very significant that an Onesimus was the Bishop of Ephesus, and the dates could fit in with the life of the onetime slave Onesimus when an older man. There is also the tradition that he was eventually martyred, and this could be the truth for there is also an Onesimus to be found listed amongst the Saints, they could very easily be one and the same. There is too a further tradition that postulates the deaths by martyrdom of Philemon and Apphia in Colossae, but of this there is no direct evidence nor have any dates been recorded.

In 2 Timothy 1, 15-18 Paul refers to those in Asia who have turned away from him and here he is referring to the report brought to him by Epaphras as to the fall from grace on the part of the Asian churches. He then remarks that Onesiphorous did remain constant. This was the Onesiphorous who came out from Iconium to offer Paul his hospitality on his first journey. Apparently hearing of Paul's difficulties he left Iconium for Rome to see him, 'For when in Rome he sought me out very diligently and found me and was not ashamed of his chains'. Paul then blesses him and his family. Onesiphorous must also have gone to see him in Ephesus to help with his work. It appears that they had a great respect for each other.

Early one morning before the heat of the day I set out with Seref and Nijat to find Colossae. Nijat had obviously spent much of the previous evening lovingly cleaning and polishing the car so that the paint was immaculate. Seref had not heard of Colossae and had little idea as to its location but I did know that it was situated on a hill overlooked by the Taurus Mountains. According to the map the nearest village was Honaz and this turned out to be at the very end of a minor road that was little more than a track. There were no signs pointing to the site and enquiries at Honaz produced little information, and the one man who might have known had gone to the market in Denizly. However, Seref did find a small holding on the outskirts of the village where the young owner thought he might know the way and offered to act as a guide.

We set off down a narrow track and in doing so stirred up a dense cloud of dust that got thicker and thicker as we progressed. As we appeared to be travelling endlessly getting nowhere and the car was becoming obliterated in a thick layer of dirt, I told Nijat to turn back and not to bother knowing that he would spend most of his evening cleaning it again. His answer was typical of the endless trouble he took to be of help 'You wish to see Colossae' he said, 'We go to Colossae', and that was that.

Luckily it was only another hundred yards or so before we came across two short lengths of decorated marble architrave lying in the ditch **(See Figure 48)**. They had obviously fallen from the truck that many years back had been instrumental in removing the treasures of

Colossae to the railway contractors, and a little further to the left was the hill. Once again we climbed up through the corn stubble to the flattened summit to see to the south the range of the Taurus Mountains and to the northern horizon a vast plain of wheat that was bustling with the harvest **(See Figure 49)**. Turning round I realised that I was standing on the rim of the theatre bowl and scrabbling amongst the weeds and the corn stalks I brought to light a few slabs of stone, all that was left of the theatre seating **(See Figure 50)**. In spite of being stripped of its accessible stone monuments a great deal must still lie beneath the site, hopefully to be uncovered eventually for nothing yet has been done. There was even less here than at Laodicea, but the City in common with most other ancient cities had once occupied a magnificent position in superb surroundings and with splendid views.

Hiding his incredulity Seref politely asked 'Why did you wish to come here, there is nothing to see', and again it was only too true. All that remained were these few stones to show that this was once the City and home of Philemon, Onesimus, and Epaphras who as Paul said in Colossians IV 12. 13: 'was one of you, a servant of Christ, saluteth you, always labouring fervently for you in prayers, that ye may stand perfect and complete in all the will of God for I bear him record, that he hath a great zeal for you and them that are in Laodicea and them in Hierapolis'. Man proposes, God and nature disposes, for here again the wheat and the weeds grow over a hill where centuries ago the streets, the villas and the public buildings of a City of no little import once stood. Standing in the stubble that now clothed the hill it was again difficult to correlate the past with the present. I told Seref the gist of the letter to Philemon and not having heard of it he was very interested and wished to have a copy. I sent him one shortly after returning home. That Paul mentions Laodicea, Hierapolis and Colossae in his letters in the manner that he does must surely be indicative of the fact that he was personally acquainted with them, for he seems to name and write only to cities that he knew personally, with the exception of that to the Romans, but here he is warning the Saints of the Church in Rome of an impending visit.

Assuming that Paul did not leave Antioch on his third journey till the Spring of A.D. 54, he could have reached Ephesus at some time in the summer of A.D. 54 when the weather had improved. It is known from Acts. XVIII. 12 - 14 that Paul spent some eighteen months in Corinth with his missionary work, and that during this period Gallio arrived in Corinth to take up his appointment of Proconsul of Archaia. When after eighteen months Paul decided to leave Corinth and go to Jerusalem before returning to Antioch, firstly he went to Ephesus with Priscilla and Aquila where the two of them intended to continue with their tent manufacturing business. Ephesus also had a reputation for its tent industry and for this reason Priscilla and Aquila might have felt that the change would give them better prospects for their work, more so than in Corinth, where it being an important harbour they could have been more occupied with the repair of sails and making the awnings for festivals. Thus they remained in Ephesus to establish themselves and the Church in their house whilst Paul went on to Jerusalem (See Acts XVIII. 21).

Figure 48: A Section of the Marble Frieze that fell from one of the lorries that took the Treasures of Colossae for hard core for the Railway that was being built through the Konya Plain.

Figure 49: The Site of Ancient Colossae.

Figure 50: Remains of the Small Theatre or Odeon at Ancient Colossae.

The exact nature of Paul's training as an artisan has been the subject of some discussion by some. He has been described as a maker of tents having been trained as a youth in the family business (See Acts 18, 3) and because he was of the same trade he stayed with them, and they worked together as tent makers. It is not likely that Paul was an actual weaver of the Cilicium cloth for this was usually undertaken by women and not thought fit for men, and as some scholars have pointed out he could not have taken a loom with him on his travels. However, he could possibly have taken the lighter tools of his craft, but when he joined Aquila and Priscilla it is obvious that they had all the necessary accoutrements for the trade and access to the raw materials, Paul need only to have had his own expertise. It has also been suggested that many tents at that time were made from leather and that Paul was a leather worker, but this is a debatable point. The procedure in the manufacture of tents would have been basically the same regardless of their being crafted in leather or textile, and it is very doubtful if Aquila and Priscilla worked in leather rather than textile either in Corinth or Ephesus[35].

The ruins of many of the fine public buildings that we see in Ephesus today, some in a partially restored state, are not those that would have been familiar to Paul for they were put up and donated to the city in the later years by prominent and wealthy families. It is their partial restoration that makes one realise, even more, that it was a City of some magnificence and one with a very sophisticated way of life that was also the case in the days of Paul. Today's Ephesus was founded on the foot hills of Mt. Pion and Mt. Koressos in the Hellenistic period by Lysimachos, not far from the sites where two earlier cities had once stood. To make sure that it had a flying start Lysimachos forcibly transferred the entire populations of the nearby towns of Colophon and Lebedus to be its citizens whether they liked it or not.

Not at any time did Ephesus, being a city state, have the status of a Roman Colony thus its administration rested in the hands of a body of Magistrates. The Town Clerk was the most important of the local officials having to be responsible for the city records and the overall administration. The Curates were priests of Artemis who had their own college and the responsibility for the celebration of the annual mysteries of Artemis. The Asiarchs were responsible for the organisation of the festivals of Diana, especially that held during the whole of the month of May that celebrated the birth of the goddess. This was not just a local festival but one that embraced the whole of Ionia and was attended by all and sundry. Its highlight being the procession that carried images of the goddess when leaving the Artemision to traverse its way through the city by the Magnesia Gate, the theatre and then back to the Temple through the Korressos Gate. This was then followed by splendid banquets and revelry.

The festival of the Artemisia took place in either March or April and was also well attended. This included games, musical festivals and gymnastic displays and was a time when the young selected their fiancés and brides. The organisation of the festivities lay in the hands of the Asiarchs. The principal towns in the province annually selected one of their wealthiest citizens, from them ten were selected to organise the Ephesian festivities and between them

---

[35] Cloth seems to have been the preferred material for tents and the goats' hair Cilicium woven by the underprivileged weavers of Tarsus would have been the material of choice. During a period of social disturbance in the late first century in Tarsus Dio, when addressing the assembly, pointed out that the citizens considered them a 'useless rabble and responsible for the tumult'. Their grievance was the fact that they were not given full citizen status through poverty. As has been said the weavers of goats' hair cloth were still in Tarsus in the nineteen thirties. Bedouin Arabs in Jordan still use cloth for their tents, but now they are used only in the summer months for the government has built them more substantial quarters where they can spend the winters.

they had to defray all the expenditure involved. The Ephesian Games were the most renowned in Asia for their day and night long revelry. Those who were nominated Asiarchs had to be wealthy and were normally individuals of influence and some moment for they usually held magistracies in their own towns, and when officiating at the festival they wore long purple capes and were crowned with garlands. During the riot of the silversmiths Luke records in Acts. 19, 31, the fact that 'certain of the Asiarchs', who were the friends of Paul advised him 'not to venture into the theatre', which is indicative of the fact that at this time he must have had some very considerable support from many of those of the City administration, and that they were sympathetic to his problems.

Ephesus did at one time come under the jurisdiction of the Kings of Pergamon, but this ended in 133 B.C. with the death of Attalus III who left the City to be a part of the Roman Empire. When Sulla was Dictator in Rome a bitter war broke out around 86 B.C. with Mithradates, the king of Pontus. That was the signal for the non-Roman population of Ephesus to rise up and slaughter their fellow Roman citizens, one of the more tragic events in its history and one that has gone down to posterity as 'The Ephesian Vespers'. Ephesus subsequently again had a large Roman population, but in spite of the City still being governed by the Magistrates and the Asiarchs, and not as a Roman Colonia, it became subject to crippling taxes that were levied under the administration of Julius Caesar between 49 - 44 B.C.

The first and second centuries A.D. could well be regarded as a golden age when the population of Ephesus could have been in the region of some 200,000. It was at this time when the trade and banking facilities were second to none that gave Ephesus prosperity and making it the Metropolis of Asia, and giving it a reputation that was to rival that of Alexandria. Undoubtedly the great temple of Diana made Ephesus more than renowned throughout the ancient world and a Mecca for the many tourists who came to gaze at its magnificence, and to fill the city coffers. It was the great centre of the Ephesian cult that was fused with that of Cybele the original mother goddess of the indigenous populations of Asia Minor. The Temple to Diana of the Ephesians, or the Artemision as it was known, would have been well known to Paul. He could hardly have ignored it for it was the outward expression of the pagan cults that were in conflict with his missionary work.

Pliny the younger visited the Artemision when Trajan was Emperor. He did so when he was on his way to take up the post of governor of Bithynia, and in his literary work he has left a detailed description of its splendours. His careful observations were confirmed by J T Wood, on excavating the site some years before Schliemann began his work at Troy, when one of the elaborately carved column bases of the Temple's once imposing entrance came to light. It proved to be exactly as described in Pliny's notes, easily recognisable for what it was, and now one of the many treasures preserved in the British museum.

Wood experienced many years of disappointment in his dogged persistence to find the Artemision. All trace of it had disappeared in spite of its massive size and its reputation for being one of the Seven Wonders of the World; however he was eventually rewarded when he stumbled on the clue that led to the whereabouts of the site. One day when excavating in the great theatre he found some gold and silver replicas of Diana that, according to an inscription left with them, were the gift of C. Vibius Satutorius a wealthy citizen of Ephesus. He donated them to the city around A.D.100 on the understanding that they were to figure in the yearly processions that went from the Temple to the Theatre, and this important event took place during the birthday celebrations of the goddess. With elaborate ceremony her wooden effigy was taken from the Artemision to process slowly with music and dancing through the crowds that lined the sacred way from the Magnesia Gate to the Koressian Gate. It was a ritual that has distant echoes in the elaborate and magnificent processions that are held throughout Spain, where during the Easter ceremonies the effigy of the Virgin, or the Saints, are taken from their respective Churches and paraded through the town on each day of Holy week.

The sacred way through Ephesus led Wood to the swamp that is overlooked by the Basilica of St John. Previously no one had thought of looking outside the precincts of today's Ephesus for when Lysimachus moved the City to its present site the Artemision remained some kilometres outside the new boundaries.

The Temple that Pliny saw and described was a larger and more elaborate version of a previous structure that a certain Herostratus had deliberately burnt down in 356 B.C., the year of the birth of Alexander the Great. His main object in perpetrating this massive act of vandalism was to ensure that his name went down to posterity, and in this he was entirely successful. When Alexander visited Ephesus in 334 B.C. he expressed the desire to participate in its rebuilding and to donate funds for its completion but the Ephesians, not wishing to be deprived of having a free hand in its reconstruction, politely refused with the ingenious excuse that 'it was not fitting for a god to rebuild a temple to a god'.

The Temple destroyed by Herostratus replaced an earlier temple that was built on marshy ground but this gave rise to numerous problems from water seepage from the swamp. Theodorus was the architect responsible for its replacement and was chosen because he had built successfully a temple on a similar waterlogged site on the Island of Samos. The destroyed Temple of Theodorus was replaced by the Artemesion that Pliny had described and the one familiar to Paul. It was the work of the architect Pythios and was built on a large podium, the entrance being reached by a flight of thirteen steps that gave onto a further impressive flight before the entrance was reached. It was the basis of the columns that graced the entrance that Pliny had mentioned.

Paul must have seen it on many occasions, he could hardly have avoided doing so. The more than life size statue of Diana stood in the cilia and was partly concealed by a diaphanous veil that was very slowly raised at the most propitious moment of a ritual, one could almost liken it to an ancient form of striptease. Copies of this statue in marble have been unearthed in the precincts of the Bouleterion, two of them now to be seen in the Seljuk museum. The concept of the Ephesian Diana was very different to that of the athletic Diana the huntress, even though she is shown in one instance on her plinth with her hounds.

The Ephesian figure had an elaborate headdress and across her bosom a striking corsage that has been likened to rows of multiple breasts, a feature that has given rise to a deal of speculation as to their significance **(See Figure 51)**. Many years ago Sir William Ramsay suggested that they could represent the eggs of the queen bee, the bee being the emblem of the City that figured on much of the silver coinage (**See Figure 52**). He concluded that the goddess was the equivalent of the queen of the hive and that her attendant priests, who undertook the everyday Temple ritual, were the drones who strangely and for some obscure reason were always dressed as women. The actual priestesses themselves were known as the 'Melissae', and they were the ones who probably had a raw deal for it fell to their lot to do the Temple's more mundane work and be responsible for the chores. However, a more recent theory postulates this peculiar corsage of Diana being a concept of virility, and does in fact represent a series of bulls' testicles.

Apart from the priests and priestesses there were many groups associated with the temple, and these were allotted various other duties, such as those who played the flutes and blew the trumpets at the various ceremonies, and those who danced at the festivals made up the formal retinue of the goddess herself. Apart from the thorn in the flesh that already afflicted Paul all this must have added up to another of a gigantic size[36].

Following the sacred way through Ephesus from the Magnesia Gate to the Koressos gate and the Stadium of Nero, there are many fine buildings to be seen that were the donations of wealthy families. In the years that followed Paul's departure, as a result of the riot in the theatre around A.D. 57-8, it is evident that Ephesus became even more beautiful and subsequently even more prosperous.

Paul would have seen the Magnesia Gate, the upper State Agora laid out by Claudius, and the Northern Stoa with its colonnade would then have been a part of the architecture. The Temple of Hestia Boulaia where the priests maintained the perpetual fire, the Heroon of St Luke, the Temple of Isis, the commercial Agora, and the Prytaneion or Town Hall would all have been familiar. But the East Gymnasium built by Flavius Damianius, the sophist and a scion of an old and wealthy Ephesian family together with his wife Vedia Phaedria had not then been built, nor had the complex of their private baths. An inscription also confirms that the Odeon, which was used as a meeting chamber for the town council and for occasional concerts, was donated to the City by Publius Vedius Antoninus, another wealthy citizen who was a personal friend of the Emperor Marcus Aurelius. It was this same citizen who built the important and prestigious Vedius Gymnasium near the Koressos gate. All these buildings were of a much later date as was the vast Temple to Domitian at the Eastern end of the State Agora. This had the Emperor's gigantic and vulgar statue in the Celia, an effigy that the Ephesians intensely disliked. But in Paul's day the nearby ancient fountain of Polio would have been much in use, the Memius monument near the entrance to Curetes street would also have been a familiar landmark and that was put up to commemorate the grandson of Sulla.

Curetes street would have been much the same as it is now (**See Figure 53**), resplendent with the statues of philosophisers, Emperors, famous athletes and the like on their marble plinths, but then in part the street would have had a series of shops on either side, and the fountain dominated by the imposing statue of the Emperor Trajan. Further on down the street the beautiful little temple of Hadrian was also an improvement of later years (**See Figure 54**).

---

[36] In spite of Paul's success in his ministry in Ephesus the cult of Artemis was not in any way affected. An inscription that dates to the time of Marcus Aurelius 162 - 164 A.D. states that 'The council of the city of Ephesus acted as the advocate of the sacred days of the month of Artemisia, to ensure that the entire month of Artemisia was sacred and dedicated to Artemis'.

Wheeled traffic was not allowed in the upper part of the City which was kept as a pedestrian precinct, and its boundary with Curates street was an arch having pillars decorated with the bas reliefs of Hercules (**See Figure 55**). This gate separated the upper from the lower town, the lower being the commercial centre and open to traffic, the ruts worn by the wheels of carts and chariots in its marble paving being a silent witness to a once bustling life.

The Baths of Scholastikia lay behind the Temple of Hadrian, a wealthy Christian woman who lived in Ephesus during the fourth century A.D. and from her own resources built this large complex on the site of a previous establishment. One wonders if Paul made use of these earlier facilities, though if he did it is very unlikely that he exercised in the Palestra. The seated figure of Scholastikia still presides over the ruins of her expertise but sadly lacks her head, one that she obviously kept during her lifetime. She was certainly a woman of considerable influence and moment for she demolished a significant part of the municipal buildings near the Odeon to furnish the material for her project. Her development not only incorporated the baths but also included the old brothel area which she made more sumptuous and up to date with mosaic floors, an atrium and a series of rooms on two stories. The figure of a handsomely endowed Priapus has been rescued from the well in the brothel courtyard miraculously undamaged and intact, it now rests in a glass case in a prime but not too prominent position in the Ephesus museum where it holds its own amongst a myriad of other antiquities. Those of a more sensitive nature are apt to give it a wide berth whilst others who are not at all bothered with such scruples ponder it more closely. Cut into the pavement of the marble street that goes on to the harbour is a sign, which clearly points the way to any stranger in Ephesus who wished to visit the establishment but was not so familiar with the city topography (**See Figure 56**). Scholastikia was a very broad minded woman[37].

The central lavatories are also to be found in this complex, quite resplendent with their row of white marble seats arranged in line against the marble walls of a large establishment (**See Figure 57**). A visit here during the winter months would have been, to say the very the least and from any aspect, a very chilly experience. It appears that life in those days had very few hang ups and inhibitions judging from a graffiti that was discovered here relating to the adjacent brothel. Scholastikia's renovations and redevelopment made a very convenient complex that not only had the facilities to cater for those who wished to disport themselves in the Baths and the Palestra, but also for those who had other diverse tastes.

On the other side of the street and facing the Temple of Hadrian and the Scholastikia Baths are a series of steps that lead to a very select residential area on the slopes of Mount Koressos, and it is here where the villas of the wealthy were built on terraces let into the hillside. Their mosaics, their frescos, and their small patio gardens with their fountains are all very much in the Pompeian tradition, the whole district being reminiscent of what could have been an ancient Chelsea.

---

[37] She was obviously a wealthy woman in her own right, not unlike Eumachia of Pompeii who inherited estates from her husband, Numistrius Pronto, and became involved with the fullers and the woollen industry to the extent that she built the collegium of the fullers and wool traders in the Forum. She also owned a brick works.

Figure 51: Statue of the Ephesian Diana.

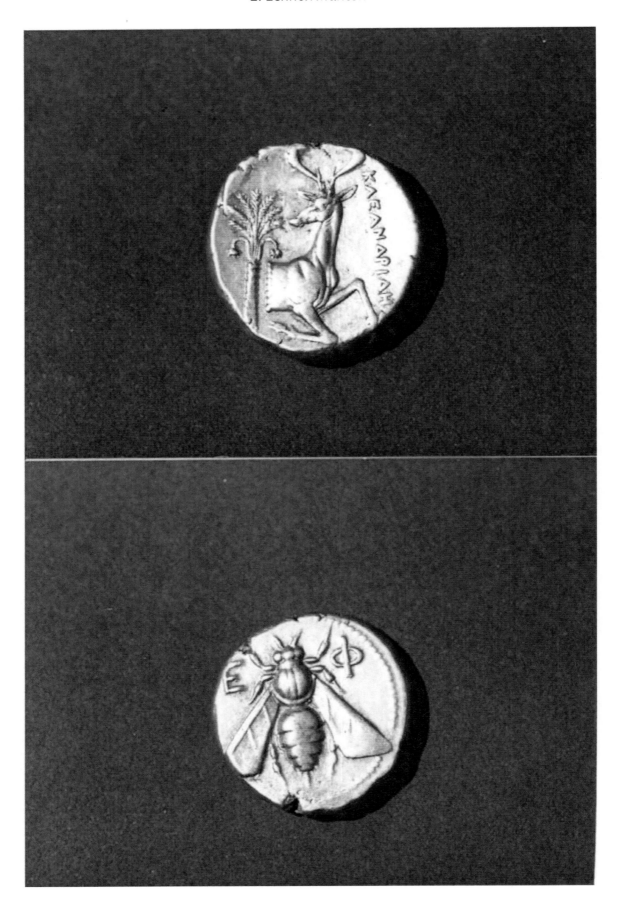

Figure 52: Obverse and Reverse of a Silver Tetradrachm Showing the Bee as the Emblem of the City, enlarged Twice.

Figure 53: Curetes Street in Ephesus.

Figure 54: The Corinthian Temple to Hadrian in Curetes Street.

Figure 55: The Gate of Hercules and the Ram that separates the Upper from the Lower Town.

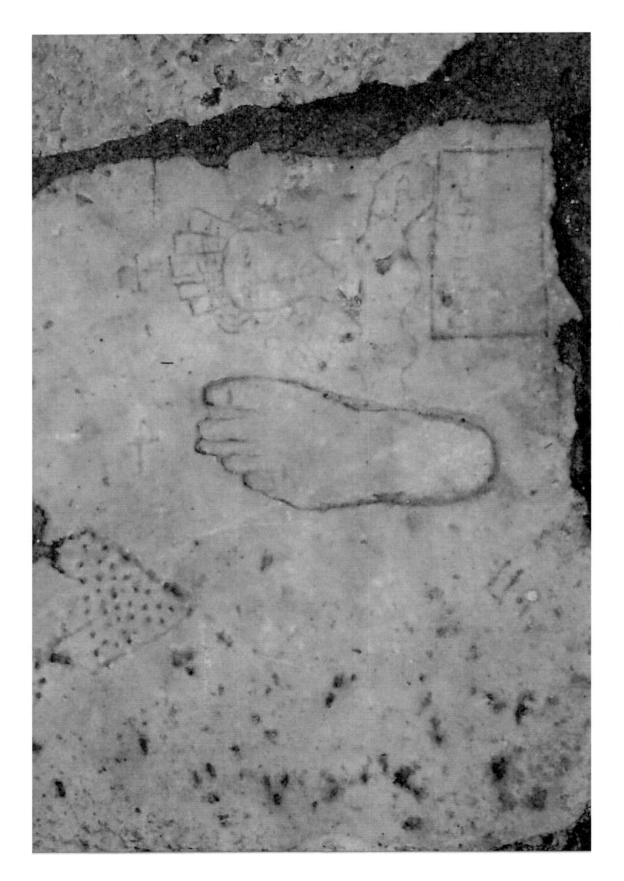

Figure 56: The Sign Cut into the Paving of the Marble Street that shows the way to the Brothel.

Figure 57: The Central Lavatories.

Figure 58: The Library of Celsus and the Triple Gate of Mazeus and Mithradates.

Those who lived here did not soil their hands with anything as mundane as work. A contingent of slaves looked after their household chores and their every want, whilst the head of the house spent his time at the baths philosophising with his friends or, more to the point, discussing the local scandals. It is not at all likely that Paul would have found lodgings in this district.

The Celsus Library was one of the finest buildings in Ephesus and its magnificent facade once dominated the junction of Curetes street with the marble road **(See Figure 58)**. The consul Gaius Julius Aquila had it built in A.D. 100 as a gift to the city and as a memorial to his father whose remains, placed in a marble sarcophagus but contained in a lead casket, still lie in a vault beneath the reading room. Aquila provided an endowment of 25,000 denarii for the purchase of books or scrolls and the upkeep of the building, and to protect them from damp and the possible ensuing damage he had the building further insulated by a second external wall. The wonderful facade of the library rose to some three storeys and has recently been restored, but the statue of its patron Athena, the goddess of wisdom and learning that once was a feature of its central arch has long since disappeared. However, it appears that recent restoration has replaced this statue.

Paul would not have seen this Library although an important addition to the City's amenities, for he died some thirty years or more before it was built, but the nearby commercial Agora was the one place that he would have frequented as a matter of course for his daily necessities, and quite possibly with Priscilla and Aquila. This covered some 110 square meters and had a row of shops under each of its four colonnades, the whole embellished like Curetes Street, with a myriad of statues standing on their plinths, whilst in the centre of the market stood the horologion, the sundial and water clock.

This Agora was a part of the Ephesus of the Hellenistic period and in 4 B.C. a triple gate to improve the entrance was built and donated to the city by two erstwhile slaves, Mazaeus and Mithridates. Both of them built this gate when gaining their freedom under Agrippa, and they dedicated it to him in gilded bronze lettering, and to the Emperor Augustus and his wife Livia. Almost every day and as a matter of course Paul must have passed through this gate, for it was as old or even older than Paul himself and though the actual date of his birth has not been recorded, though it could have been around 1 B.C., it could put his age when living here in Ephesus to be in the middle fifties.

There are certain illuminating graffiti on and near the gate. The one on the gate itself reads 'Who so relieves himself here shall suffer the wrath of Hecate'. This must have been a habit of public nuisance which was common to many Roman cities of the period for there are similar graffiti decorating the pillars of Triumphal Arches in North Africa, and especially the one in Hammam Zourka, but there the retribution against the offender is assigned to the militant god Mars. The other graffiti refers to the price of bread that was then selling for 4 obols for a 14 oz loaf of good quality, and 2 obols for a 10 oz loaf of something that was much less desirable.

Nero became Emperor in A.D. 54, an event that must have more or less coincided with that of Paul's stay in Ephesus. Nero was responsible for a number of new building projects in the city, one of them being a colonnaded pedestrian precinct that ran along the top of the East wall that separated the marble street from the commercial Agora. This was reached by a flight of steps placed at either end of the street, and it is possible that work on this could have commenced or been in hand when Paul was there. However, the paving of the marble street that we see today was not then in situ, for this was laid down in the fifth century A.D. by Eutropius, another of the wealthy citizens of Ephesus.

The commercial Agora and the shops that lined one side of the marble street leading to the theatre are a part of Ephesus that Paul would have known, together with the theatre that was built into the side of Mount Pion to overlook and dominate the broad street that went down to the harbour. This was another of the town's main thoroughfares and one that Paul must often have trod, but not as it is today, for here in the fourth century A.D. its entire length was paved with marble by the Emperor Arcadius A.D. 383-308, to become the 'Arcadian Way'.

On either side of this street were shops and mosaic pavements under roofed colonnades that sheltered pedestrians in inclement weather, they were known as Arcades after the Emperor Arcadius who had them built. A contemporary inscription records them being illuminated at night by numerous lanterns, thus making Ephesus one of the few cities to have a record of street lighting, making also the arcades an evocative picture in the evenings. Antioch of course was another ancient city to have this street lighting, but there it predated Ephesus by many years.

The sites of the shops that must have been under the Arcades have not as yet been excavated, but it is possible that some of them could have catered for the tourist trade by dealing in the silver shrines of Demetrius and his fellow silversmiths. They would have been in an ideal position to tempt the tourist with their trinkets as they visited Ephesus, and departed by boat.

The extensive Harbour Baths with their two large Palestrae were built by Domitian at some time after A.D. 81, so this establishment would not have been in operation when Paul arrived from Corinth and disembarked with Aquila and Priscilla. All those who arrived by boat in the later years were obliged to pass through these Baths as a matter of course before being allowed to enter the City.

Aquila and Priscilla must have been in Ephesus for some twelve months or more before Paul arrived from Antioch to Join them and help with the tent business, as he did when they were all in Corinth. Paul is always at great pains to stress that he kept himself by working, and he refers to this and his other difficulties in 1 Corinthians IV.11, 12, an epistle that could have been sent from Philippi:

'To the present hour we are hungry and thirsty, we are poorly clothed and beaten and homeless, and we grow weary from the work of our hands. When reviled we bless, when persecuted we endure, when slandered we speak kindly. We have become the rubbish of the world, the dregs of all things, to this very day'.

At this juncture Paul seems to have had few resources and one wonders if, by this time, his parents were dead and all connections with Tarsus severed.

These early days in Ephesus were obviously far from easy, for little headway was made over the three months that he spent preaching in the synagogue. The inevitable opposition and calumny arose from the main stream of the Jewish population, and as an alternative he managed to hire the room that Tyrannus[38] used for teaching. According to the Codex Bezae, a somewhat late manuscript he used it from the fifth to the tenth hour, which was in effect from midday till the evening. It was the custom for schools to begin their work in the early morning to avoid the heat of the day and one can again but speculate as to where it was situated, for it must have been located somewhere in the lower part of the City, and maybe in the area of Mount Pion.

Not only did Paul have to contend with the Jewish opposition, but also with the popular cult of Diana, not to speak of the many charlatans and confidence tricksters who roamed the City, including those who once practised Magic, but when converted burnt their books in public to the tune of some fifty thousand silver coins (See Acts 19, 18-20). In 1 Cor, XV.32[39], Paul talks about the 'wild animals of Ephesus', but it Is a phrase that is not likely to refer to his having confronted them at any time in the Stadium, for it is doubtful if by then the Stadium of Nero had been finished. His phrase could refer to Sceva, the Jewish chief priest and his seven sons together with the other vagabond exorcists, who were trying to undermine his teaching and influence. He remarks in verse 33, 'Bad company ruins good morals'.

The Stadium in Ephesus was another of Nero's projects and its construction must have taken some years to finish so that Paul could well have left for Corinth before its completion. Even had a smaller Stadium previously existed Paul would not have survived any confrontation with the beasts, and it is doubtful too if such events ever took place in the Stadium, as here the public were not so well protected as they were in the larger Amphitheatres. However, one end of the Stadium could be closed off and adapted to a smaller arena when gladiatorial contests were staged and there are plinths in Ephesus having bas reliefs that demonstrate their various abilities.

That Paul was aware of these displays in the Amphitheatres is hinted at when he writes in 1 Corinthians IV, 9: 'For I think that God has exhibited us Apostles as last of all - (and here he is again claiming the right to be counted as an equal to the Twelve) - as though sentenced to death, because we have become a spectacle to the world'. The Christians and the condemned were always paraded in the Amphitheatres at the end of the gladiatorial displays, and then to round off the programme were thrown to the lions, or other such beasts, as a grand finale.

It was Paul's intention to stay in Ephesus for the feast of the Pentecost for this happened to coincide with that of the Artemisia. As has been previously described the great festival of Diana was the high light of the Ephesian year when hundreds flocked into the City by sea and from the surrounding country towns. It was an occasion that Paul could not miss, for the period

---

[38] The exact nature of the hall is not known but it has been suggested by A.J. Malherbe in 'Social Aspects of Early Christianity' that it could have been a Guild hall named after the Guild's patron. On the other hand he could have been the owner of the building that was used as a lecture hall and it could have been used as a court room by the proconsul. A building that could have been the hall was sited near the Library of Celsus.

[39] The practice of magic was a part of Ephesian life and often revolved around the 'Ephesian Letters' that were six magical terms used on amulets and the like to ward off evil spirits. The burned magical books destroyed them together with other formulae such as curses and incantations. The burning of the books was not an enforced procedure but a voluntary act by their owners. However the Ephesians were wont to believe in the miraculous for articles of Paul's clothing such as handkerchiefs were often taken to the sick, often thought to be the work of demons, to effect a cure.

of the festival opened up many opportunities for missionary work, but it was Demetrius who thought otherwise, in modern parlance he was the shop steward of the silversmith's union. For a long time a great deal of hostility had been brewing against Paul amongst the silversmiths, and this due to the slump in their sales of silver mementos of Diana, a loss of trade brought about and dramatically increased as a result of his fervent missionary work. Their takings had dropped alarmingly during the previous festival and were still noticeably declining, and as a corporate body they must have wielded some influence, for not far from the temple of Hadrian in Curetes street, lying on its side, there is the plinth of a statue with an inscription that refers to the silversmith's college[40].

Their riot erupted when they took to the streets during the festival period rampaging through the city to the theatre, their passions having been whipped up by the rhetoric of Demetrius. Crowds made for the theatre not knowing what the rumpus was all about. Acts XIX, 32 relates 'Meanwhile some were shouting one thing, some another; for the assembly was in confusion, and most of them did not know why they had come together'. The fact that Demetrius and his fellow silversmiths had forcibly hijacked Gaius and Aristarchus, the two Macedonian colleagues of Paul when on their way to the theatre, is a detail in the narrative that must surely be from an eye witness account. The fracas was a heaven sent opportunity for the Jewish faction to disassociate themselves from Paul and his mission. It is obvious that they were not at all popular in Ephesus either, for when they joined the throngs in the theatre and put forward Alexander, the copper smith to speak for them, the crowds rose up and would have none of it, and led by Demetrius the roar of 'great is Diana of the Ephesians' was heard for the next two hours over the length and breadth of the City.

As has been said previously the Asiachs who were concerned for the welfare of Paul, had they possibly joined the Church, managed to dissuade him from going to the theatre, and order was eventually restored by the Town Clerk. He pointed out to those in the theatre that their assembly constituted an illegal riot[41], and that Paul and his companions had not subjected the goddess Diana to any degree of blasphemy nor he added, were they the robbers of churches. In the light of this last statement it would seem that Paul had been accused, no doubt by the Jews, of misappropriating the funds that had been collected for the yearly Pentecostal donation to Jerusalem. If there had been such a complaint the authorities must have obviously dismissed it as being untenable. To disperse the riot and bring the City back to normal the Town Clerk advised the silversmiths to air their alleged grievances in the courts. Ephesus was one of the centres in Asia for the assizes, and was visited periodically by the proconsul in this judicial capacity, and it is possible that one of these visits for the assizes could have coincided with the riot. As far as the Town Clerk was concerned good behaviour in the

---

[40] Two important festivals were held annually in Ephesus to do homage to Artemis. One held in the month of Artemision that took place in March or April, the other on the 6th of Thargelion, May to June, to celebrate the birthday of the goddess. This latter was the more important of the two when her image was taken in processions through the city.

[41] A riot in any city was to be avoided for it could result in serious consequences. Guilds at the centre of the riot, such as the silversmiths, could be disbanded and the city officials and the city lose their freedom through powers vested in the proconsul by the Emperor. The Town Clerk obviously had this in mind when he dispersed the riot in the Theatre and told Demetrius to take his complaint to the courts. As a citizen Demetrius was quite entitled to do so but it would have been heard by the proconsul and possibly with little sympathy.

city was essential and riots to be avoided at all costs, such a disturbance would not have been very acceptable to the proconsul[42].

The riot could have occurred at sometime late in the year A.D. 57, and must have given rise to a great deal of hostility and ill feeling in Ephesus, for Paul not long after said farewell to the members of the Church and left for Macedonia and Greece (See Acts, XX. 1-3).

The Acts and the letters of Paul can be more than frustrating for he gives little information as to those of his following who were with him in Ephesus, apart from Aquila and Priscilla. Neither does he give any details regarding his every day activities apart from his missionary work, though he vaguely refers to the difficulties that he encountered. He does, however, mention the fact that, before the riots began, he sent both Timothy and Erastus to Macedonia, Erastus, no doubt wishing later to return to his duties as the City Chamberlain in Corinth (See Acts, 19, 22). This quite possibly to collect the Pentecostal donations for Jerusalem from the Macedonian Churches, such as Amphipolis and Appolonia, that lay on the Via Egnatia. It is possible that Luke was with him at the time of the riot in Ephesus to record this fact, and also to have mentioned the detail of the abduction of Gaius and Aristarchus by Demetrius and the silversmiths. That Luke was with Paul at the time is born out in the description of the riot where Luke gives the correct and accurate nomenclature for the Municipal officers, that is 'The Town Clerk, the Asiarchs and the Temple Keeper', all terms that were applicable only to Ephesus.

Paul, however, did miss seeing Apollos (Acts XIX 1), a Jew from Alexandria and a devotee of St John the Baptist (See Acts XIX 25), for he had already gone on to Corinth before Paul arrived in Ephesus. Apollos came from Egypt to preach for unity in the Synagogue. In Ephesus he met Aquila and Priscilla who converted him to the Apostolic Church (Acts XVIII 24-2) and he later went to Corinth with letters of introduction to the Corinthian Church. Paul must have had a great respect for him even though he did not agree with all his views regarding the Church, for he not only refers to Apollos (in 1. Corinthians 16 12), but also in his letter to Titus (in 3. 13). By this time too it is apparent that Paul did not see eye to eye with the teaching of the Apostles in Jerusalem, for he found when he reached Corinth that there were divisions amongst the members of the Church to the extent that he remarks (in 1. Corinthians 1 12—13) , somewhat in exasperation 'What I mean is that each of you says 'I belong to Paul' or 'I belong to Apollos', or 'I belong to Cephas', or 'I belong to Christ', has Christ been divided'? (I Cor 11-13)[43].

Paul's visits to Macedonia are of interest. Whilst in Ephesus he had had reports from Apollos of the lax behaviour of those of the church in Corinth. Behaviour in general in Corinth was so licentious that those who embraced this way of life were said to have been 'Corinthianised'. These reports were later confirmed by members of the well-known Chloe family in Corinth who were visiting Ephesus, and this probably instigated Paul's first letter to

---

[42] This phrase used by the Town Clerk is interesting in that there is an extant inscription that reads, 'Agrippa to the magistrates, council and people of Ephesus, greetings. It is my wish that the Jews of Asia, in accordance with their ancestral custom, exercise the care and custody of the sacred money conveyed to the temple in Jerusalem. And those who steal the sacred money of the Jews and flee asylum be dragged out and handed over to the Jews under that law by which TEMPLE-ROBBERS are dragged out. I have also written to Silanus, the praetor, that no one should force a Jew to agree to bail on the Sabbath. 'It seems very clear that the Jews of Ephesus had taken advantage of the disturbance created by Demetrius to lay with the Town Clerk their charges against Paul citing his embezzlement of temple funds.

[43] 2 Corinthians 2. 12. relates 'When I came to Troas to proclaim the good news of Christ, a door was opened for me in the Lord.'

the Corinthians. In 1 Cor XVI 5 Paul states his intention of staying in Ephesus for the Pentecost which coincided with the Artemisia, and then leaving for Macedonia and Corinth where he intended to spend the winter. This is confirmed in Acts XIX 21, with his added intention of subsequently going on to Jerusalem. It is also apparent from 2 Cor XII 14 and from Acts XX 1 that he intended when leaving Ephesus for Corinth to go through Macedonia, and it is thought that this second letter to the Corinthians could have been written and sent from Philippi by Titus. However, in verse 14 he says 'Here I am, ready to come to you this third time. And I will not be a burden', and this is repeated in 2 Cor XIII 1 'This is the third time I am coming to you'. The first visit to Macedonia and Corinth took place on the second journey when Paul and Silas left Troas for Philippi, these verses could indicate that Paul made a second visit from Ephesus to Macedonia and Corinth at some time before the riot of Demetrius and the silversmiths. A visit that Acts has not recorded and one that could have been of a somewhat short duration[44].

Acts XX 1-3 briefly records Paul's departure from Ephesus, possibly with Tychicus and Trophemus following the riot, for Macedonia and Greece where he stayed for three months before setting out again for Syria. But Acts does not give any details regarding this period, one that could have been of the duration of some nine months. However, the letters do give some clues as to this period. Paul's first objective on leaving Ephesus would have been Troas possibly going by sea and having the Ephesians Tychicus and Trophemus travelling with him. It is known from Acts XX 4 that both Tychicus and Trophemus were with him later on in Corinth, and when Paul finally left Corinth for Syria with Sopater, Secundus, Aristarchus, Timothy, and Gaius, Tychicus and Trophemus were with the party.

From 11 Cor 2 1, it appears that Paul was expecting Titus to meet him in Troas, but when after some time he failed to arrive Paul then decided to go on to Philippi: 'but my mind could not rest because I did not find my brother Titus there. So I said farewell to them and went on to Macedonia'. Titus later joined up with Paul in Philippi, possibly bringing with him from Corinth the reply to Paul's first letter to the Corinthians (2 Cor VII)[44]. Paul's second letter to the Corinthians could then have been written and sent back to them from Philippi by Titus.

It seems that Paul then spent some time in Macedonia[45] and Illyricum before going to Corinth for he makes the comment in Romans XV 1, written after his eventual arrival in Corinth, that he has fully preached the Gospel from Jerusalem and as far around as Illyricum.

Strictly Illyria included today's Dalmatia, but in the time of Claudius the area was divided into Roman Illyricum to the north and Greek Illyricum to the south, Greek Illyricum being incorporated into Macedonia. The Via Egnatia from Philippi went through the mountains to Dyrrhachium, the port where boats left for today's Brindisi, and the Appian Way to Rome, and this district was in Greek Illyria though still in the province of Macedonia. Paul must have used

---

[44] Paul's first letter to the Corinthians is thought to have been written from Ephesus during the days of unleavened bread. 1, Cor.5,7. i.e. at Easter. 'Clean out the old yeast so that ye may be a new batch, as you really are unleavened. For the paschal lamb, Christ has been sacrificed. Therefore let us celebrate the festival, not with the old yeast of malice and evil but with the unleavened bread of sincerity and truth'. In the latter part of the letter Cor.1.16.1 be gives instructions for the collection of the monies for the Jerusalem Church - Let each of you set apart whatever his gains may enable him to spare - with suggestions as how their benevolence should be sent to Jerusalem. From 1 Cor.16. 12 it is also apparent that Apollos bad by now left Corinth to be with Paul in Ephesus and his presence is recorded in 1 Cor.1.12; 3,4; 4. 6. (J. Coynbeare, St Paul).

[45] Acts. 20. 1-2. does not record the fact that when Paul left Ephesus for Macedonia he could have gone there via Troas as has been described. It merely records that 'When he had gone through those regions and had given the believers much encouragement, he came to Greece.' It is very possible that he then spent the winter in Macedonia in visiting the local churches together with those in Thessalonica and possibly Bercia.

this route to Dyrrhachium at some time, quite possibly whilst in Macedonia when on his way from Ephesus to Corinth where he proposed to spend the winter months then to go to Jerusalem with the Pentecostal donations that he and his followers had collected from the churches of Macedonia and Achaia for those in Judaea[46].

Few travellers were in Ephesus during the summer of 1961 and it was then possible to walk in and out of the ruins without let or hindrance, it was also very evident that the Theatre had had a deal of successful restoration since Morton's visit in 1930. One morning I climbed to the topmost tier of the theatre seating, sat down and looked out over the great bowl of the auditorium to the Arcadian way, and beyond to the distant reedy marsh that was once the harbour and the sea. Reflecting in the silence how the harbour and the quays must have been in the first centuries A. D., bustling and alive with shipping unloading and loading their various cargoes and all mixed up with those who wished to embark and disembark.

It was about midday and from my seat in the Theatre I could see, way down the Arcadian Way, two other travellers sitting on a tumbled ashlar block, resting quietly in the heat of the sun and also apparently in contemplation of the past. The silence that can envelop these ancient cities helps one to visualise the greatness of their past. Here the deserted emptiness and the absolute stillness in the ruins of this vast theatre was in vivid contrast to the hubbub and clamour of those who thronged it those many centuries ago, when they listened to the harangue of Demetrius and their raised deafening shouts of 'Great is Diana of the Ephesians'. One could almost hear the dim echoes lingering on amongst the stones.

The ruins of the Theatre that we see today are, to all intents and purposes, the remains of the one that was familiar to Paul **(See Figure 59)**. Not so long before he arrived in Ephesus the Emperor Claudius had already enlarged the auditorium, and when at a later date Nero became Emperor the stage was further improved with the addition of a Scaena Frons: work that could have commenced whilst Paul was in Ephesus. Since, on my numerous visits to Ephesus I have seen the partial rebuilding and restoration of many of the other monuments. The impressive facade of the Celsus Library has risen spectacularly from its many tumbled blocks of stone and the Gate into the commercial Agora donated to the City by the freedmen Mazaeus and Mithradates has been rebuilt. The restored villas of the wealthy on the slopes of Mount Coressos, the Chelsea of Ephesus, now vividly demonstrate what was then the sophistication of an urban life for a privileged section of the community in the first centuries A. D.

Ephesus can still be silent, but only in the late evenings when the sun goes down to cast its luminous and slowly lengthening shadows across the ruins. Today Curetes street and the Marble Way no longer resound to the noise of chariot wheels but echo solely to the clack of tourists' feet for tourism has come again to Ephesus, but not to worship at the Temple of Diana. Outside the gate and the kiosk, where visitors pay their dues before entering the city ruins, are the numerous cafes, and souvenir shops that jostle cheek by jowl to display their menus and their bric-a-brac.

---

[46] It has been suggested by D. W.J. Gill that Paul, instead of going South to Corinth by the Aegean, could have used the Via Egnatia to reach Dyrrachium on the Adriatic; to then go North into Illyria and finally reach Corinth by going down the Adriatic coast through Apollonia, Oricum, and Actium. This, however, could have been a lengthy and a difficult journey with dubious coastal roads, unless he went by boat from Dyrrachium to Patras. If he did go into Illyria to preach, as he asserts In Romans 11. 19, he could then have returned by the Via Egnatia to reach Corinth by going south along the Aegean.

Figure 59: The Great Theatre.

These cafes and shops contain mementos that have taken the place of the charms of Demetrius and his fellow craftsmen, souvenirs that they once unloaded onto pilgrims and tourists of a bygone age.

They no longer come by ship and cart, but by coach and car from all the corners of the world. Not far from the Vedius Gymnasium they park in serried ranks, and in groups of all nationalities pass through the city in the wake of a waving stick or scarf held aloft by their respective guides, to stand clumped before the monuments as they listen to his, or her erudite discourse. Then, nigh on exhaustion, visit the Seljuk museum where they wonder at the statue of Diana and possibly the Priapus.

In 1988 I once again climbed to the topmost tier of the theatre to sit and look out beyond the scaena frons to the Agora and the marsh beyond the harbour, many others were climbing to the top or sitting as I had done in solitary state some twenty seven years back. The Arcadian and the Marble Way were dense with people for Ephesus was now bustling and alive, but not as a City. I preferred it as it was in 1961 clothed in its dignified and silent past.

Some interesting questions arise from Paul's stay in Ephesus, and one that has already been discussed is the possibility that whilst there he spent a part of his time in prison. Professor Duncan in his book 'St Paul's Ephesian Ministry' considers this possibility, and if true it could be inferred that Paul wrote his letters to Philemon and the Colossians from his prison in Ephesus and not, as is generally accepted, from Rome. There is no specific evidence in Acts or the letters that such an imprisonment took place, in spite of the fact that there is a building in Ephesus that is supposed to be the site of his incarceration. But in Romans 16 7 there are certain hints of imprisonment where he sends greetings to 'Andronicus and Junias my fellow countrymen and comrades in captivity'. This is the only reference to these two individuals in the letters or Acts, and as no further details of this period of captivity have been recorded it is one that could have taken place in Corinth.

Much of the hypothesis revolves around the slave Onesimus, but there are some cogent reasons that do not appear to support some aspects of the theory suggested by Professor Duncan, that Onesimus having left Philemon at Colossae, visited Paul when he was in prison in Ephesus. But if so then the long journey to Rome that Onesimus is supposed to have undertaken did not, in actual fact, take place. The journey from Colossae to Ephesus would certainly have been a far easier prospect than that of going to Rome; travelling to Rome in the first Century A. D. was a more formidable undertaking. To avoid being apprehended by Philemon, or his agents in Ephesus, it has been suggested that Onesimus claimed sanctuary in the Artemision, where the right of asylum was granted to those who sought the protection of Diana from the tentacles of the legal system.

Roman law was strict where runaway slaves were concerned, and had Onesimus on reaching Ephesus sought sanctuary in the Artemision he would then have been confined to the temple precincts, with the hazard, should he have attempted to leave them, of being arrested by the city magistrates, and moreover the Artemision was well outside the city precincts. Thus any contact with Paul in prison would have been difficult and problematical, yet in Paul's letter to Philemon he says 'I am appealing to you for my child, Onesimus, whose father I have become during my imprisonment. Formerly he was useless to you, but now he is indeed useful both to you and to me'. This would seem to confirm that Paul was then under detention in his hired house in Rome where he was allowed to have visitors, but his freedom was limited and under supervision. In circumstances such as these Onesimus could visit and see him as often as he wished and without any fear of being arrested.

The letters to the Colossians and the Philippians, as well as that to Philemon regarding Onesimus, are generally considered to have been written by Paul and sent from his house in Rome, but if they were written by Paul and sent from Ephesus, what of Ephesians; also considered to have been one of the imprisonment letters. It seems out of the question that this was written whilst Paul was in Ephesus for Ephesians VI. 21-22. records it having been sent to them by Tychicus, and in Colossians IV. 7.8 Paul intimates that it is Tychicus who is taking his letter to them. It is also apparent from Colossians IV.9 both Tychicus and Onesimus travelled back to Asia Minor together, and Onesimus bound for Colossae with Paul's personal letter to Philemon. So for Onesimus to have seen Paul in Ephesus and subsequently to have been converted to the church there seems to be a debateable point, and not very likely.

The association of St John and the Virgin Mary with Ephesus is one of the most intriguing questions of all, the strong tradition that after the Crucifixion he took her to Ephesus, where she spent the rest of her life in a small remote and isolated house high up on Mount Salmisos, and not a few kilometres away from the City, is more than suspect. St John's account of the Crucifixion recounts how, as the beloved of Christ he was present at the cross with four women. The Virgin and her sister Salome, who was the mother of John, thus John was the cousin of Jesus, Mary the wife of Cleophas who was the mother of James the less, and Mary Magdalene (St John XIX. 25—27); and this account is the only one to specifically record Jesus asking John, from the Cross, to take care of his Mother the Virgin (John XIX. 26).

Various dates between A.D. 29 and A.D. 36 have been given for the Crucifixion, but it is generally accepted that it took place around A.D. 30. According to the Gospels of St Matthew and St Luke it would appear that Jesus was born around 6 B.C., possibly at some time during the last two or three years prior to the death of Herod in 4 B.C., an associated historical event that seems to be the only one that can be taken as a definitive guideline.

The Virgin could have been some 16 years of age when Jesus was born for it was then the custom for marriage to take place, not long after puberty when girls became nubile, and this more often than not. Assuming Jesus was born around 6 B.C. the Virgin, if aged some 16 years at his birth, would herself have been born around 22 B.C. On this assumption the age of Jesus at the time of the Crucifixion would have been some 36 years, and that of the Virgin 52. John must have been a much younger man when he stood at the cross with his mother Salome and his aunt the Virgin, possibly at that time aged some twenty five years or even less.

John must certainly have stayed on in Jerusalem for some number of years after the Crucifixion, for subsequently both he and Peter fell afoul of the Sanhedrin and were imprisoned for preaching the Gospel, and healing the lame man at the Beautiful Gate. After the stoning of Stephen that could have been witnessed by Paul, the two of them left Jerusalem and went down to Samaria to help the Evangelist Phillip with his missionary work (Acts. 8.14).

Furthermore John is known to have been with the Apostles in Jerusalem at the time of the great drought in A.D. 4, when Paul and Barnabas went up to Jerusalem with the donations that the Antioch Church had collected to mitigate the difficulties of those of the Churches in Judaea. Josephus records this drought in his history of the Jews, and it was then that Herod executed James the brother of John and imprisoned Peter, who later miraculously escaped and went to see the other Apostles at the house of Mary the mother of Mark (Acts XII. 12-1).

It is clear John was still in Jerusalem about 49 A.D., for it is specifically stated in Galatians 29, that he was present when Paul and Barnabas, at the end of their first missionary journey, went up from Antioch to Jerusalem to discuss with the Apostles the vexed question of the circumcision of the Gentiles. On the assumption that the Virgin was born in 22 B.C. her age by A.D. 49 would have been 71 years, and even had she been born in 17 B.C., some five years later, her age would still have been 66 years, and that of John 44 years.

It would appear therefore that John and the Virgin did not go to Ephesus prior to A.D. 49, in spite of the tradition that she spent the last years of her life in her mountain retreat. For the Virgin to have considered the prospect of spending her last years in such a remote cottage, high up and isolated on a mountain side, does not seem to be a very practical hypothesis for what in those days was an advanced age, to say the very least it would have been a curious decision on her part.

Some have contended that they both went to Ephesus at some time between A.D. 37 - 48, but even had they done so, would the Virgin have wished to remain for long periods on her own in such an isolated locality whilst John was back in Jerusalem. Furthermore, in spite of the fact that following the stoning of Stephen, many of the disciples had gone from Jerusalem to escape the persecutions of Paul and the Sanhedrin. It would appear that, at least until A.D. 49, the majority of the Apostles were still there together. By that time James, the brother of Jesus, had taken over the leadership of the Jerusalem Church from Peter, and so he remained until he was martyred in A.D. 62 about the time when Paul was waiting to be brought before Nero in Rome.

Nothing has been recorded of the Virgin's life during the years that followed the Crucifixion, for John even if they had gone to Ephesus together, makes no reference to her being there what so ever and neither does Paul. It could be that she continued to live on quietly with her family in Jerusalem whilst under John's protection, or alternatively with them in Galilee well away from the persecutions of the Sanhedrin. In spite of those who assert that the Virgin had no other children, it cannot be proved that James who took over the leadership of the Church, was not the brother of Jesus, and as such he is categorically described on several occasions (See Gal 1, 19; 2, 1-3; and Acts 15, 4-34 21,18 – 19).

The details of the Virgin's family have been recorded definitively in Matthew XIII 55 - 56, and here the brothers of Jesus are named in their order of seniority. Matthew also mentions the sisters of Jesus but not by name, which in such a society is understandable. In those days the female progeny of a family were considered to be of an inferior status to that of the male, and of less account in the social order. Though Matthew mentions the sisters of Jesus he fails to record how many there were, but at the least there must have been two of them.

It is generally accepted that the Gospel of St Matthew as it stands today is not his original work in its entirety, but was compiled at some time between 65 - 100 A.D., from a source known as the 'logia', which could have been an original work of Matthew and from the earlier Gospel of St Mark that was based on the reminiscences of Peter's life with the Apostles, and Jesus before the Crucifixion. It is more than significant that the description of the family, as recorded by St Matthew, does correspond to a great extent with that given in the earlier Gospel of St Mark 6. 3-4. On one occasion in Nazareth Jesus referred to his family and at the time almost repudiated them by remarking 'Prophets are not without honour, except in their home town, and among their own lot, and in their own house'. That Jesus was referring to his family seems undeniable, for those in the Synagogue who listened to him preaching later on remarked, 'Is not this the carpenter, the son of Mary, and brother of James and Moses, and Judas and Simon and are not his sisters here with us', and they took offense at him.

The details of the Virgin's family as given in Matthew could have come from Mark, but Mark when writing his Gospel must have had these authoritative details from Peter, for Peter was one of the first Apostles and as an intimate of Jesus must have been well aware of his family background in Galilee. It is difficult to imagine what could be clearer, though John was asked to take the Virgin into his care by Jesus from the Cross it is not impossible for her to have wished for the comfort of her own family, in the knowledge that John would look after her overall welfare.

It was a German Nun, a Catherine Emmerich by name, who pinpointed the now traditional site of the Marymana in the hills above Ephesus. She saw in a vision a small house that she maintained was the last home of the Virgin and a subsequent search led to the discovery of some ruins that, on investigation, many thought must tally with her directions. There is, however, some considerable dispute as to the date of the foundations for though some attribute them to the first century A.D. there are many others who opt for the sixth. The traditional Tomb of the Virgin that now lies empty is at the foot of the Mount of Olives. In spite of the adamant contention of Sister Emmerich that it was to be found in the region of the house, and despite all efforts to locate such a tomb nothing has yet been discovered, which makes it dubious indeed as to the fact that one ever existed.

A small and pleasing, but not ornate, little Chapel dedicated to the Virgin was later built on the site of the old building that lay amongst the trees **(See Figure 60)**. When I first visited it in 1961 its aura of quiet devotion, its uncluttered simplicity and the remoteness of its surroundings were the epitome of peace **(See Figure 61)**. But when I left the Chapel, in a somewhat sceptical frame of mind as to the authenticity and veracity of the site, I turned into a track that led away through the woods and down the hill to immediately stumble over the root of a tree that was proud of the path, and fell flat on my face. That, I thought as I picked myself up and gathered up my belongings, will teach you to be sceptical about such matters! The Virgin however, must have been in a forgiving and merciful frame of mind, because apart from being covered in dust, no damage had been done and the cameras were still intact.

Figure 60: The Chapel to the Virgin in the Hills above Ephesus.

Figure 61: The Interior of the Chapel.

Now some twenty years on the site has lost much of its erstwhile character, and over the years has developed into a Tourist Park with the questionable amenity of a small restaurant, but the little Chapel amongst the trees, authentic or not, has happily retained its atmosphere of peace and tranquillity.

If John and the Apostles were still in Jerusalem in A.D. 49 it then follows that he must have gone to Ephesus at some time after that date. But if by A.D. 49 the Virgin was still alive, though well on in years, it is certain that John would not have left Jerusalem until after her death. After that event there would have been little incentive for him to have remained in Jerusalem, and so another question arises. Was John in Ephesus during the years 55-57, roughly at the time when Paul was there with Aquila and Priscilla, busily teaching the Gospel in the school of Tyrannus and engaged in his other missionary work?

If John and Paul were in Ephesus at the same time it is again strange that neither of them have made any reference to each other. Paul makes no reference in his letters nor is there any reference in Acts to John being in Ephesus during these years, even though Paul specifically names others such as Timothy, and of course Aquila and Priscilla. Had they been living in Ephesus at the same time they must both have been well aware of the fact, and if so one wonders if the rift between Paul and the Apostles was so marked that they refused to acknowledge the presence of each other.

In his letters Paul continually complains about his lack of recognition as an Apostle and the fact that the Twelve do not consider him as truly one of themselves. In 1 Cor. 1, thought to have been written from Ephesus, he claims to be an Apostle through the will of God. In Chapter IX 1-6 he again airs his grievances over the Apostles' attitude in not recognising his claim, and this somewhat bitterly and at some length especially in verse 2: 'If I am not an Apostle to others, at least I am to you for you are the seat of my apostleship in the Lord'. Possibly in the first place alluding to those who opposed his claims to be an apostle 'at least I am to you', to his Saints and elsewhere he states that he does not build the precepts of his teaching on another's foundations.

As Paul fails to make any reference to John being in Ephesus during the years he was there with Aquila and Priscilla, there is the possibility that John went to Ephesus after the riot of the silversmiths and Paul's departure for Corinth, but it would then have been after A.D. 57 or 58. There is little doubt that John lived in Ephesus for many years and eventually died there at an advanced age, a suggested date being in the region of AD. 98.

It is thought that John could have been banished to Patmos at some time after A.D. 81, when Domitian became Emperor, for in Revelation 1. 9 John states: 'I John, your brother who share with you in Jesus the persecution and the kingdom and the patient endurance, was on the island of Patmos because of the word of God and the testimony of Jesus'. He must have remained on Patmos, possibly writing his Gospel until the death of Domitian in A.D. 96, to return to Ephesus as an old man when Nerva became Emperor.

St Polycarp, who was born in A.D. 69, was bishop of Smyrna during the latter part of St John's life in Ephesus, and it was during this period in Smyrna when the great theologian St Irenaeus was born, and he must when a child, have seen and heard Polycarp on numerous occasions. St Polycarp according to St Irenaeus, often corresponded with St John in Ephesus, but if so St Polycarp must at that time have been a young man for he was martyred in Smyrna on the 23d Feb A. D. 155. St Ignatius, who was born in Syria in A.D. 35, and reputed to have followed St Peter as the second Bishop of Antioch, also stayed with Polycarp when on his way to his martyrdom in Rome in A.D. 107, and he too could have been acquainted with John. If at the time of the Crucifixion John was a young man of some twenty five years, and should his death have occurred around A.D. 98, his age would then have been in the region of 90 years. Irrespective though of the date of his arrival in Ephesus, be it after A.D. 49 or A.D. 57, St John must have lived in Ephesus for many years.

There are some authorities however, who are of the opinion that there were two Johns, John the Apostle and John the Elder or Presbyter. It is the latter to whom St Polycarp refers and the one who was responsible for the Epistles of St John, although the Gospel itself is considered traditionally to be by the Apostle's own hand and written on Patmos. The tradition that John the Apostle lived for many years on the Ayasoluk Hill in Ephesus, where he died and where his Basilica commemorates his death could certainly be the truth, for it goes back to the second century which in relative terms is not so long after his death. Following the death of the Virgin in Palestine it would have been quite a logical decision for John to leave permanently for Asia Minor, as it is doubtful if by then the Apostles were together as a group in Jerusalem.

The Emperor Justinian built the Basilica of St John on the top of the Ayasoluk hill between A.D. 527 - 565. This took the place of a small fourth century church that had been built previously to mark the site of his death. A great proportion of the marble that was once the fabric of the Artemision went into the construction of the new Basilica and the grave of John was located under the central dome **(See Figure .62)**. Dust that welled up through a hole in the paving over the tomb was deemed to be sacred and to have the properties of healing, which caused the Basilica in its day to become another popular and celebrated shrine that was visited by its many pilgrims.

The gleaming white marble of the ruins testify to what was once its magnificence **(See Figure 63)**, and they echo in some small way the erstwhile splendour of the Artemision. The Temple area is only a short distance away from the Basilica, and from a nearby slope one can look across a distant and dismal marsh where its foundations once competed with the waterlogged site. Now a lone marble column and some massive blocks of stone are all that remain of the great temple to Diana **(See Figure 64)**, the finest and most beautiful monument ever built for pagan worship, and an institution that must have been an anathema to Paul. Not only was the marble pillaged to build the Basilica but much of it, together with many of its magnificent columns, was used by Justinian in the building of the Santa Sophia in Istanbul[47].

---

[47] Pausanias, and Strabo in his Geographies, describes the Temple of Artemis In the first century A.D. as being a sanctuary for debtors and the helpless, and in times of political instability, for the aristocracy. There were times when the right of asylum was systematically abused to the extent that Tiberias questioned the propriety of this function and its continuance. However the Ephesians produced various dubious reasons to safeguard the rite and prevent it from being abolished. Apollonius of Tyana wrote, 'I do condemn the people who by night and day share the home of the goddess, otherwise I should not see issuing thence thieves and robbers and kidnappers and every sort of wretch or sacrilegious rascal; for your temple is just a den of robbers.' Claudius passed an edict that dates to 44. B.C. or thereabouts, that was designed to correct some questionable practices associated with the Temple; they included the sale of priesthoods by the city authorities, the purchaser then having the right to extract large sums of money from the Temple revenues, and obviously to its detriment. This situation would have been resolved by the time Paul went to Ephesus when on the third journey around A.D. 53.

Figure 62: The Tomb of St John.

Figure 63: The Basilica of St John built by Justinian.

Figure 64: The Site of Artemision.

It would seem from Acts that after A. D. 49, some of the Apostles left Jerusalem to spread the Gospel abroad, whilst James remained to lead the churches in Judaea. Peter left Jerusalem at an unknown date to lead the church in Antioch, but it is not likely that he was there in any capacity around A.D. 53, as Paul makes no mention of him being in office when he returned from his second missionary Journey. Paul left Antioch on his third and final missionary journey around A.D. 53-54 and did not return, so that Peter could have gone down to Antioch at some time after his departure.

According to Origen, Ignatius who was born in Syria in A.D. 35, succeeded Peter as bishop of Antioch, and as it is known from Colossians IV 10, that Peter was in Rome with Mark acting as his secretary around A.D. 60-61. It is possible Peter was leading the church in Antioch whilst Paul was in Ephesus, and it is possible Peter left Antioch for Rome on the appointment of Ignatius as bishop, possibly around A.D. 58-59. That Peter was in Rome with Mark acting as his secretary is confirmed and hinted at in the final verses of his first Epistle: 'Your sister church in Babylon', Peter's apt description of Rome at that time, 'chosen together with you, sends you greetings: and so does my son Mark'. At this time Mark could have been writing his own Gospel, as has already been mentioned, using as a basis much of Peter's recollections of his years with Jesus and his fellow Apostles.

The first letter to Timothy could have been written after Paul's initial trial and acquittal in Rome, and is generally thought to have been written and sent from Laodicea. It is possible that by that time Paul had already made Timothy bishop in Ephesus, with a lot of sound advice as to how he should conduct himself when leading the Ephesian Church. Amongst other things he says in chapter 3: 'now a bishop must be beyond reproach. Married only once, temperate, sensible, respectable, hospitable, an apt teacher, not a drunkard, not violent but gentle, not quarrelsome and not a lover of money'. Picturesquely described in the Authorised Version as 'Filthy Lucre', sound advice for some today.

However the reference to Macedonia in 1 Tim. 3 is obscure and may be linked to a visit Paul could have made to Macedonia after his acquittal. This letter to Timothy is interesting even if it is not the entire work of Paul, as not only in it is the general criteria for the behaviour of the bishops of the church laid down, but it also states that they should have only one wife. It is also obvious that celibacy was not then a pre-requisite for the fathers of the church, as it later became in the Catholic tradition.

It would seem that Paul also made a visit to Crete in the company of Titus, as in Titus 1, 5 - 10 he records leaving him in Crete as bishop with much of the same advice that he proffered to Timothy in Ephesus. At that time there was a considerable community of the Jewish Diaspora on the Island of whom Paul records his very low opinion in Titus I, 10, II, 16: 'There are also many rebellious people, idle talkers and deceivers, especially those of the circumcision. They must be silenced, it was one of them, their very own prophet who said, "Cretans are always liars, vicious brutes, lazy gluttons"'. This Paul says is a true testimony and goes on to say 'They are detestable, disobedient, and unfit for any good work'. But in Titus 3, 12 he writes of his intention of spending the winter in Nicopolis and sent Artemas or Tychicus to Titus to bring him to Nicopolis.

If Timothy, as bishop of Ephesus, was now conducting the affairs of the Church on behalf of Paul, it could have been between A.D. 62-14. There are no indications as to whether he and John ever met, because by this date John could have been living in Ephesus, and if so what were his relations with Timothy and the Church. Timothy must have been bishop in Ephesus for many years for the 'Acts of St Timothy' record his martyrdom on January 22nd A.D. 97, and this by the devotees of Diana for his outspoken opposition to their festivals, occasions that inevitably ended up in a permissive 'free for all' and were known as the 'Katagogia'.

Many other well-known personalities of the ancient world had connections with Ephesus. One of the great elegiac poets, Callinus of Ephesus, lived there in 650 B.C. There was the architect Paionios who was partly responsible for the temple to Apollo at Didyma. The philosopher Heraclitus was born to a wealthy family there in 540 B.C. and was greatly revered by Socrates. The birth of the celebrated artist Parrhasius took place there some centuries later, possibly around 4 B.C. but he later in his life, went on to make a name for himself in Athens. The artist Appeles also had associations with the Ephesus, and could number Alexander the Great amongst his friends, and his portrait of Alexander with Venus was the most renowned of the age. But amongst these notable personalities one must not omit to mention Artemidorus the great geographer, who was also born in the city but in his case it occurred around 100 B.C.

In all the history of Ephesus the most spectacular and celebrated event must surely be that of the visit of Mark Antony around 41 B.C. After his victories in Asia Minor, Mark Antony dressed in the garb of the god Dionysus, headed a sumptuous procession that was accompanied by a retinue of Maenads who danced to the rattle of tambourines. With a host of prancing Bacchantes they slowly made their way from the Magnesia Gate to the Koressos gate, traversing the sacred way with much blowing of trumpets, pomp and circumstance; imitating the processions of the Artemisia. However, not long after the event, in order to recoup the extravagance of his expenses, he inflicted heavy taxation upon the citizens of Ephesus and the neighbouring towns[48].

Although Aristedes recorded Ephesus as being one of the most prosperous of cities in the first and second centuries A.D., known and regarded as the Metropolis of Asia, conditions by the third and early fourth centuries were not so happy for these were periods of political strife and various other upheavals. By the fifth and sixth centuries Christianity in this region of Asia Minor was very widespread and Ephesus saw further periods of prosperity, so much so that the City became the centre of a very large diocese, where the Dogma of the Virgin was laid down in the Ecumenical council of A.D. 431., and the venue of the later council of A.D. 449.

By the fourth century A.D. problems had arisen from the silt that the river had brought down and deposited in the basin of the once busy harbour. By the seventh century this was so disastrous that Ephesus lost its maritime trade together with its erstwhile prosperity, and many were forced to leave the city to scratch a living in the districts around the Basilica. By the end of the tenth century its trade and wealth had gone forever and the former Metropolis of

---

[48] Apart from these expenses Mark Antony had not as yet paid the money that was due to his legions and demanded that the taxes that had to be paid by Ephesus and the neighbouring cities over the next nine years should be paid within two. The region was already in dire financial straits, but after the battle of Actium Augustus took measures to improve the welfare of Asia. Mark Antony with Cleopatra later spent the winter of 33-32 B.C. in Ephesus.

Asia Minor was completely abandoned, to be totally forgotten over the ensuing decades. As the centuries unfolded the sea slowly retreated leaving the harbour nothing but a marsh of reeds. The streets and the Agoras overgrown with bushes and weeds, and the once resounding shout of 'Great is Diana of the Ephesians' but a whisper in the breeze.

Paul spent three of the winter months in Corinth, after his sudden departure from Ephesus following the riot of the silversmiths, before setting out for Jerusalem to arrive in time for the Pentecost.

As has been said previously St Paul's letter to the Romans must have been written during this period, and to be taken to them personally by Phoebe of Cenchrae. In it he mentions his intention of going to Jerusalem with the Pentecostal donations before setting out for Rome, Romans XV 25, 26, and in Romans XVI 1 - 27, he lists and sends greetings to many of those of the Church in Rome. The letter must have been dictated to Tertius, Romans XVI 22, and in 23 he mentions Gaius as being his host in Corinth.

This Gaius could have been the Gaius of Derbe mentioned by Paul in Acts XX 4 and in I Corinthians 1. 14, one who could have joined Paul at Derbe when on his second missionary journey, and one of the group who left Corinth for Asia Minor and Palestine with Paul[49]. The others being Sopater, Aristarchus, Secundus, Timothy, Tychicus, and Trophimus. Though Luke is not mentioned at this juncture he must have been with them from Nicopolis onwards, because then the 'we' passages are prominent throughout the description of a journey that must be a detailed record as to the route, and the time spent at the various ports of call.

The first plan to sail from the port of Cenchrea for Syria was a project that had to be abandoned on account of the Jews who had come out in a body to picket the port, and take their revenge for their previous humiliation under Gallia. The party then had to make their way from Corinth through Thessaloniki and the Via Egnatia to Philippi, no doubt taking with them the donations that Paul and his companions had collected from the Macedonian churches and elsewhere for Judaea. There Paul remained with Luke for the Passover, the days of unleavened bread that took place in March, whilst the others went on to Troas.

After the festival both Paul and Luke set out from Nicopolis for the house of Carpus in Troas (Acts XX 6) the passage taking five days. That Luke was with Paul seems quite apparent from Acts XX 5-6, 'but we sailed from Philippi after the days of Unleavened Bread, and in five days we joined them in Troas, where we stayed for seven days'. The fact that the time taken on this occasion between Nicopolis and Troas was five days is in contradistinction to it only taking two in the opposite direction when on the second Journey, and shows how the vagaries of the winds affected the sailing times. The whole description of Paul's stay in Philippi during the Feast of the Passover and the subsequent journey to Troas must surely be an eye witness account.

The delay of seven days at Troas could have been due to the lack of a suitable boat to take them on to Miletus, for it would seem that Paul wished to avoid any vessel that might put in at Ephesus. In view of the circumstances that provoked his premature departure there is little to

---

49 Hemer, Book of Acts, has suggested that this could be an error in translation and that the Gaius of Derbe could be a Gaius from Doberus, a town in Macedonia.

wonder at his desire not to return. The detailed description of the upper room where Paul preached his lengthy sermon, the day before they were due to sail, was in the house of Carpus where those of the Church in Troas gathered.

Carpus must have been a man of some means to have lived in a house of three stories, for Luke records Eutychus having fallen from the third loft. The meagre details of the building recorded by Luke do not fit in with the life of those who dwelt in the apartment blocks that had shops on the ground floors. These were generally occupied by the less well to do and were a part of life in Rome, North Africa, and many other Roman cities. There were however, other blocks that were more exclusive and desirable from a residential point of view, and some can be seen in Ostia in a very good state of preservation, notably those known as the 'garden flats'. Others can be seen in Pompeii where their owners, having fallen on hard times, have had to convert their ground floors into shops or fullers and dye works.

The description of the upper room is fascinating for it was obviously large, possibly with no ceiling but rafters, and having a number of big windows with walls and sills which were deep enough to sit on (Acts XX 8, 9). With Paul's very lengthy, and obviously tedious sermon, together with the warm night the atmosphere in the room must have been stuffy. All this would have been enough to make Eutychus fall asleep and concuss himself by falling out of the wide open window[50].

That Eutychus had not seriously hurt himself when he fell must have been due to the fact that he was asleep and consequently very relaxed. It also leads one to suspect that the house was not in that part of the town where he could have fallen onto a hard surface, such as the paving of a street. Had this been the case and having fallen from a considerable height he would have sustained far more serious injuries. Therefore the house of Carpus could have been situated in a garden, or on the outskirts of Troas where the surrounding ground was softer: Luke could have been with Paul when he went down to see if Eutychus had sustained any serious injury for the 'we' passages recur in verses 13, 14, 15., and Paul's decision to stay behind in Troas to join them later in Assos could have been due to his immediate concern for the welfare of Eutychus, and the fact that he was well acquainted with the paved road to Assos and also the time that it would take him to cover the distance of some twenty to thirty miles possibly by horse[51].

Luke gives the sailing time between Assos and Miletus as amounting to about four days, details that must surely be accurate and a record from one who was on the journey as the map shows the distances between Mitylene and Chios, and Chios and Samos, as being practically equal. Paul must have gone aboard at Assos at some time in the late afternoon to join the others for it is only a short distance from Assos to Mitylene where they anchored for the night, and to go on to Chios the next day where they again spent the night in the harbour. Navigation

---

[50] The ruins of Troas are indicative of a Roman influence. From the description in Acts 20, 10—11, where Paul went down to Eutychus, the house of Carpus could have been a block of flats with a communal stair way, as can be seen in Ostia. If so Carpus would have occupied the third floor, but it is not known if this happened to be the top floor of the building. If the house of Carpus was in fact a block of flats it is possible that he owned the whole block and rented out the other apartments.

[51] Before reaching Assos itself Paul would have approached the city from the North West by the street of tombs that in some cases were each hewn out of blocks of granite of huge dimensions that came from nearby Mount Ida. The stone was known as 'Lapis Assius' that gave rise to the name 'Sarcophagus'. Judging from the ruins of Assos that included a fine gate to the city, a theatre with views over the sea to Lesbos, and a citadel on the summit of a cliff of granite, the City had at one time been one of some note.

at night for these coastal vessels was not practicable unless there was a full moon with a clear sky. From the fact that they put into harbour each night it could be inferred that the moon was not favourable, and Luke further remarks that the sailing time for each of these journeys was that of a day only. In addition he mentions that they put in to Trogillium before reaching Miletus, a remark that must be another accurate detail but one that appears only in the King James Version of Acts.

Trogillium was located on the headland of Mount Mycale, today's Samsun Dag, and had what must have been a sizeable roadstead rather than a large harbour, where pilgrims could land in order to visit one of the most revered and sacred of shrines to Poseidon, and by sea it was only a short course from Samos on the way to Miletus. The shrine was the focus for the great Pan Ionic festivals, one of the most important events in the calendar of the Ionic league of twelve cities that included Ephesus, Priene and Samos. Vessels that plied this route put into Trogillium as a matter of course to enable their crews to go ashore and make sacrifice at Poseidon's altar. From Acts XX 15 it would seem that a night was spent at this roadstead before going on to Miletus the next day. It is interesting that here Paul makes no reference as to the reason why they tarried. The reason was common knowledge at that time and required no explanation. Paul was merely recording that they had complied with the tradition.

Miletus had Hellenistic traditions that went back to the XIth century B.C., and could possibly have had more of an intellectual background when compared with that of Ephesus. Many erudite and able personalities came from Miletus, amongst them the philosophers Thales and Anaximenes, the historian and geographer Hercatius[52]. Apart from these intellectuals there was Aspasia, the daughter of a well to do and prominent family who became the mistress of Pericles for Pericles, who had the inspiration and the expertise to build the Parthenon in Athens also had the wit to appreciate Aspasia. Not only was she beautiful, she was also highly intelligent and for this reason was not in any way popular with the females of the Athenian Aristocracy.

Hippodamus, the father of town planning, was also a native of Miletus whose fame spread across the ages. His influence was instrumental in the layout of many of the Hellenistic cities of the VIth and Vth centuries B.C. First amongst them being that of Priene, once another busy port dating from the IV century B.C., but here again the sea has gone back to such an extent that the ancient town might never have been on the coast. Its ruins on the steep hillside now overlook the Meander River that winds its sluggish way across the plain below. The precepts of Hippodamus were followed in many of the cities of the later Roman Empire, a fine example being Timgad a city that Trajan founded In North Africa in A.D. 101, for the veterans of his legions, and this some forty years only after the death of Paul. The principles of Hippodamus are still applicable for they are reflected in the layout of New York.

Miletus was also a member of the Ionian Confederacy of Cities and one of the great trading centres of Asia Minor, being fortunate in its four harbours and prosperous enough to

---

[52] Miletus was famed for its intellectuals. Thales was the first to inscribe a right angled triangle in a circle, to calculate the height of the Pyramids of Egypt by comparing their shadow at the time of day when a man's shadow was equal to his height, and he thanked God that he was human and not an animal, a man and not a woman, a Greek and not a Barbarian. Anaximander was the first to map the world, howbeit grossly inaccurate today, and Hecataeus wrote a geography and is known for his remark 'I write what appears to be true, for the many tales of the Greeks are ridiculous'.

found several colonies, of which the most notable was Trebizond on the Black Sea coast. The city itself had two fine Agoras, the Northern **(See Figure 65)** and the Southern, and not least a splendid Theatre, which was built into the side of a hill that backed on to the main harbour. At the time this could have seated five thousand people but was enlarged during the Hadrianic period to become a massive and imposing structure that dominated the sea shore, an impressive landmark for shipping when approaching the harbour basins. Here a prestigious seat was reserved for the Emperor, or his representative, in the centre of the auditorium, and of the four columns that once held the canopy to shelter its occupant from the sun two of them to this day are still in situ and intact **(See Figure 66)**.

Two inscriptions have been found in the Theatre. One related to the Jewish community and inscribed on one of the Theatre seats reads 'Jews who are devout worshippers'. An abrupt inscription that could refer to the Jews themselves, or to 'Jews and God Fearers', this could intimate that the seats in this area were reserved for the Jewish community. The Synagogue that was situated at the end of the Harbour Stoa to overlook the Harbour Monument, was moreover one of some import having had a nave and two aisles reminiscent of a Basilica, the Jewish faction in Miletus must have been one of some moment. Paul makes no mention of the Jews of Miletus referring only to those of the Church who came down from Ephesus to see him.

A third inscription refers to an episode connected with the Theatre alterations and is concerned with the completion of certain vaults and arches. It is on the back wall of the Theatre by an upper flight of steps and is the answer given by the local Oracle to a query posed by the workmen engaged on the project. The priests of the Oracle officiated in the Temple to Apollo Delphinos situated adjacent to the Harbour Gateway, and it would seem that the workmen engaged on these particular alterations were under the jurisdiction of one of the Temple priests, one who had been 'uncivil' enough to die before the work had been completed. They then consulted the oracle as to whether they should continue with the original plans, their answer being inscribed on the Theatre wall for posterity[53].

The Southern was the larger of the two Agoras, having all four sides surrounded by colonnades of the Doric order. This was the commercial centre of Miletus and had a series of thirty nine pairs of shops in its Eastern Stoa, so arranged and built back to back that half of them looked onto the Agora square. These were apart from a further series of nineteen shops situated at the southernmost aspect. The complex as it then stood dated to the Hellenistic period and was some two hundred years old when Paul visited Miletus. From here a wide main street, known as the Processional Road, led south from the Northern gate of the Agora to another splendid gate that gave onto the marble quays of the Lion Harbour, and had sixteen columns of the Doric order in its overall design.

---

[53] This inscription is to be seen in the fifth row, another in the third row reserves the seating for the 'goldsmiths of the Blues' relating to the factions of the Blues arid the Greens of Byzantium.

Acts 20. 15-16 records Paul's decision not to break his journey at Ephesus. This has caused some discussion but it is likely that he wanted to reach Jerusalem with the minimum of delay. In view of his hurried departure from Ephesus, after the riot of the silversmiths, he could have decided that going back might involve him in circumstances that would be difficult to resolve in a hurry.

Apparently the workmen were not slaves but artisans on piece work who, due to their inefficiency, could not make it pay. The advice given to them by the Oracle in hexameter verse was, 'Get someone to teach you how to work economically by employing proper building methods and sacrifice to Athena and Heracles'. It would seem that they followed this excellent advice. See George E. Bean, Aegean Turkey.

The Lion Harbour in the Bay of Lions was the largest and most important of the four that served Miletus, and so called for it could be protected from impending hostile attack by slinging a heavy chain from the mouths of two marble lions situated on either side of the harbour entrance. But here again the sea has gone back to such an extent, as at Ephesus and likewise at Priene, that the island of Lade where the Persians in 499 B.C. completely destroyed the Ionian fleet by fire, is today but an isolated hill rising proud of the surrounding landscape. The once busy harbour now in its pervading silence is but another marsh to be picked over by storks and other water birds, watched only by the marble lions miraculously still in situ, but somewhat pathetic with their bellies wallowing in the mud **(See Figure 67)**.

Another lengthy Stoa with a colonnade of sixty four columns of the Doric order was also built in the Hellenistic period to separate the harbour facilities from the city precincts, and this sheltered a further series of thirty shops. The colonnade terminated with the Synagogue building and the very open plan of the public lavatories that accommodated about forty people at a time - the mind boggles! In the early Greek and Roman periods there appears to have been little discrimination between the sexes for it was left to the Emperor Hadrian to raise the tenets of decency as far as these essentially public institutions were concerned. In his endeavour to curb much of the unsuitable behaviour that frequently occurred in such establishments he brought in a decree that did not permit mixed bathing in the public baths, an edict that could well have extended to the other facilities.

A small square colonnaded market, also having shops, backed on to the Harbour Stoa, as did the shorter wall of the Northern Agora. The longer side of this Northern Agora faced on to the broad pavements of the Processional Road some twenty eight metres wide and some hundred metres long, the pavements themselves being about six metres. This was the fashionable part of Miletus which must have seen a continual throng of people passing up and down, a district that was enhanced with the Baths that Vergilius Capito built as a donation to the city amenities. Capito was appointed the Procurator of Asia Minor by Claudius so that these Baths must have been in use for only a short period before Paul's visit. Leading off the Processional way were the Civic Offices, the Gymnasium, the Temples, and the large ornate Nymphaeum built in the second century A.D., buildings that Paul would not have seen, nor would he have seen the well preserved Baths that Faustina, the wife of the Emperor Marcus Aurelius, built at a later date. Faustina was noted for being adept at spending other people's money.

As has already been mentioned the important Temple to Apollo Delphinos, the Delphinion, was situated by the harbour gate. It too was built in the Hellenistic period being surrounded by Doric colonnades that were converted in the Roman period to the Corinthian order. Apollo was the revered deity of the Milesians who considered the dolphin sacred to the god and regarded both as the protectors of sailors and shipping. The Temple looked across to a large circular monument erected by Augustus in the inner anchorage of the Lion Harbour, this to commemorate his defeat of Antony and Cleopatra in 31 B.C. at the battle of Actium.

Figure 65: The Agora at Miletus.

Figure 66: The Theatre at Miletus.

Figure 67: One of the two Lions still in situ at the entrance to the Lion Harbour at Miletus. A chain was slung from their mouths to protect the Harbour when Miletus was threatened from the sea.

The Temple priests, or prophets, were often the scions of upper class Patrician families who were wholly dedicated to the Temple ritual, but in some cases the interpretation of the oracle rested with the Thespode, a life appointment. The Temples to Apollo that gave oracular answers to the questions posed by all and sundry were an inherent part of Pagan life. The most spectacular and renowned being those at Delphi, Claros, and Didyma, and after the death of Paul they continued on for centuries. It would be interesting to know how he viewed their activities.

It must have been here on this marble quay of the Lion Harbour where Paul and his party landed **(See Figure 68)**. Familiar to them would have been the Streets, the Temples, the Agoras and the various other public monuments of Hellenistic Miletus, and it must have been here too where he met those of the Ephesian Church who had come to Miletus for their final meeting and to say farewell. St Luke harrowingly and graphically describes the scene of their departure in Acts XX l7 - 36, how Paul before they embarked, warned those from Ephesus that he would not be seeing them again, abjuring them not to listen to adverse teaching, and pointing out that he had not in the past been beholden to anyone for material support. By this time Paul must have been sixty years of age, but what of St John. If he was now resident in Ephesus, and it would have been around A.D. 58, he was obviously not with those of the Church who had come down to Miletus to say farewell.

It is recorded in Acts XXI 1, that after leaving Miletus they landed at Cos. The distance from Miletus to Cos is forty nautical miles due South, the prevalent wind in this region being normally to the north - west, and the duration of the voyage being in the region of about six hours. The night was spent in the harbour at Cos in order to sail on to Rhodes the following day, and from there to Patara on the south coast of Asia Minor to change ship, for what no doubt was a larger vessel to take them on to Tyre and Ptolemais, the Acre of today.

The port of Patara was the finest on the Lycian coast and had, in common with many of the major Roman harbours, a lighthouse that stood on the hill behind the harbour installations. The city was the seat of the Roman governor of Lycia and the centre for the judicial administration of the Province, it was also known for its Temple to Apollo and too, in common with Didym and Miletus was renowned for its oracles. Disappointingly very little remains of Patara today, apart from the huge granary that was built by Hadrian, no doubt as a result of the visit he made when on his State tour of Asia Minor and the fine gate that Mettius Modestus donated to the city when Governor in A.D. 100, one that he decorated with the six portrait busts of his family to ensure that the following generations of Patarans would recognise his munificence **(See Figures 69, 70 and 71)**.

The vast beach is now a major tourist attraction and the village has many little pensions. The sands of time have almost obliterated the city ruins, to the extent that the theatre, on the landward side of the hill that dominates the harbour, has been partially engulfed by their drifts and dunes. Of the harbour practically nothing remains.

Figure 68: The Lion Harbour at Miletus.

Figure 69: The Arch of Modestus at Patara.

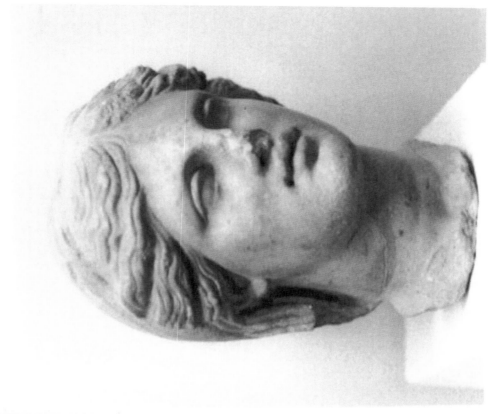

Figure 70: Two of five Portrait Busts from Ephesus that date to the first centuries A. D.

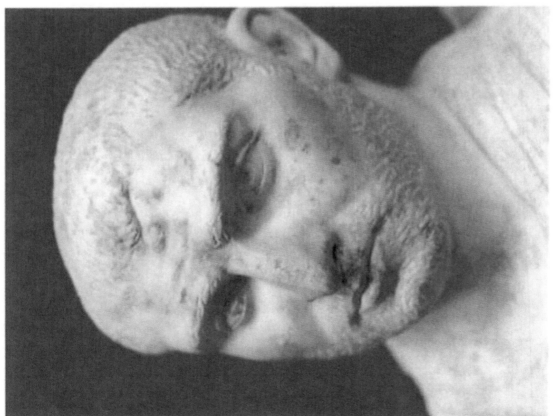

Figure 71: Two further Busts from Ephesus that date to the first centuries A.D.

The vast beach is now a major tourist attraction and the village has many little pensions. The sands of time have almost obliterated the city ruins, to the extent that the theatre, on the landward side of the hill that dominates the harbour, has been partially engulfed by their drifts and dunes. Of the harbour practically nothing remains.[54]

St Nicholas was born in Patara during the latter part of the third century A.D. to become the original Father Christmas and the well-loved Bishop of Myra, but in common with many other prelates of the Christian church his good works did not save him from martyrdom under the persecutions of Diocletian. A benevolent man who was particularly fond of children he was chosen, incongruous as it may seem, to be the Patron Saint of Pawnbrokers. An unusual profession to have such a spirit to ensure their welfare, and it came about as the result of a persistent legend that involved St Nicholas with a family of the nobility of Patara. Through undisclosed misfortune the noble father of this family lost all his wealth and inheritance, to the extent that he was left with insufficient means to provide his daughters with the dowries deemed necessary for them to marry into their accustomed elevated stratum of society.

Knowing his problems St Nicholas, incognito one night, threw three bags of gold through the impoverished nobleman's bedroom window. It is not recorded from where St Nicholas had obtained this treasure, not, one hopes, from church funds, but it did provide sufficient capital for his needs. These three bags of gold are represented in early icons as three golden apples, and hence the three golden balls of the pawnbrokers' sign.

Patara remained a busy and flourishing port for many centuries after Paul's visit, which in any event must have been somewhat brief for he makes no reference to any Christian community that might have been there at the time. From Patara they sailed on to Tyre where the ship discharged its cargoes, and they stayed there for seven days amongst those of the church who warned Paul not to go up to Jerusalem[55]. After the seven days they took a ship bound for Ptolemais, today's Acre, on the coast of Palestine, and from here they covered the last forty miles to Caesarea Maritima, taking with them the contributions that had been collected for the Jerusalem Church. They lodged there with Philip the Evangelist who was one of the seven first deacons of the Church, and the same who was with Peter and John in Samaria and responsible for the baptism of the Ethiopian Eunuch. The same Philip who had four daughters who lived an exemplary life and were credited with the power of prophesy, and one who has been confused in early traditions with the Apostle Philip who was martyred in Hierapolis in A.D. 80.

The prophet Agabus, who forecast the great famine that had not long since afflicted the whole of Judaea, came down from Jerusalem in an endeavour to persuade Paul not to go

---

[54] Hippocrates was born on Cos and the Island was also famed for its textiles and its wines. Strabo considered the city of Cos to be particularly beautiful.

Ancient Rhodes was built by Hippodamus of Miletus, and later famed for its Colossus that was destroyed as the result of an earthquake. Strabo saw the ruins.

Patara was at one time the port for Xanthos that lay some miles inland on the river Xanthos. The magnificent funerary Temple of the Nereids, built in Xanthos in 400.B.C, in the Ionic tradition, is now in the British Museum. The Nereids were water nymphs, the daughters of Cronus, and they later featured in Roman funerary art as depictions of the spirit of the deceased. Today they are featured on the doors of Orvieto Cathedral.

[55] From previous visits it is possible that Paul was acquainted with the Christians of Tyre.

further and risk confrontation with the Sanhedrin. But Paul's determination to personally take to the Apostles the contributions from the churches of Archaia and Macedonia was not to be altered.

Acts XXI 15, tells that the journey to Jerusalem was by carriage and that Mnason of Cyprus gave them lodging there, and here one speculates on the circumstances regarding the sister of Paul. She must then have been living in Jerusalem if still alive, so Paul could well have lodged with her, unless by so doing he was inflicting her with a degree of social embarrassment. It is evident though that family relations must have been cordial for her son, Paul's nephew, to have come to his help when he was again under threat from the Jews (Acts XXIII 16).

Paul and the Pentecostal donations were cordially welcomed by the Jerusalem Church, it would have been a little churlish if it had not been so, but the welcome became more restrained when they later met the Apostles. Luke must have been at the meeting for the word 'us' appears in Acts XXI, 18: 'And the day following Paul went in with us unto James, who was now the head of the Church, and all the elders[56] were present'. But does the word 'elders' refer to all the original Apostles, for by this time, around A.D. 58, John could have been in Ephesus and Peter either Bishop in Antioch or in Rome with Mark. By this time too it is very doubtful if the Virgin was still alive for by then she could have been about eighty years of age.

Whatever the situation the question of the circumcision of the Gentiles still appears to have been a matter of dissension (verses 21-22). The Apostles making it clear to Paul that his views on the subject were still not condoned by the Apostolic Church, though tolerated. In order to demonstrate his own sincerity to them and to the Law as a Jew, he was instructed to morally cleanse himself in the Temple in the company of four other individuals under a vow, who had also shaved their heads preparatory to their ritual purification. Furthermore, he was required to pay into the Temple funds their incurred expenses as well as his own[57].

On several occasions, as at Miletus, Paul has been careful to point out that he relied on his own hands for his welfare and had accepted little in the way of donations for his support. However, there were times when opportunities for work were few, especially during his journeys by sea as his expenses and keep had still to be met. This gives rise to speculations as to what were his actual resources; the improvement in his circumstances seems to have occurred towards the end of his stay in Ephesus.

---

[56] The elders of the Church would have been the Presbyters.

[57] Within the Jerusalem Church there was a faction of sectarian Pharisees whose rigid and uncompromising views could also have been held by some of the Presbyters. They had a convicted antipathy to Paul and his Gentile converts, whom they considered had flouted the Jewish traditions by not observing the Law in its entirety and not accepting Circumcision for this they blamed and heartily disliked Paul for his teaching and what they regarded as his repudiation of much of Judaism. This faction is reflected in Gal. 2 11-12, when Peter came down to Antioch to see Paul. 'for until certain people came from James, he used to eat with the Gentiles. But after they came, he drew back and kept himself separate for fear of the circumcision faction'; this in spite of the fact that the Jerusalem Church had previously decided and stipulated that some of the observances of the Law were not obligatory for the converted Gentiles Many of the Jews of the Apostolic Church in Jerusalem, in spite of James who tried to keep the balance, were mostly influenced by this sectarian faction in their dislike of Paul and the Gentile side of the Church.

In an effort to allay the hostility of those of the church, including those Presbyters who had doubts about Paul's sincerity, the assembly, possibly at the instigation of James, advised him to demonstrate his allegiance to the Pharisaic traditions by taking these four Azarite Christians to the Temple for the termination of their vow, and to pay the expenses involved Acts. 21 23-24. This took place on the day after the meeting, the day of the Feast of the Pentecost. Those terminating a vow had to go to the Temple with their expensive ritual offerings and have their hair cut off and burnt on the altar, Acts, 21, 26. (W.J Conybeare, J.S. Howson. Life of St. Paul).

When he arrived in Ephesus he must, in the first place, have joined Aquila and Priscilla to help in their work as he had in Corinth, deriving some income from this employment whilst at the same time preaching in the Synagogue to further his ministry. Later he was able to rent the school room from Tyrannus for his teaching. Latterly amongst his friends there were a number of Asiarchs who must have been wealthy enough to keep up their position in Ephesian society (Acts. XIX 31) and when he arrived in Rome it is recorded that 'he lived in his own hired house'. In Jerusalem the Apostles required him to pay the ritual expenses of those who did penance with him in the Temple, but in Jerusalem the Apostles, even though they assiduously attended the Temple rituals, in which respect James was particularly devout, were still at loggerheads with the Sadducees, the Pharisees, and the Sanhedrin. Knowing that Paul could easily attract Jewish hostility for his teaching he was advised by the Church to do penance in the Temple with the Nazarite Christians, but this did nothing to avert their anger.

The outer court of the Temple was open to any be they Roman, Gentile or otherwise, and was known as the Court of the Gentiles[58]. Anyone but a Jew to proceed further was to invite the penalty of an instant death, for the inner courts and the Sanctuary which alone was open to the High Priest, were the jealously guarded prerogatives of the Jews themselves. Paul was quite entitled to be in the Court of the Gentiles with Trophimus, one of his Ephesian converts. But the intense dislike that his reputation had engendered was such that when the Asian Jews, notably those from Ephesus, who had also come to Jerusalem as he had done for the Pentecost, saw him in the Temple they brought about a riot accusing him of defiling the precincts by bringing Trophemus, a Greek, with him having only previously recognised Paul with Trophemus in the city.

In the first century A.D., the Antonia fortress was occupied by the troops of the Legionis X Fretensis stationed in Judaea **(See Figure 72)**, and was so designed that they could overlook the Temple area, thus an eye could be kept on the activities of those in the Temple courts. At the least hint of an uprising the Temple precincts could be occupied and any disturbance put down before it escalated out of hand. The fracas that centred on the Jews attacking Paul in the Temple area ceased only when troops from the Antonia arrived to defuse the situation and take him into custody. Even then the Jews followed him in a vociferous mob and would not disperse when Paul endeavoured to conduct his defence.

The present Convent of the Sisters of Our lady of Zion is now supposedly on the site of the ancient fortress and has in its basement the 'Gabbatha', that could be the Roman pavement mentioned in John XIX, and in it can still be seen the various carved out chequer boards for the games of chance. However, there is some dispute as to the authenticity of the site, but even so it must date from the time of Pilate and the trial of Jesus. A comprehensive view of the entire Temple area as it is today can be seen from the Convent's roof, and this could be very similar to that seen by the troops when monitoring the activities of those in the Temple courts. The original fortress was rebuilt by Herod and could be reached by a flight of steps.

---

[58] This was the Outer Court that had roofed colonnades and was approached through four gates that included the Porch of Solomon, and the Shushan Gate that could have been 'The Beautiful Gate'. It was in this Court and possibly under the colonnades, where the vendors of doves did business and the money-changers had their tables. Matt, 21,13. This Court led on to raised terraces reached by flights of steps but otherwise enclosed by low stone barricades. These were the 'Courts of Israel' and of 'The Priests' that gave onto a higher terrace and the Temple itself. This contained the rooms of the Holy Place and the Holy of Holies that housed the ritual elements, The Table of Shew-bread, the Altar of Incense, The Minorah or the Five branched Candlestick and finally 'The Ark of the Covenant'.

Figure 72: The Tablet of the Tenth Legion still in situ in the ruins of their barracks by the Jaffa Gate in Jerusalem.

These steps are mentioned in Acts 21, 35,40: 'When Paul came to the steps, the violence of the mob was so great that he had to be carried by the soldiers', and in Acts 40: 'Paul stood on the steps and motioned the people for silence, and when there was a great hush, he addressed them in the Hebrew language'. The Antonia also contained luxurious apartments, cloisters, baths, and spacious courtyards that included the accommodation for a cohort of troops with their arsenal.

One very interesting reference to an historical fact occurs in Acts XXI 38, where Claudius Lysias, the Tribune and overall commander in Jerusalem, mistakes Paul for the Egyptian false prophet. This was a serious incident that must have taken place shortly before Paul arrived in Jerusalem and one that has not only been recorded by Josephus but also by Eusebius. An Egyptian posing as a seer came to Palestine with the sole intent of capturing Jerusalem, and to this effect he mustered a following of thousands of individuals. Eusebius gives a figure of thirty thousand but Acts reduces it to four, and they marched on Jerusalem from the Mount of Olives. Felix however, had had previous warning of his intentions and routed them outside the city walls killing and capturing the great majority, but the Egyptian himself escaped. For Paul to have been mistaken for a false prophet, and an Egyptian was an insult not to be tolerated, and one that led him to vigorously deny the charge with his stated credentials of being a Jew from Tarsus in Cilicia, no mean 'City' as in the Authorised version.

The recorded account in Acts of the riot in the Temple precincts is again very graphic and gives the impression that it could well have been witnessed by Luke[59], relating as it does in some detail the confrontation that took place on the following day between Paul, the Sadducees, the Pharisees, and the Sanhedrin, the latter having been summoned to the fortress by Claudius Lysias to lay their charges against Paul. The meeting is recorded as having ended in chaos when Paul was once more taken into protective custody, preparatory to being bound and flogged with the flagrum whilst under interrogation. This was normal Roman procedure to which those suspected of felony, or a serious crime such as inciting a riot, were subjected.

It is at this juncture in Acts 22 & 25 where Paul spreads consternation, but when they had tied him up with thongs Paul said to the centurion who was standing by, 'is it legal for you to flog a Roman citizen who is un-condemned'. On further interrogation by the Tribune himself it transpired that Paul's hereditary Roman citizenship was more important than his own, the Tribune having purchased his for a sum of money. This put Claudius Lysias, the Tribune, at a disadvantage having subjected a Roman of superior standing to himself regarding his citizenship, to illegal custodial treatment that would merit a severe reprimand should Paul lodge a complaint. Paul is then released from his chains and his situation eased to the extent that he is allowed to appear before the chief priests and the council to state his case: only to be taken again into protective custody having caused further dissension between the Pharisees and the Sadducees over the question of the resurrection of the dead, the Pharisees acknowledging the premise whilst the Sadducees did not.

---

[59] The hatred of the Jews for the Roman administration was such that riots often occurred at the time of religious Festival when tempers were short.

It then comes to the ears of Paul's nephew, described as a young man, that the Jews have set a plot to ambush and kill Paul. This is the only record in the New Testament of his nephew's existence and, according to Sir William Ramsay, a young man can be a 'Biblical' term indicating any age between twenty and forty years. However, some have suggested that his nephew could have been a youth which would seem to have been unlikely. As has been said Paul could possibly by this time have been sixty years of age which would indicate his sister being considerably younger. Had his nephew been in his late twenties it would still have meant a considerable gap between the ages of Paul and his sister.

At this juncture it seems that Paul was not under any close confinement in the Antonia but able to see and hear about the plot from his nephew in confidence, to the extent that he could call a centurion to take his nephew to the Tribune to warn him of the circumstances of the proposed ambush (Acts 23, 17-22). The fact that his nephew found out about the Sanhedrin's conspiracy to kill Paul has caused some to suggest that the possible family connections of Paul's sister might have had some connection with that body, but family loyalty was such that he informed Claudius Lycias of the Sanhedrin's intentions. It is also very noticeable that the Apostles and the Jerusalem Church appear to have given Paul little support during this crisis, and in his later predicaments; possibly considering that by doing so they would draw unwelcome attention to their cause and do little to help the Apostolic Church in Jerusalem.

As far as Claudius Lysias was concerned Paul, being a Roman citizen whose rights could not be violated, was now a distinct liability to his peace of mind and to the peace in Jerusalem. So to rid himself of the situation he immediately arranged for two centurions to escort Paul with horses and an armed guard of two hundred soldiers, seventy horsemen, and two hundred spearmen to go down through the hills by night to Antipas, today's Ras-El-Ain, a town some thirty five miles from Jerusalem. By now the hills had given way to the plain where the going was less hazardous, and here the guard returned to Jerusalem leaving Paul to be escorted onwards by the cavalry with the letter from Lycias to Antonius Felix, the Procurator of Judaea. It is obvious in view of the size of the escort that Claudius Lysias was taking no chances with Paul's safety, and his determination to deliver him to Caesarea without mishap. Conditions in Judaea at the time were explosive and Paul's reputation such that an ambush in the hills could not be overlooked, and hence the sudden decision to move him immediately by night. Though there is no mention of Luke being with Paul on the journey to Caesarea, the narration of events after his arrival is again very detailed. This together with the fact that his friends are allowed by Felix to visit him whilst he is technically under arrest, Acts XXV 23 points very much to the likelihood that those who went with him to Jerusalem left at some time or other to support him in Caesarea.

The letter from Claudius Lysias to Felix is in itself a little masterpiece in putting himself in the best possible light:

'Claudius Lycias to his Excellency the governor Felix, greetings. This man was seized by the Jews and was about to be killed by them, but when I had learned that he was a Roman citizen I came with a guard and rescued him. Since I wanted to know the charge for which they accused him, I had him brought to their council. I found that he was accused concerning questions of their law, but was charged with nothing deserving death or imprisonment'.

Claudius Lycias being in a difficult position regarding his maltreatment of Paul embarked on a damage limitation exercise. He omitted to mention that he firstly mistook Paul for an Egyptian agitator, and was prepared to flog him out of hand before he learnt of his true status, and because of Paul the Jews were hatching a further plot that could disrupt the peace in Jerusalem. Claudius Lysias deemed it expedient to shift the whole problem down to Caesarea and on to the shoulders of Felix, in so doing he also managed to portray himself as having handled the situation with commendable diplomacy and tact.

Felix does not figure too well in the affair either, and this is not surprising for Tacitus on one occasion described him as being arrogant, used to acting in a regal manner, cruel in the extreme and lustful, not exactly a eulogistic description of his character[60]. His brother Pallas gained his freedom to subsequently amass great wealth and influence when Claudius was Emperor, and it was he who paved the way for Felix to become the Procurator of Judaea in A.D. 52. By the time Paul arrived with his escort at Herod's Palace in Caesarea it had been taken over by the Romans as the official residence of the Procurator, and Felix had been in office living there for some four years or more.

The first wife Felix had was the granddaughter of Antony and Cleopatra but now he was married to Drusilla, the young sister of Agrippa 1, which demonstrates that many who had a family background of freed slaves did well for themselves. This was certainly the case as far as Felix was concerned for he was now moving in the most rarefied of circles. The Sanhedrin in Jerusalem were persistent, if nothing else, in their efforts to lay hands on Paul. Within five days of his arrival in Caesarea the high priest Ananias, who had been appointed by Herod to that office in A.D. 48, together with Tertullus and other notables of the Sanhedrin, arrived hot foot from Jerusalem in an effort to persuade Felix to hand him over to them for trial. The Jews had hired in Tertullus, an able prosecutor, who endeavoured to strip the charges against Paul of their religious context, and present them more with a political bias in that he was a threat to the stability of the civic administration, and if proved could merit a heavy sentence even death. The Indictment is recorded in Acts. 24.5: 'We have found this man a pestilential fellow, an agitator among the Jews throughout the world, and a ringleader of the sect of the Nazarenes. He even tried to profane the Temple, and so we seized him'. However Felix, because of Paul's defence in proving that these charges could only be brought by the Asian Jews who were not represented, and that the only charges against him could be of a disputed theological nature, and no doubt taking into account the fact that Paul was a Roman citizen, shelved the issue on the excuse that Lysias was not present to give his account of the episode[61].

---

[60] Tacitus has described his character thus 'in the practice of all kinds of lust and cruelty he exercised the power of a king with the temper of a slave'.

[61] In his defence Paul also stated that only twelve days had elapsed since leaving the house of Phillip the Evangelist and his hearing before Felix at the Instigation of the Jews. The possible sequence has been suggested by Wieseler: Day 1. Departure from the house of Phillip in Caesarea; 2. Arrival in Jerusalem; 3. Meeting of the Elders; 4. Arrest in the Temple on the day of Pentecost; 5. Trial before the Sanhedrin. 6. Departure from Jerusalem for Caesarea under guard at night; 7. Arrival in Caesarea; 8. On the twelfth day Ananias left Jerusalem for Caesarea to be present at Paul's trial before Felix on the thirteenth day.

Paul was now being held in custody under the guard of a centurion (Acts. 24.23), who was instructed by Felix to allow him some liberty. It was a few days after the hearing when Drusilla expressed a wish to see Paul and so he was brought before them. Felix showed little umbrage when Paul took him to task for his way of life, but when Paul discussed justice, self-control, and the coming Judgement, Felix became frightened and said, 'go away for the present; when I have an opportunity I will send for you'(**Acts 24. 25**). It was the first of several meetings and not in the character for Felix to have shown such affability without some very good reason, and this becomes clearly apparent in his hope that Paul would proffer some monetary consideration for his release. When after two years Felix was recalled to Rome and it was very obvious that no such bribe was forthcoming, and furthermore was not likely to be proffered, he confined Paul to prison to await the arrival of Festus, his successor, and left him to deal with the problem.

Nemesis had recently caught up with Felix for his deplorable handling of a full scale riot in Caesarea that had involved the Syrians and the Jews, a situation where many of the Jews had lost their lives with the destruction of their property. The event gave rise to serious political repercussions in Rome that ended in the immediate recall of Felix to answer charges of disgraceful incompetence. His eventual fate is not known, though it is thought that Drusilla and her son lost their lives in Pompeii when Vesuvius obliterated the city in A.D. 79[62].

It was a little while before Festus, the new procurator of Judaea arrived to take up his appointment in Caesarea, but within three days he went to Jerusalem to be greeted by the High Priest and the Jews who then requested he send Paul to them for trial, but with the intention of having him killed in an ambush on the way. Festus was not so gullible, and arranged for the Jews to bring their complaints before him in Caesarea, where their treason charges were so ridiculous he realised the root causes lay in religious disputes, and suggested that Paul should appear before their court in Jerusalem under his supervision. It was then that Paul, realizing what the inevitable outcome would be, appealed as was his right to go before Caesar in Rome. It was Festus who was now in an unhappy position. The appeal had to be granted in accordance with Roman Law and documents prepared concerning the nature of Paul's indictment but, revolving as it did around a dispute over Jewish doctrine brought by the Jews themselves, it was of little import not being classed by the Romans as a criminal offence. The dilemma of Festus is well described in Acts XXV 25-27 and finally summed up when he says 'For it seemeth to me unreasonable to send a prisoner and not withal to signify the crimes laid against him'[63].

---

[62] From Acts. 24. 23. it appears that Paul was lodged in Herod's Palace, the Praetorium, under the guard of the Centurion who had brought him from Antipatris to Caesarea. Normally prisoners under the guard of a centurion were chained to them by the right band. However Acts 23. records Felix instructing the centurion 'to keep him in custody, but, to let him have some liberty and not prevent his friends from taking care of his needs'. No doubt in these circumstances Paul would have had the help of Luke with those from Jerusalem, from Phillip the Evangelist and his household, and from the other Christians of Caesarea. It is possible too that in this case Paul was not chained the whole time.

Albinus succeeded Festus as procurator of Judaea and is said to have made a habit of giving prisoners their freedom in return for a bribe (Josephus Antiquities).

In this case Paul would have been in chains being of no further use to Felix.

[63] During the two years of Paul's detention in Caesarea the political climate under the maladministration of Felix had gone from bad to worse. There were periods of unrest in Caesarea itself that reflected the mood of the people.

When Agrippa with Berenice arrived in Caesarea to welcome Festus in his new appointment Festus took the opportunity to discuss the problem of Paul. Agrippa was the great grandson of Herod the Great, and though a Jew had been educated in Rome, and spent much of his early life in the milieu of the Roman aristocracy. As such he was not impressed by the fanatical activities and the murderous intent of the Sanhedrin in Jerusalem.

In a brief passage in Acts XXV 23, Luke conjures up a scene of great splendour and protocol when describing Paul's appearance before Agrippa: 'So on the next day Agrippa and Berenice came with great pomp, and they entered the audience hall, no doubt the hall of the Praetorian, with the military tribunes and the prominent men of the city'. Festus then gave the order for Paul to be brought in before he informed Agrippa of the circumstances of his detention, and the difficulty he had in framing the indictment that had to be forwarded to Rome. It must have been a very humiliating experience for Paul to stand before Agrippa chained by the hand to his custodian (Acts 26.1). Paul's defence of the charges against him to Agrippa were spirited and again centred around his teaching of the resurrection, and the efforts of the Jews to kill him. Festus, who could not understand this theological testimony of Paul's argument with the Jews, in a fit of exasperation exclaimed (Acts 26. 24): 'You are out of your mind, Paul! Too much learning is driving you insane'. However Agrippa understood the situation and ruled that he saw no reason in Roman law why Paul was detained and that he could have had his liberty had he not appealed to Caesar (Acts 27. 32). It was ironic that Paul had so recently elected to be tried before Caesar in Rome, and had he not done so the course of history might well have been changed.

There is no indication of the attitude taken by the Apostles, or those of the Judean Churches, as to Paul's difficulties over the years spent under arrest in Caesarea, and subsequently in prison before the arrival of Festus. Acts makes no reference to any of them during this period, in spite of the fact that Paul was initially allowed to have visitors, but Luke certainly must have been with him as also was Aristarchus from Thessalonica (Acts XXVII. 2).

In the late nineteen thirties the village of Kaisereeyah on the site of ancient Caesarea was isolated and accessible only by a track that wound its way through shallow sand dunes, patches of coarse grass and clumps of cactus that were always bright with yellow flowers and globular fruits. The track was one that camels and donkeys had worn to the village. One morning I managed to find an Arab with little else to do but look after two donkeys in a nearby settlement. He agreed to act as a guide and at a slow pace we set off down the sandy track through the scrub and the cactus clumps. The animal I was allotted had little stamina and was quite diminutive, obviously under nourished so needed very active encouragement, a difficult proposition without the attention of a pointed goad! My guide was much better off. His choice was a great deal more sturdy and robust, but as he was distinctly on the corpulent side his need was a lot greater than mine.

In common with many other sites that are associated with St Paul there is little that remains of the ancient Caesarea. What was once an important city and port is now an Arab village that is clustered behind a broad expanse of golden sandy beach, its low houses brightened with the glow of warm red tiles. This ambitious project of Herod the Great, who having spent some twelve years on its construction and on a site of some 164 acres, dedicated it to the Emperor Augustus. The only significant remains of the harbour, from where Paul left on his final journey to Rome, are the remnants of a mole made up from massive ashlar blocks that curve out into the bay. It is possible to tread over them carefully and see many others that have tumbled through the blue green crystal depths to strew the sandy bed below.

The ruinous debris of ancient Caesarea lies behind the village, a litter of oddly shaped boulders and stones that extend for acres, the vestiges of its municipal buildings, villas, streets, shops and temples. Many of their ancient columns and stone blocks have been incorporated into the village dwellings which is not unusual. Once it was a city of boulevards and avenues that went down to the harbour, together with subways built to link up the various city districts that had their sewage systems. A Temple of massive proportions was a well known landmark that dominated an expanse of waterfront notable for its grandiose architecture. But it was the Palace of Herod that outshone all other buildings to become in the Roman period the seat of the government of Judaea, the official residence of Pontius Pilate, of the slippery Antonius Felix, and his successor Porcius Festus. Recent excavations have uncovered the ruins of a large palace with a dining room that looks onto a swimming pool that could rival that of the Olympics. This structure, called the Promontory Palace, could be the remains of the Praetorium and possibly where Paul was kept under guard on first arriving in Caesarea (Acts 23.35). Certain inscriptions on pedestals found on the site relate to past governors of the province, and suggest that this could well be the ancient Palace of Herod and the later residence of the procurators of Judaea.

The Amphitheatre at Caesarea had the capacity to seat twenty thousand spectators and gives some indication as to the size of the population. In his 'History of the Jews' Josephus recorded it being built into the side of a hill that lay to the South of the city and behind the Port. It is still there, and in its day was the venue for the chariot races, that were so popular throughout the Empire as to cause as much rivalry and mayhem as do the football matches of today. One of the granite obelisks that once marked the starting point still lies where it tumbled to the ground. The amphitheatre in itself was not a lavish structure built in marble, but relatively simple as in Olympia, where spectators found their seats on the raised perimeter bank. A more prestigious place was reserved for Herod and the subsequent procurators of Judaea to enable them to view the proceedings with some dignity.

Caesarea was a wealthy city in the days of Paul, which brings one back to the hypothesis that during the two years he was there awaiting the pleasure of Felix, he must have had some degree of financial security. Luke, as has already been suggested, must have been there with him to have recorded this period, and the question of his financial circumstances would not have been a problem as he could have relied on his profession as a physician.

The great Eusebius was born there in A.D 264, and was consecrated Bishop in A.D. 315. In A.D. 325 he played a significant role at the Convocation of Nicaea in formulating 'The Nicean Creed', and was also responsible for a vast output of religious works that included his valued 'History of the Church', and his death occurred in Caesarea in A.D. 340. Origen, reputed to have been born in Alexandria in A.D. 185, was another outstanding father of the church who went to

Caesarea in A.D. 231, and there established his renowned school of theology, but he too suffered under the persecutions of Decian and died in Caesarea in A.D. 254.

The Cathedral dedicated to St Paul was built over the traditional site of his imprisonment by Felix, but only the remnants of the original apse, and a long vault that was once part of the cathedral crypt remains. It is this crypt that is thought to be the site of the actual prison where Paul was at one time incarcerated. A small and simple church now stands on the ground plan of the ancient Cathedral, and here it preserves the Christian tradition on the site of what once was the seat of the well-known Bishops of Caesarea.

The bowl of the partially restored theatre, which looks across the sandy shore to the backdrop of the sea, could also seat some thousands in its capacity, but now does service as a playground for the village children. There amongst the dark skinned Arab boys frolicking away their idle hours was one with very fair skin, having clear blue eyes and flaxen hair, was he by chance a throwback of some ancient Crusader stock, another lingering echo from the past.

As I made my way back from the theatre in search of the corpulent Ahmed and the donkeys, a long camel train slowly and silently plodded across the expanse of the bright yellow sand of the bay to disappear into the distant scrub. I watched them till they were out of sight, and later found Ahmed in deep conversation with some soul mates, all squatting and earnestly gesticulating with their hands and arms. The donkeys stood by with expressionless faces, drooping necks, and dejectedly immobile, it did not augur at all well for the return journey.

CHAPTER 5

The Final Journey to Rome

Before Paul was summoned to Caeserea to have his indictment heard by Agrippa he had already decided to take his appeal to Nero in Rome, and from Acts it is apparent that, because of this decision, Agrippa was not then in a position to release him from custody; this in spite of Agrippa's considered opinion that the Jew's complaints were of a theological nature and, as such, were not applicable for trial in a Roman court. Agrippa had thus, in spite of his better judgement, to put Paul into the charge of the centurion Julius for his journey to Rome. From the detailed account of the journey it would seem that Luke and Aristarchus, the Macedonian, were with him at the time; Aristarchus being one of the original party that left Corinth with Paul in order to celebrate the Pentecost in Jerusalem, Acts XI 4. It is possible that Aristarchus could also have been in the custody of Julius for Paul mentions in Colossians IV 10, written from Rome, 'Aristarchus my fellow prisoner greets you'. It is, however, a little ambiguous, Aristarchus could have gone with them but of his own volition as suggested in Acts XXVII, 2[64].

The details of the voyage again appear to be accurate (**See Map**). The boat was one of the local vessels based on Adramyttium, a port not many miles from Assos that has its ruins not far from today's town of Edremit. These smaller boats hugged the coast keeping it well in sight, and for this reason they sailed only during the daylight hours to the various ports of call with their cargoes, and chiefly in fine weather In order to navigate by the local landmarks. This being the case it is not at all likely, and very problematical, that the vessel carrying Julius with Paul and the others would have ventured on a direct course from Sidon to Paphos and thence to Myra on the Lycian coast, but would have opted instead to sail the longer voyage by the Cilician and Pamphylian coasts[65].

Myra was an important harbour where grain ships from Alexandria put in regularly for provisions and water before going on to discharge their cargoes in Italy. The Egyptian grain amounted to a third of Rome's yearly requirement, some 200,000-400,000 tons, and its delivery was essential in keeping the populace of Rome well fed. Many of these ships sailed together in convoy from Alexandria, and were originally under Imperial or governmental control, but in the time of Claudius Rome was once hit by a serious shortage of bread that precipitated a riot against him in the Forum. To prevent the occurrence of such shortages in the future it seems that Claudius, in order to ensure regular supplies, put the transport of the grain and the building of the grain ships out to public enterprise[66]

---

[64] Apart from Paul there were others going to Rome for trial and in the custody of Julius and some of his troops. Those to be sent to Rome were probably kept in custody till a number of them could be dispatched together under the one escort.

[65] From Caesarea to Sidon is a distance of some sixty seven miles and could have been covered in a day's sailing, they either put into Sidon for cargo or because of adverse winds.

[66] An edict of Claudius is extant that states "Likewise, under an edict of Claudius Latins gain the right of Roman citizenship if they build a seagoing vessel capable of carrying at least 10,000 modii of corn and if that ship, or one substituted in its place, carries corn to Rome for six years".

THE FINAL
JOURNEY TO ROME
ACCORDING TO
GROLLENBERG

Julius could have requisitioned accommodation for himself and his charges in a vessel in private ownership, a fact that appears to be confirmed in Acts XXVII, 11, 'but the centurion paid more attention to the pilot and to the owner of the ship than to what Paul said'.

The site of ancient Myra is the Demre of today, a small town situated on the coast some little distance East of Patara, the birthplace of St Nicholas. In the first century AD, Myra was the capital of the district of Lycia and in the later centuries became a well known centre of Christianity when Theodosius was Emperor; and this due to its associations with St Nicholas and the high regard that the Byzantines had for the Saint. His empty tomb was vandalised in the distant past but it can still be seen with a gaping hole in the restored remains of his Basilica near Demre **(See Figure 73)**: many of his looted bones found their way to Bari in Italy where they are now regarded as venerable relics.

All this transpired long after Paul's visit with the centurion Julius, but even at that time Myra was a city with an ancient Lycian heritage. Hewn into the precipitous cliffs that overlook one aspect of the ruins are a series of beautiful tombs that mostly date from the 4th century B.C. **(See Figure 74)**, impressive monuments that Paul must surely have seen. He could hardly have failed to do so for their facades make up a spectacular necropolis, and even though a few of them date from the early Roman period the greater majority were antiquities when Paul was there with Julius the Centurion, awaiting a grain ship from Alexandria.

Being remote they are a splendid reminder of a past culture that has been disregarded by the world at large and for hundreds of years have suffered only from the weather and time. But when I last went to Demre to see them they appeared to be pickled with a plague of coloured insects that, on closer inspection, turned out to be an infestation of a so called cultural tour. Not content with viewing their magnificence from the paths they were clambering over the pediments to take photographs of "Annie", or whoever, astride a pinnacle, pictures that, if not thrown away or lost, might find their faded way to a dubious posterity.

Having quietly survived the passage of centuries these historic monuments are now the subject of the unmitigated onslaught of tourist pollution, one that must inevitably bring about an even further and more rapid destruction. Also built into the cliff near this cluster of tombs are the well preserved remains of the theatre that dates to the Roman period. The spacious auditorium has twenty seven tiers of seating that can still he reached through covered flights of grandiose steps and passages, all a part of the integral structure. Paul must have seen this theatre when waiting in Myra for the grain ship to Italy, and it could well have been his last contact with this part of Asia Minor[67].

The weather must have been deteriorating well before they set sail from Myra for Luke records their progress from Myra to Cnidus a distance of some hundred and thirty miles, having taken several days sailing and tacking into the increasing strong winds from the West; the rough weather being such that they were unable to take shelter in the harbour at Cnidus but were forced to make for Crete, Acts XXVII 7.

---

[67] It seems that the Alexandrian grain ships put into Myra, where there was a good harbour, when the winds were blowing from the West.

Figure 73: The Vandalised Tomb of St Nicholas at Demre.

Figure 74: The Lycian Tombs at Demre, the Ancient Myra, that were antiquities in the days of St Paul

Mercantile shipping that included those carrying corn usually sailed during the summer months, navigation ending about the end of the Autumnal Equinox, the end of September or early October, but some masters did risk sailing during the winter months. With the weather conditions being such as they were in this case it would seem that the master was pushing his luck when he set sail with Julius and Paul. Pliny In his writings observed that 'not only the fury of the storms closes the sea but avarice invites compulsion to venture on them in the winter, and Vegetius noted that 'the greed of private merchandising causes hurried voyages'.

The largest grain ships, like those of the Isis class, carried three masts and could carry a cargo that varied from 1000 - 3500 tons, and could often accommodate up to 600 passengers. Josephus has described his experiences aboard one that unhappily foundered in the Adriatic when on a ill fated journey to Rome in A.D. 63, he fortunately being rescued and eventually taken to Puteoli. Claudius laid down the minimum tonnage carried by a grain ship to be not less than 68 tons. These were smaller vessels that had either one or two masts, those having two had one for the mainsail and one that could be used to help steer and control the vessel with the aid of two primitive rudders (Acts XXVII 40), not unlike oars that could be removed when necessary and lashed aboard. Luke records the vessel that carried them having two hundred and seventy six souls on board together with the cargo of grain, which must indicate that it was not one of the largest carriers but one of a lesser tonnage. Ships of the period are depicted on Trajan's column in Rome.

It was unfortunate that they could not put into Cnidus for the city had two excellent harbours, one for the Naval triremes and one a good deal larger for commercial shipping, the two separated by a short isthmus that joined the main peninsular with a small rocky island having a lighthouse. The commercial harbour had an extensive quay, and for those coming into the maritime anchorage the view was that of a city climbing steeply up the hills of the peninsular, terrace upon terrace of narrow streets with marble colonnades, temples and municipal buildings, all rising up behind a theatre that had commanding views across the harbours[68].

The focal point of Cnidus was the circular Temple. The ruins can still be seen and it overlooked and dominated both the anchorages, and had within it the Venus of Praxilities. This was the greatest treasure the Cnidians possessed, a life-size Venus that was sculpted in the nude from a flawless white marble, known to have been the work of Praxilities for be also sculpted a draped version. The Cnidians, however, were not in any way a collection of prudes for they lost little time in rejecting the draped version. A wise decision for the Venus of Cnidus soon became famous throughout the ancient world, and the Temple a major attraction for tourists who came expressly to see it; indeed legend has it that one impressionable youth became so enamoured of the figure that he managed to secrete himself in the temple one night, to leave the spotless white marble with an irremovable stain. Again Paul must have seen the statue, though he makes no mention of it, for it seems that he landed for a short time at Cnidus when on his way back from Cenchrea to Caesarea and Antioch.

---

[68] The harbours of Cnidus are still in use and overlooked by the splendid ruins of the Theatre.

St Luke's impressive description of the disastrous voyage has many features of a journalistic and eye witness account, especially when he gives details of the storm and the winds that forced them to sail to the South of Crete. Luke has described it as 'sailing under the lee of Crete off Salmone - the Cape Sidero of today - to the city of Lasea near Fair Havens, a voyage that took longer than anticipated, and there they debated as to whether they should spend the winter in that small harbour or sail on to the anchorage at Phoenix'[69]. Paul, having already had past experience of being shipwrecked on more than one occasion, and on another occasion adrift for a day and a night (2 Cor XI 25) was of the opinion that they should stay and spend the Winter in the Fair Haven anchorage 'as the Fast had already gone by'; this being the Fast of expiation that took place on the tenth of Tisri; a date applicable to the beginning of October when seafaring became hazardous. However, as the weather was showing some signs of improvement the blame can hardly be put on Julius for taking the professional advice of the ship's master, rather than that of Paul, to make for the larger and more sheltered harbour of Phoenix in Crete and to spend the Winter there, an anchorage that could be identified with the Lutro of today.

In the narrative of the disaster there are many other detailed observations that give the account a deal of credence, for Luke describes in Acts XXVII 14 how the wind Euroclydon drove them to the island of Clauda, almost opposite Phoenix. This could well have been a gale of some ferocity that suddenly swept down from the region of the Mount Ida range on mainland Crete in a North- Easterly direction; to hit the vessel as it hugged the coast when rounding Cape Matala and subsequently drive it under the lee of the island of Clauda. At this juncture they all endeavoured to bring aboard the ship's boat that was being towed and had by now, no doubt, shipped a great deal of water.

It was then that they lowered the sea anchor to prevent the possibility of the vessel running aground on the sandbanks of Syrtis that lay some 400 miles to the S.W. of Clauda and not far from the African coast; to help their position they then trimmed the sails and lowered the helps to undergird the ship's timbers and prevent them from springing a leak, Acts XXVII 17. This practice of frapping, as it was then known, was used to prevent the timbers springing apart in severe weather; it involved the passing of ropes beneath the ship's hull from port to starboard and keeping them taught with a windlass. Some with considerable seafaring expertise have suggested that the vessel could then have been laid into the wind on the starboard tack and, if brought into this position and allowing for all eventualities, could then have drifted to the W. by N. at the rate of some thirty six miles in each twenty four hours. With the wind staying in the E.N.E. direction it has also been calculated that this could have brought the vessel on an approximate bearing from the South side of Clauda to the North coast of Malta at the time of the shipwreck. Acts XXVIII gives a graphic description of the event.

Other passages are equally descriptive in their detail, such as when on the third day they cast all the unnecessary tackle overboard to lighten the vessel. Unfortunately the exact nature of the unnecessary tackle has not been recorded, but could have included some of the sails.

---

[69] For the vessel to have made the lee of Crete by Cape Sidero it has been calculated that the winds must have been coming from the North-West. These North-Westerly winds were common at this time of the year. The 'Etesian Monsoons' described by Pliny are thought to be one and the same.

However, it seems unlikely that It would have included the main spar as suggested by Smith in his Voyage and Shipwreck of St Paul written around 1850; if so It would have taken the efforts of all on board to jettison It into the sea. The vessel by now would have been leaking to a great extent requiring everyone over the following eleven days endeavouring to keep it afloat. Luke records in Acts IXVII 21, that nothing was eaten during that time; apart from having little time to eat the leaking sea water could have destroyed the greater part of their provisions. The text suggests that on the fourteenth night the crew could have suddenly been aware of the noise of the sea dashing against a rocky coast; soundings of 20 then 15 fathoms confirming that land was near and necessitating the dropping of four anchors from the stern to prevent a drift onto the rocks during the night. This was followed by the crew endeavouring to leave the ship by letting down the boat that had been brought on board, a project that was foiled by the troops of Julius who cut it adrift before it was properly lowered.

Before daybreak Paul appears to have exhorted everyone to greater efforts of survival, and after some food they opened the hatches and began to cast the grain overboard. This could have shifted position to the extent that the vessel had now a dangerous list. If this had been the minimum cargo of 68 tons it would still have been no mean feat. The grain was usually transported loose in the hold and thus had the disadvantage of being able to destabilise a vessel by shifting position in rough weather. There was also the added hazard of a grain cargo in a leaking boat swelling to the extent that it could split its timbers and cause it to founder.

When the morning dawned the crew hoisted the mainsail, slipped the anchors and prepared to run the ship aground onto a small beach, where much of it broke up under the pounding sea, Acts 27, 14[70]. Julius then prevented his men from killing all those in his custody should they escape, normally they would have answered with their lives for such an occurrence so that, one way or another they all got ashore[71]. It seems to be indisputable, though questioned, that the Island of the shipwreck was indeed that of Malta[72]. After having got into difficulties when nearing Phoenix the drift of the vessel would have covered some 468 miles at the rate of thirty six miles in each twenty four hours, this in its West by North direction over thirteen days. The actual distance from Malta to Clauda is something less than 280 miles. Rather more than a coincidence. The whole is an absorbing and dramatic account that has too much factual detail in it to be the product of a fertile imagination.

---

[70] Smith has suggested that the clay like deposits of mud in this area of the coast where the vessel could have run aground would have held it firmly by the bow, to then be broken up by the waves beating over the stern.

[71] They would have been chained by the right hand to their guards. For their own survival they would have slipped the chains and killed the prisoners. For a guard to lose his prisoner meant the forfeit of his own life. Julius could have waived this principle and let each endeavour to save themselves otherwise chained few would have survived. Acts.27. 42-43.

[72] Reasons given by Conybeare, Howson, and Smith, appear to confirm the fact that St Paul's Bay could have been the site of the shipwreck. They suggest a vessel drifting W by N in this region in a gale would approach Koura point on the Eastern boundary of the Bay, and that the crew that night would have heard the roar of the breakers on this part of the coast. Soundings taken within a quarter of a mile of the point give the readings of twenty fathoms and then fifteen fathoms, and at this juncture the vessel could have anchored. This appears to confirm the description given by Luke and that the vessel could have drifted that night some quarter of a mile from Kourous point towards the beach. However, there has been in the past a dispute as to the site of the wreck, for some have held the opinion that it took place on Melida in the Gulf of Venice. Smith, though, has maintained that, to reach Melida in the circumstances described with the inconsistencies that would have obtained in the position of the vessel's drift and the record of the soundings as described by Luke, all would seem to negate the hypothesis and that Malta was the actual site of the disaster.

The Winter storms that caused the shipwreck on the coast of Malta must have been unusually severe for in Acts XXVIII 11-13, Luke records the fact that the Castor and Pollux, another grain ship from Alexandria, had already taken shelter in the harbour where it had to remain for three months until conditions were suitable enough to undertake the relatively short passage to Puteoli; and Acts XXVIII 8-10, also recounts the detail of the healing of the father of Publius of a 'bloody flux', obviously dysentery; Publius being the chief of the community then living on Malta. That Luke was indeed with them on the voyage is hinted at in verse 10 'they bestowed many honors on us, and when we were about to sail, they put on board all the provisions we needed'[73].

After leaving Malta on the Castor and Pollux they spent three days in Syracuse and then one in Rhegium where they had to wait for the South winds to take them on to Puetoli, a port a little to the South of Ostia where the grain ships from North Africa discharged their cargoes into large granaries. Luke is meticulous and again accurate in recording, as he did on the third journey from Corinth to Caesarea, the time taken when sailing between their various ports of call and the time spent before moving on. The Castor and Pollux was well named for they were the gods and the patrons of sailors and shipping, another detail that could hardly have been fictional.

Puteoli had a particularly fine harbour where the populace came down to watch the grain ships come in. Seneca writes:

'Unexpectedly, today, Alexandrian ships appeared within sight, those which are usually sent ahead and announce the arrival of a fleet behind them; they call them the mail boats, a welcome sight in Campania. A vast mob stood on the docks of Puteoli and spotted the Alexandrians from the configuration of their sails, despite the great mob of ships. They alone use their topsails then in the way that all ships do in the open sea: nothing helps them to cut through the water as much as their topsails, that is what drives the ships most. All ships apart from the grain ships were obliged to strike their top sails when they rounded the promontory prior to coming into harbour. In the midst of the turmoil I took great pleasure in my leisure, because I was about to receive letters from my people'.

Suetonius recorded an occasion when 'Augustus once watched the corn ships arrive and was delighted when they paid him homage with garlands and incense'.

The environs of Puteoli were very beautiful and in those days very fashionable. There are many frescos in Pompeii that illustrate the sumptuous villas that the wealthy had built up and down the coast line and in and around Puteoli itself. An amusing graffito that refers to the delights of Puteoli can be seen on a wall of what was obviously a not very salubrious lodging house in Pompeii. Apart from some single rooms the establishment mainly had dormitories taken up by actors with touring companies when on their regular visits to the town. One, Julius Speratus, who was not an actor but happened to be in Pompeii for some unstated reason, seemed not to be in the least impressed with the town and its facilities. For on a wall that must have been next his bed he questions 'What on earth possessed me to visit the town when there

---

[73] Publius owned much of the land in the region. His people regarded Paul as almost a god in that he survived the bite of an adder that came out of the blazing wood he had gathered for a fire. A cave in St Paul's Bay is traditionally where they sheltered after the wreck.

is nothing so beautiful as Puteoli'. Man has long been inspired to inscribe on walls his thoughts and shafts of wit, and these graffiti are to be found in all the Greco - Roman cities of the day. Especially are they numerous in Pompeii and Herculaneum where they have been preserved in their entirety by the volcanic ash, and it is these scribblings that do more than anything to bring these ancient cities back to life.

The grain from North Africa destined for Rome, and known as the Anona, was loaded at Carthage to be shipped and stored in large granaries in the Port of Ostia, where they can still be seen in the well preserved ruins of the harbour facilities. Not only did Ostia import these grain stocks for Rome, essential in keeping the Capital supplied for the greater part of the year, but private enterprise also brought in a multitude of other goods from the colonies of the Empire, luxuries such as carbuncle stones, ivory, together with quantities of high grade olive oil and fruit, all destined to satisfy the demands of the Patrician wealthy. The offices of the various shipping lines that specialised in these imports were congregated in the Piazza of the Corporations behind the theatre; their business titles and emblems of trademark still extant in their mosaic floors. The elephant being that of the company trading with the provinces of North Africa, and in so doing responsible for the import of the carbuncles, ivory, fruit and olive oil.

It has been recorded that a Marcus Vettius Latro, one who might have had Libyan forbears, spent a significant part of his life in North Africa as the procurator responsible for the collection of the 'Anona' the grain tax, and for the regular shipments to Italy. His ability and competence proved such that he was later sent to Sicily to organise their grain imports and finally, at the peak of his profession, he ended his career in Ostia with the crucial task of supervising the grain stocks for Rome, and it is likely that Puteoli had the same arrangements for grain control.

Some of the coins of Nero show the harbour at Ostia having ships of only one mast in the anchorage, and it is possible that the Castor and Pollux was a similar vessel; it has also been estimated that these were capable of around seven knots an hour. Had the Castor and Pollux been such a vessel sailing from Rhegium, before a South wind, it would then have been feasible for it to have covered the distance of some 182 miles to Puteoli in twenty six hours, which would agree with Luke's statement in Acts XXVIII 13, 'After one day there a South wind sprang up, and on the second day we came to Puteoli'.

That there was a Christian community in Puteoli seems very evident for Luke records in Acts XXVIII 14, the fact that they gave them a warm welcome and considerable hospitality over the week that they had to stay before setting out for Rome. Doubtless this hospitality also extended to Julius, but it is possible that lodgings were requisitioned for the rest of the party under the supervision of his troops. In view of the extent of the luxury trade that Puteoli had with Egypt it follows that there could also have been a significant colony of Jews in the population, and it would appear that the Christian communities at this time were not under any direct threat from Nero.

The few brief details of the journey from Puteoli to Rome, as given in Acts XXIII 15, are also accurate and again appear to testify to the truth of Luke's record of the Journey. The great

Appian Way that stretched from Rome to Capua, and was broad enough for two vehicles to pass each other, was built by the censor, Appius Claudius. It was the oldest, the finest, and the most celebrated of Roman roads that were extended in the later years to Brundusium, today's Brindisi on the Adriatic. In the time of Paul the only road between Puteoli and the Appian Way at Capua was by the one known either as 'The Consular Way' or the 'Campanian Way, and this must have been the route used by Julius and his contingent when they set out for Rome. In the time of Domitian a road was built along the coast from Puteoli to Sinuessa where it joined the Appian Way, and had this been so in the time of Paul the journey would have been considerably shorter.

Julius Caesar raised Capua to the status of a colony and it became the most important city to lie on the Appian Way, From Capua the road went some twenty one miles to Sinuessa on the coast, and from there through Minturnae to Formiae a pleasant town where Cicero spent his retirement, until being murdered by assassins when on a journey in his palanquin. From Formiae the road passed through the Caecuban Hills to Fundi and Terracina on the Southern aspect of the Pontine Marshes. To drain the Marshes Augustus built a canal that went some twenty miles from Terracina to its terminus at the Appii Forum, and this was used by barges dragged by mules that took merchandise and people. Luke mentions the Appii Forum together with the Three Taverns. The Appii Forum was the town at the end of the canal where the barges were unloaded and one where the taverns were very suspect, the Mecca of the bargees and the haunt of what has been described as a vulgar and motley crowd.

Though a road of sorts went part of the way across the Marshes it is more than likely that Julius made use of the barges. The distance from Puteoli to Terracina was in the region of some sixty five miles, did Julius requisition transport for this part of the journey where he could, and did he have power to do so? Otherwise they would have had to walk the whole distance. There is a lengthy inscription of about A.D.14, from Sagalassos, that is in the region of Pisidian Antioch, where the powers of requisition of transport are laid down and to whom it is entitled. An excerpt states:

'The people of Sagalassos should provide a service of ten wagons and the same number of mules for the needs of those passing through and should receive from users 10 asses for each wagon over each shoenus and 4 asses for each mule over each shoenus. A shoenus was a unit of distance and two donkeys could be supplied for one mule. In addition, the right to use is granted to those on military service, both to those who have a warrant and to those on military service from other provinces who pass through'.

Could Julius by any chance have profited from a similar regulation?

The news of Paul's arrival in Italy must have been sent at once by the Christians of Puteoli to those in Rome, for many from Rome set out to cover the forty odd miles to the Appii Forum in order to give him an ecstatic welcome. It is speculation as to whether Aquila and Priscilla were amongst them. After the death of Claudius in A.D. 54 Aquila and Priscilla, together with many other Jews, went back to Rome for the former edict of Claudius was then no longer applicable. The Christians then followed him to the Three Taverns on the Appian Way, some ten miles from Rome, where they were joined by others of the Christian community who were waiting in eager anticipation to give him a further welcome.

This open display of affection and welcome for Paul, as he was about to enter Rome with his escort, must also indicate that the Christians in Rome, like those in Puteoli and elsewhere in Italy, were then living an organised and more or less open existence and not subject to any marked political hostility. It is also clear that Paul was not coming to Rome as a common felon, but was afforded some degree of consideration and preferential treatment in that he was eventually allowed, even though under the supervision of a guard, to hire his own house and have some considerable freedom. He must then have had adequate funds at his disposal to rent such a house. Was it by chance an inheritance from Tarsus?[74]

The nature of Paul's hired accommodation in Rome has given rise to some speculation, as suggested above. Apart from the villas and palaces of the wealthy there were numerous districts of badly built tenement blocks, called insulae, that were little more than slums and liable at times to collapse. These were used mainly by the more impecunious of the citizens of Rome as places in which to sleep, spending as they did the better part of the daylight hours on the streets or in the baths. As has been said the Satrycon of Petronicus gives a vivid description of the way of life in Rome as it was in the time of Nero. Certainly Paul did not have his lodgings in these districts.

However, apart from the wealthy[75] and in view of the cost of accommodation it seems that the greater part of Rome's population existed in rented rooms above shops and other commercial establishments. Examples of this state of affairs can be seen in the streets of Pompeii where some had to live above establishments given over to local fullers and dyers. That Paul fell into this category does not seem possible either, being in the charge of and no doubt lightly manacled to his guard. The Christians in Rome, many of them with means, must have congregated in each other's houses. Aquila and Priscilla obviously had some form of housing; no doubt it was the Christian community that arranged Paul's accommodation. Luke is specific in the fact that it was a hired house where Paul was detained and could not leave without escort, but those of the Jewish community, and others, could visit him there, as they wished. It has been estimated that, from the time of Augustus, there could have been some 40,000 Jews living in the Transtiberium region of Rome; that there was a large Jewish colony in Rome at that time, many of them having Roman citizenship, has been substantiated by Philo, the Jewish historian.

It is thought that Julius entered Rome through the Porta Capena, to take his charges to the Headquarters of the Praetorian Guard on the Palatine Hill where Paul was handed over to the Captain of the Guard. This interpretation was based on the Greek version of Acts where the Captain of the Guard is described as being a Stratopedarch, or Chief of the Camp. However, the researches of the historian Theodore Mommsen have revealed that the old Latin version for 'Captain of the Guard' translates into the title Princeps Peregrinorum, the Chief of the Peregrini.

---

[74] The question again arises as to Paul's means of support during this period. Was he entirely dependent on the Christians of Rome or did he have by this time some means of his own? By this time his parents in Tarsus would have passed on.

[75] Many of the Christians in Rome were wealthy, for example Pudens.

The Peregrini were an elite force that had their own commandant and barracks on the Caelian Hills; not subject to every day military duties they were more entrusted with assignments that included the conveyance of urgent dispatches to the various Colonial governors. He concluded that Julius of the band of Augustus (Acts XXVII 1) was in all probability one of the Peregrini who had gone to Caesarea on a mission to Festus, and happened to be there when Paul was brought before Agrippa and then detailed to take Paul and the others back to Rome.

In Rome the legal machinery must have been as ponderous as it can be today, for it seems to have ground exceeding slow for Paul to have spent two years waiting in his hired house for his trial by Nero. It is also strange that Luke fails to refer in any way to Paul's trial and its eventual outcome, but somewhat abruptly ends 'Acts' at this juncture, In view of the Pastoral letters it is possible that Paul won his appeal and was released, for in his second letter to Timothy, presumably written in the Mamertine prison in Rome when awaiting his second trial, Paul mentions the fact that Luke was still with him.

Paul must have had considerable freedom during the years he was waiting to have his appeal brought before the courts. He could air his views with the Jewish hierarchy, who came to see him at his request, 'And some believed the things that were spoken, and some believed not'. Many others came to see him, and it is logical that the Captivity Epistles were written during this period for it is known from Colossians IV 14 that Luke, the beloved physician, was still with him as was Aristarchus. Paul refers to Aristarchus as a fellow prisoner, but it is questionable if he too was to be brought before Nero there being no reference to the nature of any indictment, and there is no hint that he was under any restraint when he left Caesarea with Paul.

Colossians IV. 12.13 also states that Epaphras came from Colossae to express his concern over the behaviour of many of the church, not only in Colossae but elsewhere in Asia Minor, for it would seem they were far from conducting themselves in as Saintly a manner as befitted them as Saints. The slave Onesimus from Colossae was another to arrive in Rome, on the money that he had 'borrowed' from Philemon and this on a visit that could hardly have been accidental. Tychicus was a constant companion, until he went back to Asia Minor taking with him Paul's letters to the Ephesians and the Colossians that exhorted them to mend their ways; as did Onesimus with the one from Paul to his master Philemon and it would appear that both of them went back to Asia Minor together. Demas was another of the faithful in Rome until he deserted the cause for, as Paul remarks with some disappointment in his second letter to Timothy, 'a life that embraced more worldly things'[76].

It is significant that there are no intimate references whatever to Peter in the pastoral letters, apart from those made by Paul in Galatians where he recounts the disputes that took place in Jerusalem and Antioch over the question of the circumcision of the Gentiles. Other passing references are recorded in 1, Corinthians III, 22 where Cephas is mentioned in conjunction with Apollos, and in 1 Corinthians IX 5 where he considers his status is quite the equal to that of Peter and the other Apostles.

---

[76] It is thought that Paul's letters to the Colossians together with that to Philemon, to the Ephesians and to the Philippians, were written from Rome during the first year of his captivity. It seems too from Philippians 4. 22., that Paul was instrumental in the conversion of many in Caesar's household. "All the saints salute you, chiefly they that are of Caesar's household".

Some authorities are of the opinion that Peter went to Rome at some time in A.D. 42, but this seems hardly logical for Peter would then have been in Rome for at least some three years or so prior to A.D. 45-46, around the date when Paul went down at the request of Barnabas to help him establish the Church in Antioch. Though it has been disputed it appears that Peter was the first to lead the Church, to become at some time the first Bishop in Antioch, but at what period and for how long is not known and is difficult to ascertain; it may have been subsequent to Paul's departure from Antioch on the third missionary journey. Paul's stay in Antioch at the end of his second journey was his final visit and he makes no mention of Peter being in Antioch at that time, either as head of the Church or as Bishop, nor does he mention Ignatius as having taken over the Church from Peter. The life and movements of Peter are mostly conjectural and not well documented for the years subsequent to the quarrel with Paul over the circumcision of the Gentiles.

Mark must have gone to see Paul on many occasions during the two years he spent in his hired house in Rome, for Paul refers to him with some degree of warmth in Colossians IV 10. The antipathy that he had previously felt for Mark must have been resolved, an antipathy that stemmed from the first journey when Mark decided to leave them in Perga and go back to Jerusalem.

Peter was certainly living in Rome whilst Paul was awaiting the pleasure of Nero and in 1 Peter V 13. there is the suggestion that Mark was acting as his secretary, and possibly writing at the same time his own gospel based on Peter's recollections of life as it was in Galilee and Judaea with Jesus and the other Apostles. In Peter's letter addressed to the peoples of Pontus, Galatia, Cappadocia, Asia, and Bithynia, all of them Provinces in Asia Minor, he exhorts them, in 1 Peter IV 3, to avoid amongst other things lusts, excess of wine, lasciviousness and idolatries, and in this, together with much other advice, he echoes and supports Paul's teaching. Silas, who took the place of Barnabas on the second journey, was also in Rome during this period, for it is he who takes Peter's first letter to Asia Minor, 1 Peter V 12.

The Rome of Paul and Nero was not the Rome that we see today. Nero was mainly then preoccupied with satisfying his colossal vanity, very often with his solo performances in the theatres that the aristocracy of Rome were constrained to attend, and any who ventured to leave before these lengthy and boring occasions came to an end were apt to suffer the consequences. He was also besotted in the building of his sumptuous Golden House in the heart of Rome, a project that included the creation of its gardens and a vast ornamental lake, all of which took some precedence over state affairs. The Golden House was one of the splendours of Rome and its gardens and lake must have been a familiar part of the landscape when Paul was there.

It was Titus who drained Nero's precious lake, not so long after the fall of Jerusalem in A.D. 70, and a few years only after the death of Paul. On its site he built the enormous edifice of the Coliseum, and the labour required for this grandiose project came from the thousands of Jews he brought back from Jerusalem as prisoners of war. What Paul would have thought of that, had he then been alive, is open to conjecture. The spoils that Titus took from the Temple of Solomon are depicted in a sculpted frieze on the Arch of Titus near the Forum Romana and here, prominently displayed amongst the loot, is the Arc of the Covenant and the five branched candelabra, the sacred Menorah, both of them being filched from the Temple of Solomon's Holy of Holies. In spite of the persecutions that Paul had sustained at the hands of the Jews he would not have approved of the looting and the destruction of the Temple.

The Pastoral letters could indicate the fact that Paul had won his appeal before Nero, and though various dates have been put forward there is the possibility that it took place between A.D 61 - 63. The letters to Timothy and Titus are not considered to be the entire work of Paul, but as they stand today could date from a decade or two after his death, even so they may well contain a lot of detail that has been derived from an original source.

There is nothing to suggest that he later went to Spain as he had once intended, apart from his statue in a Piazza in Tarragona. That may or may not be significant, but from his letter to Titus there is the inference that he visited Crete, to leave Titus there to organise and maintain the Church. He has very harsh words for the Cretans calling them habitual liars, evil beasts, slow bellies and much too fond of filthy lucre; his reactions to the life style and conduct of some of today's tycoons would be more than interesting! He also has very little to say in favour of those of the Diaspora, considering many of them to be unruly, vain talkers and deceivers; if indeed these are his sentiments they do not exactly reflect his earlier discourses on charity. In view of the never ending difficulties and the continual rebuffs that he had had from the majority of the Jews of the Diaspora it is not surprising that he became somewhat Jaundiced in his outlook. It is also evident that this letter to Titus was written from Nicopolis in Macedonia where it was his intention, after leaving Crete, to spend the winter.

From his first letter to his beloved Timothy it is clear that Paul left him in Ephesus to lead the Ephesian Church, but here again he makes no reference to John who must, by now, have been resident there for some little while and also concerned with the Church. Some authorities consider his letter to Timothy was written and sent from Laodicea, if so, it could point to the fact that Paul did visit Philemon in Colossae after winning his appeal in Rome, an intention expressed in his letter to Philemon when he requested that a room be prepared for him should he be acquitted. In view of the reports regarding the lax behaviour of those of the Churches in Asia Minor, brought to him by Epaphras from Colossae, Paul may have felt it essential for him to visit them personally, and this could have taken precedent over any visit that he might have had in mind to go westwards into Spain[77].

In this letter to Timothy, in which he still emphasises that he is the accredited Apostle of Christ unto the Gentiles, he has more harsh words to say about those in Ephesus, complaining

---

[77] Conybeare and Howson have suggested that after Paul's successful appeal before Nero, he firstly went back to the Churches of Colossae, Laodicea, and Colossae, by leaving Brindisi for Dyrrachium and the Via Egnatia for Asia Minor. He then went to Spain to return to Ephesus around A.D.66 and be disappointed at the lax behaviour of the Ephesian church; to leave Timothy there as bishop to cope with the situation whilst he went on to Macedonia; from there to write the first letter to Timothy with further advice as to how he should behave as bishop. 1, Tim, 1-3, "I urge you , as I did when on my way to Macedonia, to remain in Ephesus that you may instruct certain people not to teach any different doctrine". He later went to Crete with Titus where, according to Philo, there was a large colony of Jews of the Diaspora, to leave him there whilst he returned to Ephesus. From Ephesus he wrote his Epistle to Titus before leaving for Nicopolis in Epirus where he intended to spend the winter. Titus 3.12. "When I send Artemas to you, or Tychicus, do your best to come to me at Nicopolis, for I have decided to spend the winter there".

The possibility that Paul was denounced by an informer during this visit and then arrested by the Magistrates of Nicopolis, to then be taken back to Rome has been put forward by Coynbears and Howson. However, there is still the question as to why Paul left his intimate possessions at the House of Carpus. Troas and Nicopolis are not that far apart and there could have been a reason for Paul being with Carpus in Troas at that time. The speculation is endless and much depends on the question as to the genuineness of the Pastoral Epistles. However, even if they are not entirely authentic much in them must derive from an authentic source.

that many of them have turned aside unto vain jangling. There are distinct comparisons in these letters to Timothy and Titus for he castigates those of the Churches that have fallen from grace in both of them, and for good measure he denounces the general populace for their deplorable behaviour.

The worst catastrophe in the time of Nero was the fire that broke out in Rome in A.D. 64, one that caused devastation in many large districts of the city and an event that made his administration even less welcome to the citizens than it was already. To divert and distract the attention of the populace from this national disaster Nero resorted to an age old political trick, and what could be handier as an alternative 'cause celebre' than the wholesale persecution of the Christian scapegoats. The people of Rome, however, were not to be hoodwinked and widely considered the Emperor to have engineered the conflagration in order to destroy those parts of the city that were not particularly desirable, for those living in these districts had long felt it was Nero's intent to knock down their homes and rebuild the area more to his liking.

Many Christians were covered in tar and burnt as human torches to light up his Circus, not the Coliseum but the amphitheatre that he had built in the region of the present Basilica of St Peters. Peter was detained and Paul sought out, arrested, and brought to the Mamertine prison to be held in chains to await a second trial. It is a tantalising fact that no details of this period have been recorded, but it is still intriguing to speculate on the various events that might have occurred, one of them being, as has already been discussed, his possible detention at the House of Carpus at Alexandra Troas. That he went to Asia Minor after winning his appeal before Nero is suggested in his second letter to Timothy in chapter IV verse 20, 'Erastus remained in Corinth, Trophimus I left ill in Miletus'.

This second letter to Timothy from the Mamertine Prison in Rome is full of sadness as he recalls the days of their first meeting in the house of Timothy's grandmother Lois and his mother Eunice in Lystra. The letter must have been written when Paul realised that he had little hope of being released for the second time. He mentions that no one came forward to support him during this hearing, and there is little doubt that the Jews in Rome considered this a heaven sent opportunity to be rid of him. Many of those of the Christian communities in Asia Minor, such as Hermogenes, also abandoned him, but others in Rome such as Onesiphorus came regularly to the Mamertine to see him.

Paul is emphatic that Luke is the only one who is still with him, an observation from which it could be inferred that he was the one who came regularly to the Mamertine to look after his needs and to see to his welfare. This passage confirms Luke being in Rome at this time, and seems to rule out the suggestion that both Paul and Peter were imprisoned in the Mamertine together. In this last letter to Timothy there are still no references to Peter, but from 11 Tim IV 11, it seems that Mark had already left Rome to join Timothy in Ephesus; no doubt he went from Rome to avoid the persecutions that had also brought about the arrest and detention of Peter. It does not appear that this was also in the Mamertine; Paul makes no reference to him being there with him.

That Timothy was in Ephesus is apparent from 11 Tim IV 19. In this letter Paul passes on to him the salutations from Aquilla and Priscilla, and from the family of Onesiphorus, all of them then still in Rome. He concludes with the greetings from others of the Roman church and of these he especially names Pudens, Claudia and Linus, one who became first Bishop of Rome after Peter: but many of them did not survive the persecutions of the later years.

Paul is in no forgiving mood, however, where the coppersmith Alexander is concerned; he was obviously a bad hat for Paul to have delivered him unto Satan for heresy (to have excommunicated him), and for Paul to have fervently hoped that, according to his works, he should get from the Lord his just rewards; Paul rarely expresses such animosity and must have been sorely tried. Was this the same Alexander who was summarily rejected by the crowds in the theatre in Ephesus, when the Jews put him on the stage to speak up for them.

One of the most moving things in this last letter, and one that must have some basis in fact, is the request that Paul makes of Timothy to bring him his cloak and parchments from the house of Carpus in Troas. The possible reason for Paul having left them there has already been discussed[77], and the plea that Timothy should endeavour to bring them before the onset of winter is also significant, for one has only to set foot in the cold marble dankness of the Mamertine to appreciate the request. This passage also confirms both Timothy and Mark being in Ephesus together, for Paul asks Timothy to bring Mark with him to Rome.

Traditionally St Peter and St Paul were martyred on the same day in Rome in A.D. 67, though this has been open to dispute. St. Peter, not having the advantage of Roman citizenship, was crucified in the Circus of Nero where others had died as flaming torches, head downwards at his own request. He was an old man, and a rare and interesting fresco depicting his crucifixion can be seen in the crypt of a Romanesque church in the village of Tavant in the valley of the Loire.

Having full Roman citizenship Paul could not be crucified and was led down the Via Ostiensis, the highway to Ostia that left Rome by the Ostian gate near the pyramid of Cestius, a monument that Paul must have seen as he was taken from the City precincts to a pine wood near the third milestone on the Via Laurentina. Here he was beheaded on a spot called the Aquae Salviae, a site now known as the Tre Fontana where the Abbey of the Three Fountains commemorates the site, and here the Salvian springs still flow. That a pine wood did exist on the site was confirmed in 1875 by the Trappist monks who used to maintain the Abbey; when digging in the grounds to build a new cistern they uncovered a mass of calcified pine cones together with a hoard of Nero's coins, tragic reminders of the past.

It was Constantine the Great who removed Paul's remains from a Roman tomb near the Via Ostiensis and had them reinterred in a metal coffin emblazoned with a golden cross, and above the new grave he built the first of several Basilicas dedicated to the Saint. One was destroyed by fire in 1823 but the tomb remained intact, and the Basilica of St Paul without the walls that stands today incorporates much of the original design, the tomb itself lying beneath the high altar, The fire that destroyed the Basilica in 1823 revealed the slab that protected the tomb, but the intense heat damaged an inscription that now reads 'Paolo Apostolo Mart'. The word 'Mart' should have read 'Martyri', the last three of the letters having disappeared in the fire. Under the high altar a small window gives on to the slab that is now hidden in the darkness below. This was examined by Professor Lanciani in December 1881, who concluded from the style of the lettering that it must date from the period of Constantine and be indisputably authentic.

Pudens, mentioned by Paul in his last letter to Timothy was a prominent Christian in Rome, and one who must have been well known to Peter; the site of his house is thought to lie in the crypt of the Church of St. Pudenziana, and in the Church are the portraits of Peter and Paul, reflecting the appearance of the two Saints that have come to light in the Vetri Cemeteriali, glasses that were buried with the dead in the catacombs of Rome during the second and third centuries. Depicted in gold leaf on these glasses are the images of the two Apostles that can give an indication of what could well have been their likenesses.

There are some interesting facts that have come to light regarding the family of Pudens. In 1892 Rodolfo Lanciani wrote a book on 'Pagan and Christian Rome' and In it he records a discovery made in 1776 of an oratory near the church of St Prisca on the Aventine, the discovery being noted in the Codex 969 of the Bibliotheque Nätionale In Paris. In the Codex Lanciani he found that an individual named Carraras had found an underground chapel near St Prisca that was decorated with fourth century paintings of the Apostles. The church of St Prisca is thought to have been on the site of the House church of Aquila and Priscillaa, who returned to Rome at some time after the riot of the silversmiths when Paul left Ephesus for the last time. Below the church of St Prisca is a small museum and in the wall by the stairs down is a broken plaque with the words Placidvs Prisci.

In the excavations of 1776 a bronze tablet was also found with the following inscription 'to Gaius Marius Pudens Cornelianus by the people of Clunia, near Palencia in Spain, as a token of gratitude for the services he had rendered them during his governorship of the Romanised province of Tarragona' and dated 9th April A.D. 222. Did he put up the statue to Paul in the Piazza in Tarragona? It would seem that the house of Aquila and Priscilla, or Prisca, later passed into the hands of Cornelius Pudens who must have been some later descendant, or from another branch of the family of the Pudens referred to by Paul in Timothy 11 4 21.

The Pudens Puedentinus of the New Testament was the son of the wealthy senator Pudens who was a friend of Claudius and had a palace situated on the Vicus Patricus, today's Via del Bambin Gesu on the slope of the Viminale; part of the palace now lies under the church of St Pudentiana and the rest under subsequent developments on the Viminale and Esqueline Hills.

Claudius gave Pudens Pudentinus the title of 'Aulus' before he went to Britain in A.D. 43 in the legion of the second Augusta commanded by Vespasian, and under the overall command of Aulus Plautius. When Claudius went to Britain in A.D. 47 to receive the homage of the vanquished chieftains, Cogidubnus, who had built a palace at Fishbourne near Chichester, was one of them. He had a daughter named Claudia, and it transpires that Pudens Pudentiana, who became the commander of a garrison of the second Augustan legion stationed on Cogidubnus's territory, on returning to Italy took Claudia with him and married her. The harbour at Bosham near Noviomagnus, the Roman for Chichester, was Vespasian's choice for leading the attack on this part of Britain.

Excavations in the ruins of the palace of Cogidubnus have shown that he was in no way a barbarian. It was built in the Roman fashion with elaborate mosaic floors, not only that many of the potsherds recovered from the ruins have Latin inscriptions. This though is not the only artefact of importance that was discovered. In the front wall of the Council Chambers in Chichester there is a slab of marble with an inscription in Latin that is known as the Pudens stone. This is a fragment that was unearthed when the Chambers were being built in 1723. It reads:

'To NEPTUNE AND MINERVA: THIS TEMPLE FOR THE WELFARE OF THE DIVINE HOUSE: BY THE AUTHORITY OF TIBERIUS CLAUDIUS, COGIDUBNUS: LEGATE OF AUGUSTUS IN BRITAIN: THE GUILD OF SMITHS AND THOSE OF IT WHO MINISTER IN SACRED THINGS: HAVE AT THEIR OWN COST DEDICATED THE SITE: BEING GIVEN BY PUDENS THE SON OF PUDENTINUS'.

The stone is four feet by two and originally stood in front of a temple, the ruins being some three feet thick and running from East and West. The stone was unearthed when the foundations of the Council Chambers were being excavated. What could be clearer? Pudens had paid for the site of the Temple when commanding the garrison of the second legion that was then stationed on Cogidubnus's lands and Claudia was obviously named after Claudius.

Claudia became very popular in Rome being well educated and of Kingly birth. She had sons as well as her two daughters Pudentiana and Passedes, both of them remembered by churches dedicated to them. Cardinal Baronius, who was responsible for the Martyrologie Romain, Ecclesiastical Annals 1848 records, 'it is delivered to us in the tradition of our forefathers that the house of Pudens was the first that entertained St. Peter at Rome and that there the assembly formed the church, and that of all our churches the oldest is that which is called after the name of Pudens'. The wooden altar in the early church of St. Pudentiana, one that was traditionally used by St. Peter, was later transferred to the Lateran Basilica by St. Sylvester, and is now only used by the Pope when celebrating Mass. The oldest mosaic to be seen in any church in Rome is also to be found in St. Pudentiana. It depicts the sisters Pudentiana and Prassedes holding crowns with the Lord and the Apostles in the foreground.

Martial describes Claudia in an epigram thus: 'Though Claudia Rufina, the tribal name of the Pudens family, has sprung from woad stained Britons, how she possesses the feelings of the Latin race! Mothers of Italy may deem her Roman and those of Attica her own'. In others he not only extols her disposition but hopes further that the gods will bless her and make her fruitful to her husband. From a humble beginning Martial had acquired a reputation that spread throughout the Roman world and his epigrams were composed with a critical eye to be satirical, serious, or faintly obscene. When he first came to Rome as a young man in straightened circumstances he lived in a tenement block on the Quirinal Hill, and from there could visit Pudens by going down the Via Depretis that then went through the Pudens estate. He must have know Pudens well over the years for he writes 'You urge me Pudens to take pen in hand and prune these epigrams of mine; how much thou lovest them now I understand when thou would'st have each quip a faultless line'. In his last letter to Timothy in II 4 21 Paul also mentions Linus whom Peter made Bishop of Rome, and he is thought to have been the brother of Claudia. Most of them suffered a sad end for St. Linus was martyred in A.D. 90, St Pudens the father of Aulus Pudens in A.D. 96, St Prudentiana in A.D. 107, St Prassedes in A.D. 104 and St. Timotheus, one of the sons of Claudia, in A.D. 104.

St. Peter and St. Paul, having spent almost a year in prison, were taken in A.D. 67, traditionally together, to their Martyrdoms and they are said to have parted company at the Ostian Gate, St. Paul to go on to the Salvian Springs and St. Peter to the Circus of Nero. But St. Peter was an old man and the distance from the Ostian Gate to Nero's Circus was lengthy and circuitous, so that this tradition could well be questionable[78].

Of the two Apostles it was St. Paul who had had the better education in Tarsus, for St. Peter came from the background of fishermen of Galilee. It is the rhetoric of St. Paul, his letters, his abrasive character and drive, and his single mindedness that brooked no tolerance or deviation from his views that over shadowed much of the work of the Apostles after the Crucifixion, especially that of Peter, but of the two one cannot help but feel that it was Peter who might have been the better loved in Rome.

The Jews' rejection and hatred of Paul is clearly put in Acts XXIV 5, 'We have, in fact, found this man a pestilent fellow, an agitator among all the Jews throughout the world, and a ringleader of the sect of the Nazarenes', and it was this wholesale rejection on their part that made him turn his attention to the Gentiles who, in the main, were the more receptive of his mission. Romans XI 13, 'Now I am speaking to you Gentiles, in as much then as I am an apostle to the Gentiles, I glorify my ministry in order to make my own people jealous, and thus save some of them'. It was his genius in realising very early on in his ministry that the dietary laws and the rite of circumcision, considered essential by the Jews for their salvation but rejected by the Gentiles was of no importance to the Christian teaching (Acts XV 1). The crucial argument that took place with the Apostles in Jerusalem as to whether the Gentiles on being converted to the Church should, or should not, be obliged to submit to the rite of circumcision went in Paul's favour, and was a watershed regarding the development of the Christian Church.

Paul discusses the subject at length in Romans and finally sums it up in Romans III 3 'Then what advantage has the Jew or what is the value of circumcision'?, and concludes in verses 29-30 'Is God the God of Jews only? Is he not the God of Gentiles also? Yes, of Gentiles also. Since God is one; and he will justify the circumcised on the ground of faith and the uncircumcised through that same faith' (See Figure 75).

Had it not been so the Gentiles of all the facets of the Christian Church today could well have been subject to ritual circumcision, and obligatory quirks of diet; rituals that are still essential for the Jews and Moslems who are strictly observant of their tenets. Some years ago a retired Baptist missionary discussed with me his experiences in India, and remarked on the

---

[78] It has generally been accepted that St Peter and St Paul were not martyred on the same day, a tradition that possibly arose during the persecutions of the Emperor Valerian who sought to desecrate the Christian tombs. For safety the remains of Peter and Paul were then removed to a region of the Appian Way known as the 'Ad Catacumbas' on the 29 June A. D. 258. Those of St Paul were taken eventually to the Basilica erected by Constantine that is now the site of St Paul without the walls, whilst the present tomb of St Peter under St Peter's in Rome has every indication of being authentic. Eusebius gives the date of St Peter's death as A.D. 68, during the persecutions of Nero whilst others have opted for A.D. 64 or 65. That of St Paul is said to have taken place in A.D. 67, when still under the Neronian persecutions. Should this have been the case then Peter should have died when Paul was no longer in Rome but being sought out to be brought back for trial. It would also explain why Paul was on his own when confined to the Mamertine pending his last trial: 'Only Luke is with me' (2 Tim, 4, 11). Before his death it is more than likely that Peter too was confined to the Mamertine.

occasion when, after having given a small dinner party for his friends, he went into his kitchen to find his servant Ali tucking into what was left of the pork and crackling. On expressing his profound surprise that Ali should be so enjoying himself he was informed with a broad smirk that 'Mahomet didn't know it all, even though he was a Prophet'.

Figure 75: The Statue of St ~~Paul~~ PETER in St Peters in Rome.

POSTSCRIPT

St Paul lived through the administration of five Caesars. He was born during that of Augustus and survived those of Hadrian, Caligula and Claudius, to then be martyred by Nero. The dates of his Missionary Journeys cannot be accurately determined but the opinion of some authorities contends that the first Missionary Journey could have begun in A.D. 46-48. However, Metzger is of the opinion that it began in the spring of 44 to return to Antioch in 47.

It is now contended that the letters of Paul to Timothy and Titus are not by his hand. One must then question who was responsible for there are references in them that relate to Onesophorus who came out from Iconium to offer him hospitality when on the first journey. He must have been well known to Paul for they later discoursed on Charity when in his garden to be overheard by Thecla who later found them hiding from the Jews in a cave. Though the stories relating to Thecla are now considered as being more legendary than factual and her tomb at Silifke to be regarded with some scepticism, there must have been a Thecla to have attained the sanctity of Sainthood and to have had a Basilica erected and dedicated to her memory.

Later when in the Mamertime Prison Paul blesses him and his house. The first letter to Timothy was written in Laodiciea and the second from Rome when in the Mamertine. In 11 Timothy IV 9-22 he asks him to bring him his cloak and books from Troas and sends him greetings from Claudia, and others in Rome. Claudia was the daughter of Cogidubnus who built the sumptuous villa at Fishbourne near Chichester. Pudens was Aulus Pudens of the Pudens family and her husband and Linus her brother. The fact that these letters are not now considered to be the work of Paul they have been dropped from some versions of the New Testament which is a pity.

The 'We' passages have also come under scrutiny by Prior and Rogers who have put forward theories as to why they too are not the work of Paul. However, their lengthy reasoning has been largely discounted by Stanley F. Porter who is still of the opinion that they could have come from an earlier source which indicates that he too does not consider Paul as being the Author of Acts, but if not then again who was? If Luke was not the author of Acts whoever was must have been using an earlier source to have been so well aware of many aspects of the period such as the vagaries of the winds that blew from Troas to Neapolis and vice versa, this being recorded as two days from Troas to Neapolis and five days back from Neapolis to Troas. There is too the remark of Paul that when on the way to Jerusalem they 'tarried' awhile at Ttrogillium. No mention is made as to why they tarried because at that time it was common knowledge, and thus no need to record the reason. Would this eye witness detail have been known by an author writing at a later date?

Ephesus was the premier city of Asia Minor and designated itself in an inscription as 'The finest and greatest Metropolis in Asia'. It was well situated for communications by sea and roads and was the centre for Roman administration and jurisdiction. Apart from its magnificent theatre that could seat some two hundred thousand, it had the Temple to Diana and many other fine buildings. Paul spent more than two years in Ephesus and appears to have had considerable success in spite of considerable opposition from an indigenous population of devotees to the cult of Diana. Over the years many tourists of the day visited Ephesus, those coming by boat having to pass through the harbour baths before entering the city. Those arriving during the time of Paul could also have been influenced by his rhetoric for it is recorded that Demetrius, at the time of their riot, addressed those in the theatre saying 'You also see and hear that not only in Ephesus but almost in the whole of Asia this Paul has persuaded and drawn away a considerable number of people'.

Side was a coastal city lying East of Antalya and according to Strabo, the principal slave market of the time. Judging from its impressive remains it was at that time very prosperous, and this no doubt due to its slave trade. It has the ruins of a large Agora that had surrounding colonnades, a marble lavatory that could seat fourteen at a time. It was also lined with shops and it was here where the slave auctions were held. The Agora was approached through an impressive main gate that gave onto a main street of columns and shops that went down to the shore, and here there were Temples to Apollo and Athena together with another smaller Agora. Not far from the main gate are the well preserved ruins of a large theatre that once had a scena and façade that was profusely decorated. There was also a large Nymphaeum and fountains all demonstrating that Side had been a city of some moment. It is not beyond the bounds of possibility that it was from here where Philemon obtained his slave as a youth and gave him the name Onesimus. Today Side is a fashionable resort with fine hotels; the ancient Street to the shore has lost its colonnades but is now lined with various boutiques.

ABOUT THE AUTHOR

I have long been interested in the ramifications of the Roman Empire and to this extent have visited, over the years, the Roman sites in North Africa. I was asked then by Seabys to write a book on the Roman occupation of North Africa. This was published in 1988 and subsequently became a part of the bibliography for the Degree in Archaeology at Leicester University.

Also being an artist I exhibited regularly in the R.O.I and in the Paris Salon to be awarded the Certificate of Honour in 1977. As such I was interested in the Byzantine murals to be seen in the frescoes in the Cappadocian rock hewn churches in Turkey and I spent some years in recording these frescos. This resulted in my giving papers to two international conferences, one in Niece held by the French and one held by professor Marinelli in Orvieto. As a result Rex Morgan, from Australia, asked me to write two monographs on the frescoes. This I did and one is recorded on the internet under the title The Cappadocian frescoes and the Turin Shroud Lennox Manton, Illustrated in colour. It was as a course of doing these journeys that I became more interested in St Paul's Journeys in Asia Minor and over the years visited the sites associated with his journeys doing them all by car

On these journeys, three as a guest of the Turkish Government, many interesting facts turned up which seemed to substantiate many of the observations of St Paul and St Luke to be found in the New Testament . The book endeavours to show how life under the Roman administration could have affected the course of his life and his journeys. The book is not in any way evangelical but in the past I have had help from Professor Stanton, late of London University, and an authority on the Mark Gospel. Professor Marinelli now has my archive of the Cappadocian frescoes on some forty discs held for reference at the Institute for Sindonology in Rome. An exhibition of some of the frescoes was held in Piccadilly and opened by the Cultural Minister from the Turkish Embassy. The enlarged prints were done by Kodak. The frescoes also featured in two television Epilogue programmes put out by what was then Southern T.V.

CHRONOLOGY OF ST PAUL'S MISSIONARY JOURNEYS

Start of first missionary journey	spring of 44
Mission to Pamphylia, Pisidia and Lycaonia	44-47?
Stay at Antioch	47? – 49
Start of second missionary journey	spring of 49
Macedonian mission	winter of 49-50
Corinthian mission	spring of 51
Start of third missionary journey	spring of 52
Sojourn in Galatia and Phrygia	52-53??
Ephesian mission	spring of 53 to Spring 56
Macedonian mission	summer to Autumn 56
Second stay in Corinth	Winter of 56-57
Journey from Corinth to Jerusalem by way of Macedonia and Troas	
	Spring of 57
Arrival in Jerusalem	Pentecost of 57
Departure as a prisoner to Rome	September 59
Winter in Malta	Winter of 59-60
Arrival in Rome	February of 60

INDEX

Adana, 3, 7, 118

Ahmet Uner, 106

Alexander, vii, 2, 10, 24, 30, 70, 87, 94, 118, 122, 123, 126, 138, 170, 185, 204, 247

Alyana, 3

Antalya, i, iv, 2, 3, 70, 71, 78, 86, 87, 90, 254

Antioch, iii, iv, x, 1, 2, 3, 10, 20, 24, 46, 47, 48, 49, 50, 51, 52, 53, 54, 56, 57, 58, 60, 62, 63, 66, 70, 80, 86, 89, 90, 91, 92, 93, 94, 95, 99, 104, 105, 115, 116, 118, 119, 122, 124, 125, 126, 128, 129, 138, 139, 141, 142, 143, 148, 160, 161, 163, 183, 193, 199, 203, 220, 236, 241, 244, 253, 256

Artemesion, 170

Athenodorus, 12, 16, 32

Augustus, iv, vii, 7, 8, 12, 30, 51, 52, 69, 87, 90, 91, 92, 95, 96, 104, 123, 125, 126, 182, 204, 210, 229, 239, 241, 242, 243, 253

Baal, 38

Baalbek, 23

Bagkonak, 120

Barada River, 21

Bassianus, 124

Beroea, 107, 131, 133, 138

Beth She'an, 20

Bethlehem, 8

Bithynia, 6, 71, 123, 125, 126, 127, 133, 143, 169, 244

Bodrum, 2

Burkhardt, 37

Buyukbenli, i, 86

Cappadocia, i, ii, 2, 3, 7, 128, 142, 244

celibacy, 5, 6, 203

circumcised, ix, 11, 115, 116, 119, 251

Commagene, 2

Cydnus, 16, 142

Cyrene, 9, 51, 52, 69, 138

Damaris, 132

Damascus, iii, ix, x, 6, 18, 19, 20, 21, 22, 23, 24, 25, 26, 27, 28, 29, 30, 31, 36, 37, 39, 46, 99

Darius, 24, 118

David, i, 8, 32, 36, 52, 87, 90

Delphi, 137, 214

Demetrius, 139, 183, 185, 186, 187, 188, 191, 254

Demre, vi, 233, 234, 235

Derbe, iv, 90, 99, 105, 106, 107, 109, 110, 112, 118, 119, 125, 138, 142, 153, 205

Diaspora, viii, ix, 8, 9, 10, 20, 36, 50, 51, 69, 101, 104, 122, 125, 130, 131, 133, 137, 153, 203, 245, 246

Didyma, 204, 214

Diocletian, 36, 127, 148, 219

Dionysus, iv, 80, 85, 125, 204

Dogubayazit, 1

Domitian, 70, 157, 171, 183, 198, 241

Dorylaeum, 122, 125, 127

Doummar, 21

Dr French, i, 127

Drusilla, 226, 227

Dunuk Tas, 17

Edomites, 32, 36

Egridir, 80, 86, 142

Epaphras, x, 153, 157, 161, 162, 163, 243, 245

Ephesus, 1, 176

Epidaurus, 128, 129

Epiphania, 54

Esdraelon, 20, 22

Eskisehir, 122, 125

Euphrates, 21, 119, 153

Eutropius, 183

Ezekiel, 24, 25

Ezion Geber, 31

Felix, ix, 224, 225, 226, 227, 228, 229, 230

Festus, ix, 227, 228, 229, 243

Fethiye, 2

Fitzwilliam Museum, 124

Flaccus, 51, 52

Fortunatus, 134

Forum, iii, 30, 34, 130, 172, 231, 241, 245

Fundi, 241

Furies, 132

Gaius, 51, 107, 119, 137, 138, 182, 185, 186, 187, 205, 248

Galen, 129, 150

Galilee, 20, 21, 29, 40, 193, 194, 244, 250

Gallia, 205

Gallipoli, 1

Gamaliel, 17, 18, 19, 46

Ganymede, 153

Germa, 123, 125, 142

Gethsemane, 19

Golan Heights, 20

Gordium, 2, 122, 142

Groves of Daphni, 55

Hadrian, v, 9, 69, 71, 144, 153, 172, 173, 177, 185, 209, 214, 253

Hadrianutherae, 127

Hannibal, 124, 125

Hebron, 31, 32

Heraclitus, 204

Herculaneum, 49, 61, 240

Hermon, 21

Herod, 7, 8, 24, 29, 30, 32, 51, 52, 61, 123, 138, 192, 193, 222, 226, 227, 228, 229, 230

Hierapolis, iv, v, 124, 143, 149, 152, 153, 157, 159, 161, 163, 220

Hippodamus, 49, 207, 208, 219

Honaz, 162

Ibis, 150

Iconium, 87, 93, 99, 100, 101, 104, 105, 107, 112, 119, 123, 125, 142, 143, 162, 253

Idumea, 31, 32

Illyricum, 188

Ionian, 209

Ionic, 71, 91, 125, 133, 207, 219

Ipsos, 142

Isis, vii, 171, 236

Issus, 24, 48, 118

Istanbul, i, 2, 86, 199

James, ix, 18, 29, 39, 46, 52, 116, 141, 192, 193, 194, 203, 207, 220, 221

Jebel Haroun, 37

Jerusalem, i, vi, viii, ix, 6, 8, 10, 17, 18, 19, 20, 22, 26, 29, 31, 32, 36, 37, 39, 46, 47, 51, 52, 61, 80, 91, 115, 116, 117, 118, 133, 138, 139, 141, 153, 157, 163, 185, 186, 187, 188, 193, 198, 199, 203, 205, 208, 219, 220, 221, 224, 225, 226, 227, 228, 231, 244, 251, 253, 256

Job, 32

John, v, 2, 5, 7, 8, 21, 37, 52, 54, 69, 80, 149, 150, 170, 186, 192, 193, 194, 198, 199, 200, 201, 204, 214, 219, 220, 222, 245

Joppa, 115

Josephus, ix, 8, 21, 51, 52, 123, 138, 193, 224, 227, 229, 236

Judas, 22, 23, 25, 141, 194

Julian, 104

Julius Frontinus, 157

Jupiter Gate, 24, 25

Justinian, v, 16, 199, 202

Kara Dagh Mountains, 106, 111

Karaman, i, iv, 3, 99, 106, 107, 110, 111, 118, 119

Kasneh, 38, 39

Kasr el Bint, 33

Kedron brook, 19

Kemal Ataturk, 100

Kepeniklers, 149

Konya, v, 3, 86, 93, 99, 100, 101, 104, 105, 106, 149, 165

Koressos, 168, 171, 173, 204

Kumeileh, 24

Kutahya, 127

Labranda, 99

Laodiciea, 50, 253

Laranda, iv, 106, 110, 119

Lebanon, 21, 139

Levites, 5

Lion Harbour, v, 209, 210, 213, 214, 215

Luke, x, 5, 7, 10, 17, 20, 29, 36, 39, 46, 53, 92, 107, 112, 118, 119, 122, 123, 126, 128, 129, 131, 139, 157, 161, 169, 171, 186, 192, 205, 206, 207, 214, 220, 224, 225, 227, 228, 230, 231, 233, 236, 237, 238, 239, 240, 241, 242, 243, 247, 250, 253

Lyaconia, 101, 122

Lycia, 70, 214, 233

Lycias, 46, 225, 226

Lystra, iv, x, 7, 87, 100, 101, 103, 104, 105, 106, 107, 112, 119, 123, 125, 142, 153, 246

Macedonia, 125, 126, 129, 138, 139, 186, 187, 188, 203, 205, 220, 245, 256

Macellum, 79, 127, 148

Maenad, 80

Mamertine, 148, 243, 246, 247, 250, 253

Mary Magdalene, 192

Maximus, 24, 30, 87

Medusa, 71

Midas, 2, 122

Miletos, 49

Mithradates, v, 169, 189

Morton, 9, 22, 49, 54, 60, 91, 101, 102, 104, 106, 137, 148, 188

Nablus, 4, 5, 21

Nag Hammadi, 141

Narbonius, 51, 52

Narcissus, 138

Nazareth, 20, 194

Neapolis, 5, 21, 126, 129, 253

Nebuchadnezzar, 32

Necropolis, 139, 157

Nicaea, 3, 230

Nicephorus, 7

Nicodemus, 6

Nymphaeum, iii, iv, v, 11, 31, 35, 71, 77, 153, 156, 209, 254

Nymphas, 143, 153

Nyssa, 80

Obodas, 32

Octavian, 52

odeon, 12

Odeon, v, 31, 132, 153, 167, 171, 172

Olives, 194, 224

Onesimus, i, x, 160, 161, 162, 163, 191, 192, 243, 254

Onesiphorus, 93, 246, 247

Optimus, 91

oracle, 133, 208, 214

Orontes, 48, 50, 53

Ostia, 11, 61, 206, 239, 240, 247

Ostiensis, 247, 248

Ottoman, 9, 100, 101

Parthenon, 130, 131, 207

Patara, v, 130, 214, 217, 219, 233

Perga, iii, iv, 70, 71, 73, 74, 75, 77, 79, 80, 85, 86, 87, 90, 106, 244

Peter, iii, vii, 7, 18, 39, 46, 52, 53, 54, 58, 59, 115, 116, 117, 138, 141, 193, 194, 199, 203, 219, 220, 243, 244, 246, 247, 248, 249, 250

Pharisees, viii, 4, 9, 17, 46, 52, 115, 220, 221, 224

Philemon, x, 149, 160, 161, 162, 163, 191, 192, 243, 245, 254

Philippi, 23, 69, 91, 123, 126, 128, 129, 130, 131, 183, 187, 188, 205

Phrygia, 92, 122, 124, 142, 143, 153, 256

Pilate, 21, 222, 229

Pisidian, iv, 70, 80, 86, 87, 89, 90, 91, 92, 93, 94, 95, 99, 104, 105, 119, 120, 122, 125, 126, 142, 143, 160, 241

Pompeii, vii, viii, 49, 61, 123, 153, 172, 206, 227, 239, 242

Priapus, 172, 191

Ptolemais, 214, 219

Qatrana, 37

Qatraria, 37

Quartus, 134

Queen of Pontus, 94

Queen of Sheba, 31

Quirinal Hill, 250

Qunaytirah, 20

Rabban, 17

Rabbath Amon, 31

Rabbell II, 36

resurrection, viii, 224, 228

Rhegium, 239, 240

Rhegma, 16, 142

Rhoda, 53

Rodolfo Lanciani, 248

Rufus, 138

Sadducees, viii, 4, 5, 52, 221, 224

Sanhedrin, viii, ix, 5, 6, 18, 19, 20, 22, 23, 29, 31, 36, 193, 194, 220, 221, 224, 225, 226, 227, 228

Scholastikia, 172, 173

Sebaste, 87, 90, 93, 99, 100, 104, 105, 119, 142

Seleucia, iii, 68

Senneca, 137

Simeon, 17, 51, 124

Simon, 9, 138, 194

Smyrna, 143, 150, 153, 198

spikenard, 5, 150

Stephen, 6, 10, 19, 20, 22, 23, 51, 193

Strabo, 11, 12, 32, 36, 70, 92, 93, 122, 150, 199, 219, 254

Tarsus, iii, 1, 3, 7, 8, 9, 10, 11, 12, 13, 14, 15, 16, 17, 18, 19, 20, 39, 46, 47, 118, 142, 144, 148, 168, 183, 224, 242, 250

Teresa, 23

Tetrarch, 29

Thecla, 6, 7, 93, 94, 99, 253

Tiberias, 4, 20, 30, 91, 200

Tiberius, viii, 29, 30, 249

Titus, x, 4, 7, 61, 116, 124, 153, 186, 187, 203, 244, 245, 246, 253

Trachoma, 150

Trajan, iii, 9, 36, 68, 69, 126, 169, 172, 208, 236

Troas, vii, 122, 123, 126, 127, 128, 129, 131, 148, 149, 161, 186, 187, 188, 205, 206, 246, 247, 253, 256

Trogillium, 207

Turner, 21

Tychicus, 138, 160, 187, 192, 203, 205, 243, 246

Unal, 153

Upper Pannonia, 48

Urban Council, 104

Urbane, 138

Urgup, 3

valley of the Agora, 132

Venus, 54, 55, 69, 130, 133, 134, 204, 236

Vespasian, 4, 249

Vesuvius, 153, 227

Via Egnatia, 127, 130, 161, 186, 188, 205, 245

Viminale, 249

Virgin, v, 170, 192, 193, 194, 195, 196, 198, 199, 204, 220

Vitellius, 30

Wadi Musa, 31

William Ramsay, 7, 18, 100, 106, 171, 225

Wilson, 8, 21

Wood, 169, 170

Wordsworth, 132

Xenophon, 10

Yalvac, 90, 92, 120

Zeus, 80, 122, 127

Zion, 222

Zourka, 182